Global Business Citizenship

Global Business Citizenship

A Transformative
Framework for Ethics and
Sustainable Capitalism

DONNA J. WOOD • JEANNE M. LOGSDON
PATSY G. LEWELLYN • KIM DAVENPORT

M.E.Sharpe
Armonk, New York
London, England

Library of Congress Cataloging-in-Publication Data

Global business citizenship : a transformative framework for ethics and sustainable
capitalism / by Donna J. Wood ... [et al.].
    p. cm.
Includes bibliographical references and index.
ISBN 0-7656-1626-2 (cloth : alk. paper) ISBN 0-7656-1627-0 (pbk. : alk. paper)
    1. International business enterprises—Management. 2. Social responsibility of business.
3. Business ethics. I. Wood, Donna J., 1949–

HD62.4.G535 2006
658.4′083—dc22   2005017676

Printed in the United States of America

The paper used in this publication meets the minimum requirements of
American National Standard for Information Sciences
Permanence of Paper for Printed Library Materials,
ANSI Z 39.48-1984.

∞

| BM (c) | 10 | 9 | 8 | 7 | 6 | 5 | 4 | 3 | 2 | 1 |
| BM (p) | 10 | 9 | 8 | 7 | 6 | 5 | 4 | 3 | 2 | 1 |

Contents

Preface

Globalization is perhaps the most challenging development of modern times. It has pushed the stark economic contrasts of poor and rich nations to center stage. It has weakened nations and governments without creating a replacement institution to look out for the public good. It has revealed both the astonishing successes and the destructive impacts of capitalist business.

In the last two decades or so, few other topics have commanded more attention worldwide. We have all learned a great deal about multinational corporations, balances of trade, tax havens, transfer payments, economic development, sweatshops and child labor. We've learned about cross-border political conflicts, immigration patterns, ethnic and cultural minorities and majorities, unstable or indifferent or corrupt governments. We've learned about multilateral efforts to contain the disruptions of globalization, such as the World Trade Organization and the Kyoto Protocol on Global Warming.

Through the magic of video, the Internet, the business press, and the efforts of global NGO participants, we've also seen the human faces of globalization. We've seen busy young executives in Prague and Guang-Zhou; we've watched efforts to merge cultures as the European Union expands and consolidates; we've worked along with the trash-pickers of Indonesia and the cocoa plantation workers of Côte d'Ivoire; we've mourned with Texas workers as their factory moves to Puerto Rico, and we've celebrated the arrival of new jobs with the Puerto Ricans; we've learned about the call center workers as well as the basket weavers of India. We've watched the native peoples of central Africa suffer from the horrible effects of river blindness, curable by a single oral dose of a Merck medication, and we've seen their wide-eyed gratitude when help arrives. We've watched the pride and amazement on the faces of Bangladeshi college graduates supported by Grameen Bank. We've felt the suffering of AIDS victims who have no access to the medical treatments that could ease their pain, and we've learned about company efforts in Africa to get appropriate help to HIV-infected employees.

What can we make of all this raw information, all these faces, all this new hope and deep despair?

Globalization Is Inevitable, But Its Outcomes Aren't

Most people who write about globalization are taking sides for it or against it. We are keenly aware of the pro and con arguments, though we aren't enthusiastic about them.

For example, some maintain that globalization is the ultimate "rising tide" that will bring opportunity and prosperity to all the world's peoples. Others claim that globalization is the ultimate greed-grab of corporations that care only about their own profit. Some believe that globalization will result in industry monopolies and the consequent death of capitalism; others suggest that globalization offers entrepreneurial wealth-building for anyone and expands the realm of economic possibility. Some propose that businesses are good "corporate citizens" and that this will only get better with globalization; others point out that "corporate citizens" are not enacting duties but are voluntarily participating in community affairs, and that their support can be withdrawn at a moment's notice. Some argue that global companies have no grounds to be "citizens" in any meaningful way; others argue that if they do have such grounds, it can only spell trouble for democracy and human well-being.

We acknowledge these claims and arguments, but we have a different take. We don't think it matters a bit how anyone feels about it—globalization is an implacable, unstoppable process. We do think it matters a great deal, however, that business leaders and managers understand the processes of globalization and the crucial role they themselves play in shaping its directions and consequences.

Most of the nay-sayers in the globalization discourse are frightened or furious about the current visible abuses of human capital in the service of financial capital. They believe that globalization leads inevitably to giant corporations that assume the powers of government and then use those powers to further their own ends rather than the public good. Given all that we have learned about global business in the last 25 years or so, it is not hard to see why this view is so prevalent and powerful.

Our view, though, is different; and it is not a view that unduly praises the corporation and its capitalist environment. We believe that globalization can yield the very best that capitalism has to offer—rapid innovation, technological progress, rising quality of life, more choices for all, equal opportunity to share in society's benefits, and equal protection from its harms. And most importantly, following decades of study of the political, legal, social, and ethical environments of business, we are convinced that *it will be businesses themselves that lead the way to a new negotiated order, a widely accepted set of standards on human rights, labor conditions, the environment, corruption, and economic development.*

We are not arguing that this *should* happen; we are arguing that it *will* happen. Global business citizenship, we argue, is the right way for managers and companies to steer their own courses through these rocky shoals of globalization. Global business citizenship is the path to sustainable capitalism, bringing innovation and wealth creation to all.

In this book we lay out our argument, present the evidence, and examine the available tools and the efforts already underway. We ask you, the reader, to walk with us in the hope that globalization will not destroy the many benefits of capitalism, but that capitalist enterprises will do what is needed to sustain an environment in which they—and everyone else—can thrive and profit.

A Note on Language

You might find the language of this book to be a bit more breezy than the ordinary business text. We use some colorful metaphors and even tell a few jokes. We have done this on purpose—to get your attention and keep it as we develop some very important ideas.

We are all perfectly capable of writing pedantic scholarly prose. But we are serious about wanting you to read this book and think about how to apply its messages in your organization, so we have written it more as a conversation than a lecture. Enjoy!

Themes and Levels of Analysis

Table P.1 illustrates how the book's major themes are presented and discussed over three levels of analysis—the individual, organizational, and systemic levels. This table is your roadmap through the many topics and tools in the book.

You'll see that not every topic in every cell is included systematically in the book, but we've offered the complete matrix of ideas so you can see how and where the book's themes and messages can be pushed further. For the most part, we have focused most heavily on the organizational- and individual-level themes. There is so much that individual managers and specific organizations can do to steer the processes of globalization toward sustainable capitalism—and our goal is to encourage you, inform you, and stand beside you as you see how this can happen in your life and your company.

Table P.1

Themes and Levels of Analysis

Themes	Chapters	Individual	Organizational	Systemic
The status quo isn't so great.	1, 2	Managers are stuck in a performance vise with too many challenges and responsibilities; they feel trapped and powerless; faced with fear, uncertainty, doubt.	Firms face ever-harder competitive pressure in a more complex and turbulent environment. Bad actors in the global economy—the ruthless rule-breakers—are hard to rein in.	Problems abound within and across nations: shrinking governments, cross-border economies, massive poverty, a growing divide between rich and poor, violence, environmental degradation.
Trust is essential, but easily lost.	2, 3	Trust makes life easier for managers. To keep trust alive, agreements must be kept, duties fulfilled, and expectations met.	Trust lowers transaction costs and earns social capital for the firm. To keep trust alive, stakeholders must be satisfied.	Trust makes the social system possible. To keep trust alive, institutions must permit and support its fulfillment by persons and organizations.
Ethics and values make a difference in business.	2, 3, 4	Personal character: Most managers aren't evil and want to do the right thing. Ethics belongs in business decision-making and action.	Organizational guidance: Vision, mission, values, principles, codes, and policies all help a firm's employees develop and use good ethical judgment. (Ch. 4)	Institutional enforcement: Law, regulation, courts, and even industry self-regulation can and do support ethical conduct for individuals and organizations, for thebetterment of societies and institutional systems.
The GBC process gives firms a hybrid strategy.	3		GBC—global business citizenship—offers a hybrid strategy for firms to help them be trustworthy on standards, adaptable in implementation, systematic in their learning. (Ch. 3)	

We already have the tools for achieving nation-level GBC benefits.	5, 6, 7, 8, 9, 10	Personal tools: Buy-in, commitment, courage; the language of rights, duties, and justice; management communication and authority channels; peer support; knowledge of planning and decision-making.	Organizational implementation tools: • Stakeholder engagement (Ch. 5, 6) • Organizational development and change management (Ch. 7, 8) • Accountability and sustainability reporting (Ch. 9, 10)	Systemic tools: Stakeholder activism; investor/customer pressures; supranational regulatory agreements; stable civil institutions.
Applying these tools to GBC promises to change the status quo.	11, 12	For people, and especially managers: A better and more moral life, a sense of efficacy, a solid reputation, and an ability to learn and grow. (Ch. 11)	For companies: A good reputation based on earning stakeholders' trust; the creation of sustainable businesses; the possibility of competitive advantage; and organizational learning. (Ch. 11)	For the globe: Global business citizenship is the path to sustainable capitalism, to bringing innovation and wealth creation to all. (Ch. 12)

The Bottom Line

Sit back, relax, and enjoy the flight. Then put on your superhero gear and get out there and save your own corner of capitalism. Adopting the principles and processes of global business citizenship is something that any manager can do, any corporation can do, and any industry can do. Stay with us for the why and the how.

Acknowledgments

We owe a large debt of gratitude to all the managers, companies, government agencies, nonprofit organizations, and supranational bodies that have been actively trying to think through the issues of global business citizenship and experiment with solutions.

Getting a book like this from concept to conclusion involves a number of key players besides the authors. We certainly thank Harry Briggs, the executive editor at M.E. Sharpe, as well as Elizabeth Granda, Amy Odum, and Carmen Chetti, who designed a number of our graphics. Over the course of our research we have had numerous wonderful student assistants who have tried to keep us sane and organized. Kim Parker earns a special thank you for managing the permissions process and other extraordinary efforts.

All of us want to thank our dear friends and colleagues Steve Wartick and John Mahon for their unflagging support despite skepticism about our core idea of global business citizenship. We thank the Sloan Foundation and our program officer, Gail Pesyna, for a seed grant that got us going on this work. In addition, funding for a mini-conference on the topic of global business citizenship was provided by chaired professorships at the University of Northern Iowa, the University of New Mexico, and the University of Maine, held by Wood, Logsdon, and Mahon, respectively.

Donna wants to thank lifelong mentors, students, friends, and family for all the usual reasons. Her position at the University of Northern Iowa, the David W. Wilson Chair in Business Ethics, provided significant financial support for the project as well as a fabulous work environment. Imagine—a workplace where everybody's got your back! Donna dedicates her contributions to this book to her two sons, Jacob and Sam Wood-Bednarz, and to her "adopted" mom, Lois O'Connor.

Jeanne expresses appreciation to the deans and her department chairs in the Anderson Schools of Management at the University of New Mexico for encouragement and research support in writing about global business citizenship over the past five years. She especially values the contribution by Jack and Donna Rust to create the Jack and Donna Rust Professorship in Business Ethics, which has provided financial support to write this book. She thanks her MBA and Executive MBA students for providing vibrant discussions about how to design practical ethical approaches to complex business situations. Jeanne dedicates her contributions to the book to her husband, John E. Young.

Patsy is grateful for research support from the University of South Carolina Aiken School of Business through the John M. Olin Chair in Enterprise Development. She thanks her family and friends for their patience and unfailing support, and her students and colleagues for stimulating and challenging her thinking on the subject of business citizenship and accountability. Patsy dedicates her contributions to this book to her husband, Ron Lewellyn, and their daughter Casey.

Kim is appreciative of her educational experiences at the Gestalt Institute of Cleveland, American University (the AU/NTL program), and the Fielding Institute—they each shaped her view of the world in profound ways. Kim thanks AT&T, BellSouth, and First Data Corporation for providing exceptional career opportunities to learn and grow. Kim dedicates her contributions to this book to her family for modeling a strong work ethic, compassion, and treating people fairly.

Finally, we each want to acknowledge our teammates on this project. Good work is always fun, but good work with great colleagues is simply the best.

Global Business Citizenship

An Invitation to Global Business Citzenship

"You want me to do WHAT???"

For today's manager, just getting through the workday can be tough enough. The pace is implacable; there is extraordinary pressure for performance in a risky, turbulent, globalizing environment. This requires difficult trade-offs and good explanations for the paths taken and not taken. Dangers loom large, and rewards sometimes seem distant. Increasing demands and higher risks, decreasing time and head count, hypercompetition, and always the pressure to meet earnings projections—all these challenges can make many managers' lives something less than truly satisfying.

Scared yet? You should be. Yet fear can be a friend if it steers us away from disaster. A wise and courageous person is not unafraid.

Now add in new demands for stakeholder accountability, global social responsibility, ethical conduct, and transparency, spurred in large measure by globalization and communications technology. Then consider how much weaker many governments have become in regulating conduct for the safety and well-being of citizens, both individual and corporate. Next, contemplate the vast economic and social inequities among the world's nations and the derivative threats and opportunities. Finally, reflect for a moment on what all this might mean for your work life, your chances of having a happy retirement, and the prospects for your children and grandchildren.

If you're like most managers, you face competing stakeholder demands, you're up against ethical problems regularly, and you may lack a framework or a language to address them. Like people anywhere, managers are self-interested *and* concerned for others. They want to do good *and* they are very

Exhibit 1.1

What Is a Global Business Citizen?

A **global business citizen** is a business enterprise (and its managers) that responsibly exercises its rights and implements its duties to individuals, stakeholders, and societies within and across national and cultural borders.

practical. They have big dreams and irksome constraints. Herein lies the biggest dilemma of modern global management.

The good news is that most people—managers certainly included—*want* to do the right thing. The desire for ethical conduct and ethical treatment is built into the fabric of human character. The bad news is that so far there has not been a good template for incorporating ethics and responsibility into the fabric of management practice—at least not a model that the average manager feels can be "worn out of the store" and put into action.

This book offers you a beacon through the fog surrounding responsible management practice via the process of *global business citizenship*—a new way of thinking about ethical and responsible global management.

In practical terms, we want to help you negotiate the rapids of the social, cultural, and political change that accompanies globalization. We want to give you good reasons for making the effort to do the right thing every day in every way. We offer a framework for seeing that ethical, responsible business practices transcend cultural and religious boundaries, and that such practices are good for the firm and good for business as a whole. The global business citizenship process will help you design your organization and your worklife in a more sustainable—and personally sustaining—way.

Linking Ethics to Business Practice

Here's a little quiz to test your motivation to manage ethically. You leap out of bed in the morning and go off to work, thinking with great enthusiasm:

    A. Hey, I'm going to do a lot of good for a lot of people today!
    B. Maybe I'll get lucky and won't have any big problems today!
    C. Wow, this looks like a great day to exploit some workers!

Sure, there are some "immoral" or sociopathic managers, the ones who look for new ways to cheat, lie, and steal, and who don't seem to care who gets hurt in the process. We see their handiwork in some of the big scandals and disasters of the corporate world. And there are some managers who thoroughly infuse their business practices with deeply held religious or philosophical principles—the founding executives at Johnson & Johnson or Levi Strauss might come to mind. In the middle, however, are the managers who lack the awareness, the vocabulary, or the framework for relating *what they believe is right* to *what they believe is necessary in business.*[1] Not having good tools can make even the best-intentioned manager frustrated, ineffective, and distrustful.

These "amoral" managers do have values, and typically very good ones. But for a variety of reasons, those values are difficult for the managers to apply to and implement in business practice:

- They may separate their private behavior from their business behavior, believing that business is a "game" with its own rules and that "real-life" rules do not apply.
- They may be afraid for any number of reasons to raise ethical issues, to expose problems, or to champion social responsibility.
- They may not be sufficiently tuned into the long-term and broad-based consequences of business decisions, focusing instead on the narrow, short-term performance goals that are familiar and comfortable.
- They may lack the analytical skills, the experience, and the vocabulary to conduct ethical analysis alongside economic or technical analysis.
- Responsibility and accountability in organizations are so often diffused across levels and functional silos; the process of how work actually gets done often "hides" any real sense of control or impact for managers.

So, if you find yourself among or reporting to or supervising that large middle of "amoral" managers, how's that workin' for ya?[2]

Here are just a few examples of the difficulties that managers have stumbled into for lack of skill—or will—to act upon values they already hold:

- A young engineer hesitates to tell his boss about a design problem he believes can lead to great customer harm; he is afraid of his boss's temper, or he just doesn't know how the information will be received. And he is concerned about what his expression of concern might mean to his own job security.
- A CPA is told by her managing partner that her client demands that his gambling wins and losses not be recorded on his personal tax return, even though the law requires reporting. It's a wash; there's no tax liability anyway, so what's the problem?

- A federal contracts manager is told by superiors that if prototype testing doesn't entirely pan out, he should "smooth the curves" on the report to avoid raising questions about potential product limitations.
- Threatened with job loss if her unit doesn't cut costs, a manager chooses to overlook safety violations and routine maintenance of security systems.
- A newly minted MBA is promoted too fast. Flattered, he fails to see that he has been chosen because he is inexperienced and will be set up as the fall guy if the major corporate fraud is discovered.
- Forced to downsize, a manager is tempted to place older employees on the lay-off list, given they lack "runway" potential.

Almost all of the thousands of managers we have met intend to do the right things for their families, communities, employees, and companies, as well as for themselves. They mean to cause no harm, and they feel good about helping those in need. They obey the law (most of the time) and keep a wary eye out for those who don't. They participate in community affairs and societal governance, and they "give back" in gratitude for what they have been given. In short, they are good folks.

But—and isn't there always a "but"—the new realities of global business are presenting managers with problems and dilemmas they never dreamed about. It's more than the common (and false) wisdom that business and ethics are unrelated—it's a whole new world of challenges for the manager.

Globalization and the New Pressures on Managers

The pressures on managers haven't changed so much because of globalization, but they have become much more intense and time-constrained. There are huge pressures to ensure company financial performance and success. There are equally strong pressures for individual managers to get good evaluations, bonuses, and promotions, enabling them to experience personal success.

But managers today are between two worlds in terms of knowing how to achieve these goals. What worked well 10 or 20 years ago doesn't work so well anymore; the standards of success for the organization and individuals may be similar, but the paths to achieving them are not clear. New stakeholder expectations and processes for meeting them are not yet well defined. It may seem at times unrealistic to expect ethical conduct of oneself, much less of colleagues, business partners, and competitors. Indeed, in some situations, it seems impossible to even understand what the right course of conduct is. Consider these examples:

- Marlene arrives in Haiti where her company contracts with a local supplier who subcontracts with small manufacturers. She meets with the supplier's senior executives and requests a final schedule of the previously arranged tours of production facilities. She is told that unfortunately, because of local flooding, the facilities are undergoing renovation and cannot be toured at present, and she is then urged to approve the anticipated three-year supply contract quickly, before competitiors move in to appropriate the supplier.
- Stefan from Internal Audit at headquarters discovers that his company's Pakistani chemical factory is surrounded not by the required buffer zone, but by makeshift neighborhoods of workers and their families living in shacks of tin and cardboard. Following the plant disaster in Bhopal, India, in the mid-1980s, Stefan's company developed detailed standards to prevent exactly such an occurrence. He finds, however, that local plant managers, workers, and officials seem to have only a vague awareness of Bhopal or of the company's safety standards.
- Jim has been sent by his company to a Middle Eastern country where he is to investigate some new business opportunities. After settling into his hotel, he decides to take a walk. Within a few blocks he comes upon a woman being assaulted by a group of men. He tenses, looks around for help, and finding none, moves to intervene. As he steps in to offer assistance, Jim is grabbed by two of the men and soon realizes that he is being arrested. His passport is taken and he spends the night in jail, missing an important business meeting. Released the next day with stern warnings not to interfere with local Islamic law, he must explain to his boss and ask for guidance.

Most managers are familiar with the language of *costs* and benefits, and are typically able to decide which of several courses of action is economically best *for the firm*. But what can a firm-centric economic analysis tell us about how a manager *should* behave in situations like those above? Instead, the broader ethical language of *harms* and benefits, voluntary versus involuntary participation, rights and duties, just processes and fair distribution is required.

- Marlene has to be aware that the supplier may be trying to manipulate around her company's express desire to uphold workplace safety and labor standards. Will she offend the local supplier if she refuses to sign until the inspection has been done? What will happen to the subcontractors' workers if her company cuts its ties with the supplier? What if she signs, and the subcontractors are exposing their workers to very hazardous chemicals?

- Stefan is faced with implementing headquarters standards in a situation that is, in utter contradiction, both unthinkable and locally acceptable. He knows all too well what happened at Bhopal, but if no one at the Pakistani plant seems to know or care, how is he going to enforce required safety standards? What if he enforces the standards strictly and is accused of cruelty to poor workers just looking for a place to live? What if he lets things slide and a major disaster occurs?
- Jim has landed in a theocracy that throws into immediate clarity his own cultural beliefs and assumptions about individual freedom, equality, and rights. Everything in his character tells him to stand up for vulnerable people, to oppose abuse and violence, *and* to respect the values and beliefs of other cultures. Nothing in his management education has prepared him, however, for the experience of legal, socially accepted violence against women. Without breaching his own integrity, how can he conduct business in a culture where such customs assault his sensibilities?

Each of these managers is experiencing a clash of values, beliefs, and practices that has the potential to cause great harm to vulnerable stakeholders. There is also the possibility of creating great good—but how is that defined, and by whom? The problems here are ethical, and therefore require a shift in language and an adeptness and comfort level that managers already have with traditional business analysis.

Global managers know they have an obligation to abide by legal and ethical principles, and they ordinarily want to do so. But how often do the ethical problems involved appear to be too confusing and perhaps insurmountable, because of competing pressures? Standard guidance is reflected in the adage, "When in Rome, do as the Romans do." But when is the "when-in-Rome" approach appropriate, and when should it be rejected? What should the firm's relationship be to various types of governments? How many managers have a clear reading of their stakeholders' interests and of the consequences of their daily business operations? The global business citizenship process offers answers and—more importantly—ways to evolve to next year's answers, not just today's.

Countervailing Forces

Sure, there are opportunists who can make big bucks today by exploiting human suffering and using the world's poor as expendable labor units. There are those who can make a killing by manipulating small corners of global financial markets. There are those who feel free to trade in toxic wastes,

entire regions at great risk in the absence of any governmental or
overnmental oversight. In the short term, it might indeed benefit these
o be crooks and scoundrels as long as they don't get caught.

e convinced, however, that most managers do not want to live their
lives as opportunists, manipulators, thieves, or agents of environmental destruction. Quite the opposite, in fact—most managers we know would like
to ensure a legacy of opportunity for their children and a reputable name
for themselves. They want their lives and their efforts to count for something important, and they want to retire with dignity and financial security.
All of these high-value objectives are at great risk in a world where opportunism reigns.

But what can one person or one organization do in the face of intense
pressures for consistent short-term growth in market share, revenue, profit,
stock price? What are the countervailing pressures to act responsibly, and
how strong are they? In the modern world of instant communication, there's
no place to hide—but is anyone watching?

Government as Regulator

A significant source of control of business opportunism[3] in democratic societies is government. Traditionally, its roles include being a guarantor and
enforcer of citizens' rights and privileges as well as a provider of the institutions and infrastructure necessary for business to thrive. Within industrialized nations, there are many cases in which stakeholder and public concerns
have been addressed via the legislative and regulatory apparatus of the state.
In some cases, government intervenes in business affairs to favor and support a particular industry or set of businesses.[4] But in large measure, democratic government involvement has emerged to *sustain* business enterprise
and all the public benefits it provides by correcting market failures of ineffi-
ciency, externality, and inequity.[5]

Antitrust law is an example of enhancing market *efficiency* by strengthening competition through prevention of monopoly, industry-wide price-
fixing, and other anti-competitive practices. Insider trading prohibitions
are another example of efficiency-related regulation. Adam Smith's capitalist theory assumes that investors have complete access to information
that could materially affect a firm's valuation. In practice, however, we know
that information is sometimes parceled sparingly to the popular press and
thus to the ordinary investor, and we know that brokers, fund managers, bank-
ers, and a host of other financial professionals have private access to material
information before anyone else does. Therefore, laws and regulations to pro-
hibit insider trading are meant to improve market efficiency by forbidding

those "in the know" from acting first to buy or sell stock that is rising or falling, before the general public is aware of the information.

Laws and regulations correcting for *externalities* are intended to reduce harms to involuntary stakeholders or to society as a whole. For example, pollution control regulation restrains the ability of an upstream papermill to dump toxic wastes into the river. If this behavior were not regulated, the toxics would eventually kill the fish in the river, harming the fisheries downstream (involuntary stakeholders of the papermill) as well as destroying any collective benefits such as clean water the river provides to the entire society.

Finally, *inequities* occur in market transactions when there are big differences in people's access to information, opportunity, and bargaining power. Adam Smith's theory of market competition assumes that consumers have full information about products and services so that they can evaluate which is best for them and choose accordingly. In practice, however, sellers have information that they don't want to share voluntarily, for example, the actual miles per gallon or kilometers per liter that a vehicle gets in normal use, or the true rate of interest to finance a purchase. Therefore, laws and regulations are meant to reduce the market contract inequity by requiring that relevant and timely information be provided to customers.

Government Regulatory Failure

For at least two decades, there has been a trend in many industrialized democratic nations toward less government, fewer restrictions on business, and more reliance on markets to correct themselves. To those who really believe in capitalism, this trend raises serious questions—not because government waste is a good thing (it isn't!), but because government plays several vital roles in creating an environment where the best that business has to offer can thrive. The question is how to find the optimal balance between freedom of action and control of market abuses.

Globalization trends have added to the difficulty of governments to adequately control the excesses and failures of capitalism while nurturing its many benefits. National governments cannot easily regulate businesses when capital, goods, information, and even labor flow so freely across borders. Too many nations feature weak, corrupt, or oppressive government officials who are more interested in private graft than the public good. Supranational institutions that would foster *sustainable* capitalism[6] are nonexistent or barely emergent. Meanwhile, business power and influence have grown tremendously, alongside increasingly unacceptable inequities in wealth distribution, access to education, human health and welfare, use of technology, and life opportunities in general. These inequities and power asymmetries have

Exhibit 1.2

Stakeholder: Any person, group, or organization who can affect or is affected by the organization's actions. Traditionally, a company's stakeholders include investors, employees, customers, suppliers, and local communities. Others—governments, NGOs, activists, the media—are also considered stakeholders today.

For the earliest popular discussion of business stakeholders, see R. Edward Freeman's book, *Strategic Management: A Stakeholder Approach* (Marshfield, MA: Pitman, 1984).

always existed, but in modern times they are contributing to a dangerously unstable world.[7]

Accountability to Stakeholders

To some extent, stakeholder groups serve as regulators of global business conduct. In many ways, NGO and market-based stakeholders are better able than governments to intervene in undesirable business behavior. No corner of the globe is without satellite communications, and thus visibility and multidirectional knowledge transfer are virtually immediate. On the one hand, this can make it much easier for a business to coordinate its activities and to increase its efficiency. On the other hand, it makes every business activity more broadly transparent and more instantly vulnerable to massive stakeholder pressures.

Customer stakeholders can be mobilized in a flash to buy certain goods or avoid certain others, based on non-economic values and objectives. Employee stakeholders are able to compare their situations with those of their peers around the world. NGO stakeholder groups like Greenpeace, Human Rights Watch, or OxFam now have virtually instant knowledge of incidents related to their concerns, and they have rapid communication tools permitting real-time cross-border organization and action. Thus, the visibility ensured by modern global communications lessens the control that business organizations can exert over their image, identity, and reputation, and raises the stakes, encouraging managers to pay stricter attention to the stakeholder impacts of their actions.

Firms and Their Managers

The fact is, in the absence of effective national and supranational governance of business's social and political impacts, firms and individual managers by default take on greater responsibility and a greater monitoring role for

11

their own actions and with each other. Every business needs to internalize a bigger sense of responsibility for creating and sustaining a stable world, a "level playing field" for capitalist enterprise, a baseline of dignity and opportunity for all people, a greater respect for the natural environment.

These are not merely stretch goals; they are becoming the system norms that make it possible for capitalism to thrive in the long term—to be sustainable well into the future. For those who believe that capitalism is the best system for economic welfare, these goals are imperatives.

"But It's Not My Job!"

So true—you aren't getting paid the big bucks to reform the world. So whose job is it to make sure that globalization doesn't cause more harms than benefits? Whose job is it to help your organization prosper in a bewildering environment? Whose job is it to be responsible for the impacts as well as the productivity of your department or function?

Okay, maybe it is your job, and theirs, and ours too. We want to help you think differently about individual responsibility for business citizenship. So how, in this morass of confusing messages, can managers make good judgments?

The Promise of Global Business Citizenship

This book provides practical and thought-provoking guidance on the ethical challenges of managing global business. By *global* we do not mean strictly cross-cultural, although many of the examples we use in the book involve doing business across borders. One of the many intriguing features of globalization is that it has crystalized ethical conflicts and contradictions by expanding the range of behaviors to which people are exposed, forcing us all to view the extremes of human conduct and to experience empathy for previously unknown or unnecessary suffering. Along the way, each of us is exposed to values, beliefs, and practices different from our own. Some of them are intuitively appealing; some violate our sense of fairness or our belief in human dignity. Greater cross-cultural awareness has allowed people all over the world to uncover many hidden assumptions of their own cultures, and to question whether those assumptions actually support human welfare. This means, however, greater turbulence and uncertainty for managers.

Managers are responsible for an enormous range of business decisions and are accountable to a number of individuals, groups, and organizations, who expect and demand different outcomes. Some of managers' responsibilities seem clearly governed by legal standards and the judicial process, others by market conditions, political processes, or ethical and community norms. But often the governing mechanism isn't simple and clearcut. The long-term consequences of short-term decisions can come back to haunt companies in liability judgments, regulatory burdens, failed reputations, and ultimately profitability declines and threats to survival.

To top it all off, the daily problems of managers are now global as well as local, cross-cultural as well as intra-country, and correspondingly difficult to grasp and to solve. "Muddling through" is not satisfactory; the stakes are much higher, the issues deeper, and the players so diverse. Standards of behavior and performance, and their enforcers, are less clear, often contradictory, or even nonexistent. Conflicts have become the norm, a particularly difficult situation for those well-meaning managers who prefer consistency and predictability in order to do their jobs well, be successful, and enjoy a good life.

In this book we offer you the process of *global business citizenship* (GBC), a conceptual approach to identifying principles of ethical management and then applying them concretely and with cultural respect. The GBC process requires:

1. a set of fundamental *values* embedded in the corporate code of conduct and in corporate policies that reflect universal ethical standards (sometimes called hypernorms[8]);
2. *implementation* throughout the organization with thoughtful discovery of where the code and policies fit well and where they might not fit (say, because of changing social expectations or local cultural variations);
3. *analysis and experimentation* to deal with problems of fit, conflicts, and contradictions; and
4. *formal, systematic processes* to organize and communicate organizational performance and the specific results of implementation and experiments in order to facilitate learning both within the organization and for its stakeholders and other organizations.

Our goal is to support executives and functional leaders in making good choices by offering a clear rationale for citizenship behavior and a practical set of analytical and implementation tools. To do this, we use the language of business citizenship and a variety of examples from traditional business issues as well as extraordinary social and environmental problems, and we examine how business leaders can rely upon good principles and implement good practices for managing across borders and cultures.

We want to encourage and empower you, and to increase your understanding of how capitalism can sustainably meet its promise of wealth creation and just distribution. The theory and practice of global business citizenship provide, we believe, the best path currently available to help managers solve many of these challenging problems. GBC gives managers a lens to clarify the nature of problems, a compass to point toward sustainable global capitalism, and a machete to maneuver in the global jungle.

Even more importantly, GBC offers a logical, practical framework for addressing social responsibility and ethical problems in a way that allows managers to *manage intentionally with integrity*—to meet your business obligations and maintain self-respect, to pass the profitability *and* the front-page tests, to act upon your best intentions, and to work toward your noblest dreams.

We are walking with you on this journey. We invite you and your company to become *global business citizens,* and to learn how social responsibility and ethical conduct can be embedded in your firm's daily practices and decision-making processes. We give you good arguments about why this path is best for you, your company, and your society. We encourage you to look at the imperatives of global strategy and the trap of ethical relativity in a new way. We urge you to think big about what capitalism means, what it has to offer, and what threatens it. Equally, we will help you stay grounded in the real daily problems and opportunities of managing ethically and responsibly in a chaotic global environment.

In short, GBC is theory and practice with promise. Stay with us to learn the theory, observe the practice, and think about applications in your own company. We believe that you will come to a new and more effective understanding of the impacts and opportunities of globalization. You will see that global business citizenship offers a promise of capitalism in full flower, to the greater benefit of all.

► 2 ◄

What's Wrong with the Status Quo?

Some days and for some managers the status quo seems mighty fine. Just getting through the workday without disaster is a major accomplishment. It is natural, and certainly understandable, that managers might resist one more "new idea" that promises greater organizational and personal success, but requires a lot of change to make it happen. It can seem too hard to embrace a new way of thinking about doing business that accepts greater ethical obligation and more responsibility for the results of business decisions.

But there are good reasons for managers not to be satisfied with the status quo of business values and practices. The changes taking place in today's world are profound, and they open up new worlds of risk and opportunity. Managers, their firms, and their industries all are facing challenges never before imagined, and even capitalism itself is under siege. In this chapter we'll briefly examine the modern business environment in terms of the challenges and threats it holds for social systems, companies, managers, and capitalism. Then we'll explore how the path of global business citizenship changes the view—from the thickets and thorns of ordinary practice to the inspiring vista of a better life in a better world.

Why spend time struggling with cultural value clashes when you could just apply headquarters' standards everywhere the company operates? Why worry about worker safety or pollution problems in countries that don't seem to care themselves? Why even try to keep jobs in the home country when customers apparently want ever-cheaper products? Competition to grow and to keep market share can be so tough that it's often difficult enough just to *maintain* the status quo, much less improve on it.

15

Exhibit 2.1

Levels of Analysis

In this book we lean pretty heavily on something the social scientists call "levels of analysis." We want to explain this device so you won't feel like we're jumping all over the place as we talk about the global economy, societies, industries, companies, and individual managers.

The main idea of "levels of analysis" is that at any particular point we are focusing on a particular kind of entity—an individual, a company, a group of companies in an industry, a national economy, a cross-border economy, the world society. Each kind of entity represents a portion of the human experience, and each has attributes that are unique to it. A society, for example, can't be "motivated" like an individual can be; an organization can have goals but an industry ordinarily wouldn't. Going from the other direction, we can see that world society necessarily contains much diversity of belief and action, but individuals usually seek a certain degree of consistency between their beliefs and their actions.

There are many ways to think about "levels of analysis," so here we're going to review just four of the main categories that we use—individual, organizational, systemic, and suprasystemic. You'll easily be able to spot the level we're operating on—language such as "you," "your company," "this society," or the "global economy" will tip you off.

Individual level of analysis: We're always aiming to reach you, the reader, the manager. We want to address the problems you face and offer you encouragement and motivation to walk and talk the GBC path. At the individual level we are concerned with perception and awareness, interpretation, decision and action, and consequences as they involve you personally, as a human being.

Organizational level of analysis: We know, though, that you don't do business all by yourself. You are most likely working in a company—a collection of people, perhaps a great many people—which can make your life infinitely more complex. So, we focus also on organizations, their structures and processes, their challenges and decision-making methods, their outputs and outcomes.

Systemic level of analysis: And we know that neither you nor your firm could do business if there weren't institutional structures such as a functioning economy, government and a rule of law, an educational system, and a "voluntary sector" or set of organizations devoted to fun, enlightenment, service, meaning, and all the other things that people do. Normally we'll be working at a systemic level when we talk about the social, political, and economic institutions within societies.

Suprasystemic level of analysis: These institutions, made up of organizations and individuals and their actions, form a tremendous overlapping network that we might think of as "society" or, at a more complex level, "global society." When we talk about "capitalism," for example, we are usually working at the suprasystemic level, thinking about the institutional structures and processes of capitalism across and regardless of borders.

Systems Are More Complex and Turbulent

Complexity and *turbulence* are words that organization theorists love to use. Their meaning is simple, though dealing with them is not. In any system under observation:

Complexity is the number of units and the relationships among them;

Turbulence means simply the rate and volatility of change.

Theorists make predictions about how organizations will structure themselves under different conditions of complexity and turbulence. For example, in a simple, placid environment, one might expect a business to . . . well . . .

Okay, these ideas were developed in the 1950s, when there might have been such a thing as a simple, placid business environment. In today's world, there's no such thing. Instead it's rapid, often unpredictable change, along with complicated, shifting networks of relationships and transactions. The manager's task is to try, try, try to keep the effects of complexity and turbulence from spinning out of control. It's a monumental challenge.

Global Competitive Pressures Are Ratcheting Up the Pace of Change

Technological "creative destruction" has always threatened mature industries and their steady stream of revenues and profits. But now the high-growth technologically advancing industries, like software and information processing, are moving through the product life cycle much more rapidly. It's almost no joke that this year's pricey miracle gadget is next year's loss leader at the local electronics supermarket. And in virtually all industries, the search for cost reduction strategies is pushing companies to use suppliers from far-flung parts of the globe or to set up their own plants there. Next year these business arrangements may become less competitive, so there will be new pressures to renegotiate and relocate.

More People Can Play, and Interdependencies Are Tightening

In current iterations of physics' chaos theory, the flapping of a butterfly's wings in Taipei can eventually result in a tornado in Kansas.[1] The reality of intricate patterns of global interconnectedness is unmistakable. In current global economics, Tom Friedman has written compellingly about the vast interdependencies among nations, cultures, and industries. In fact, he defines globalization in terms of interconnection:

> the inexorable integration of markets, nation-states and technologies to a degree never witnessed before—in a way that is enabling individuals,

17

corporations, and nation-states to reach around the world farther, faster, deeper and cheaper than ever before.[2]

In the introduction to his book, *The Lexus and the Olive Tree,* Friedman illustrates this definition by exploring the causes and effects of the 1997–98 Asian financial meltdown. Thailand's private banks closed abruptly when the Thai government was unable to maintain a fixed currency exchange rate. Frightened capital flew out of other Asian lands, causing a crash in global commodity prices, including oil, which caused Russia to default on its high-interest bonds, which caused global hedge funds to sell off liquid assets to pay their own debts, which crashed other successful emerging markets such as Brazil, which caused extreme volatility in U.S. Internet/tech stocks, which. . . . But you get the idea. Globally, interdependencies are tightening, and this cannot help but change the way business operates.

Societal Needs That Affect Business Are Increasing Everywhere, but Many Governments Seem Less Able or Willing to Address Them

Populations are growing and increasingly are concentrated in urban areas. Basic infrastructure is crumbling in many industrialized nations, and it is vitally needed in the developing world. For example, access to clean water is threatened in many urban areas that lack sewage systems and waste treatment plants. Roads and bridges need to be built or replaced. Social needs, such as education, health care, police and fire protection, and old age security, need to be provided. Net job loss exacerbates pressures on governments because tax revenue falls and government expenditures rise.

In the last two decades of the twentieth century, a worldwide trend could be seen toward reducing the size and importance of government. There are good arguments to be made for reducing government waste, of course, but it is possible to go too far. There are some tasks in the collective interest—including the interests of the business institution—that are simply handled best by a well-functioning government. As governments worldwide are weakened, no other institution is able to step into the breach. This creates challenges for businesses that thrive when conditions are lawful, safe, and politically stable, and where regulations ensure that all businesses play by the same rules.

Global Stakeholder Groups Enforce Demands

At the same time as governments have lost much of their power to meet public and business needs, stakeholder expectations of businesses have ratcheted up more than a notch. Global communications make it possible for corporate scandals and disasters to be seen instantaneously, with all the attendant pathos and emotion. Naturally, the media do not favor the "happy news" of corporate successes in improving social welfare by raising standards of living, preventing child and forced labor, improving drinking water supplies, or lobbying for government acceptance of basic human rights. Instead, the public learns about sweatshops, plant explosions, oil tanker accidents, destruction of valuable environmental resources, and more routine commercial practices that can spread harm to vulnerable populations.

It's no wonder, then, that global stakeholder groups have sprung up in the wake of business's globalization. Rising stakeholder concerns and expectations have materialized in a variety of ways. Boycotts and consumer actions, long a staple of consumer protection groups, now have the potential to circle the globe in a flash, as market leader Nike, Inc. discovered in the late 1990s when it was targeted by global human rights and religious groups. Environmental protection and human rights interest groups make use of the Internet, cell phones, and fax machines just as business executives do, and they can mobilize an attention-grabbing demonstration, a powerful lobbying campaign, or a proxy resolution drive in mere hours. Labor unrest in developing nations, such as Malaysia, the Philippines, and Indonesia, has grown, expressed in human rights language, though this sometimes comes as a surprise to companies that have settled in these countries in part because of the "quiet" and subordinate behaviors of labor.

Even if these activist stakeholders have little direct influence on the corporation, they are often able to convince core stakeholders—customers, suppliers, employees, stockholders, and other capital providers—that the company must address the group's concerns or face serious consequences. Investors supporting socially responsible investing have become a permanent legitimate segment of the shareholder community, accounting for over 11% of professionally managed portfolios in the United States in 2003. Approximately US$2.14 trillion is invested in socially responsible funds and initiatives, according to the Social Investment Forum. The rapid growth in social investing is astonishing: this figure is up from US$640 billion in 1995 and from only US$65 billion in 1985.[3]

Firms Face More Threats . . . and Opportunities

Competitors Play Hardball on an Uneven Playing Field

There are vast differences in the quality of life as well as the cost of living among the countries and regions of the world. Great efficiencies in transportation and communications have made it possible for manufacturing facilities to locate profitably in developing areas where the workforce is trainable and eager to work for low wages. Resulting changes in nations' balances of trade put stress on developed economies because of the flight of skilled and semi-skilled jobs and consequent loss of income. It simply isn't possible for an American or European or Japanese worker to survive on 30 cents an hour, but this is the nature of the competition from developing regions.

In addition, the larger the company, the more able it is to put downward pressure on the prices it pays its own suppliers. Wal-Mart is by no means the only example; in fact, General Motors started the trend toward squeezing suppliers in the early 1980s. This trend is a happy one if you're working at Wal-Mart or GM, but if you're one of their thousands of small and mid-sized suppliers, your life could become more and more miserable.

Cultural Differences Are Confusing

Lack of clarity about which cultural differences are critical to an organization's success, which threaten it, which are irrelevant, and which are problematic makes decision making complicated. Local managers may know the best way to satisfy local concerns, but they must defend their decisions to distant regional or central headquarters personnel who don't understand local norms and customs and who are focused on company-wide goals rather than local harmony. It is even more challenging when those distant regional or central headquarters executives must make the decisions and local managers must implement them, whether or not these decisions are consistent with local values and practices.

Short-Termism Is Rewarded

Publicly held companies have yet another challenge that their privately owned competitors do not face. Stock markets seem to resonate to promises of smooth growth in revenues and earnings from quarter to quarter. The reward is growth in stock price. Analysts and brokers expect *their* targets to be met or exceeded, and a company's stock can be trashed if those targets are missed.

These pressures encourage short-term thinking on the part of executives. Creating revenue for next quarter becomes more important than sustaining the enterprise for the next twenty years. One well-known way to boost a company's stock price is to lay off a substantial percentage of workers. Remember the consultants' admonition to become "lean and mean" as a response to global pressures? So often, however, it's not "dead weight" that's being cut, but productive workers who make contributions that simply can't be covered by the remaining workforce. Such short-termism can boost this quarter's stock price, but at a very high cost in years to come.

There are even cases where the top management team has decimated the workforce, piled up debt and spent cash on acquisitions and reorganizations, and boosted the stock price just in time to cash out their options and move on. What's left behind? A quivering fragment of a formerly good company, without the necessary resources to meet the challenges of the future.

Big Corporations Aren't Trusted

Too many large firms have reputations for unethical and irresponsible behavior. Sometimes these reputations are deserved, and sometimes not. But the costs of a bad reputation can be quite high. The demise of Arthur Andersen is an extreme example. A reputation for integrity is essential for public accounting firms, so the rapid loss of clients after its association with Enron and indictment for destruction of documents triggered dissolution of the firm.

Cynicism about big business increases with headlines about extraordinary executive compensation and board cronyism. Mutual funds are under scrutiny for giving a few clients (or their own managers) preference in trading to earn a better return on their accounts. Other clients are deciding to move their funds. The scandalous falls of Parmalat in Italy and of Ahold in the Netherlands generated massive ripples among the European Union and its trading partners.

Anyone who has read just a bit of business history knows that scandals come and go, and that some time periods—particularly those with minimal or no government oversight—are more inviting of fraud. We seem to have hit one of those time periods in the late 1990s and early 2000s. A consequence has been a huge decline in the public's willingness to trust businesses and their managers. Without trust, can an economy and its companies thrive?

Managers Are Caught in a Vise

The ever more complex global business environment offers new twists on the old management problem of simultaneously meeting multiple goals. Now there are more goals, set by more stakeholders with louder, more persistent, and more insistent voices, who work effectively together with the media to exert worldwide pressure. Too often, stakeholder expectations conflict, and managers are left to figure out which way to react to minimize damage to their organizations and their own careers. Pharmaceutical companies, for example, must manage conflicting demands of shareholders and analysts for profits, and the expectations of world health organizations and activists who advocate the donation of drugs to developing-world populations suffering from HIV/AIDS and other virulent diseases.

Figure 2.1 **The Manager's Vise**

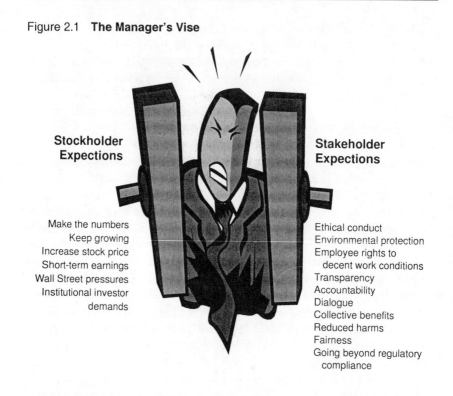

Stockholder Expections

Make the numbers
Keep growing
Increase stock price
Short-term earnings
Wall Street pressures
Institutional investor
  demands

Stakeholder Expections

Ethical conduct
Environmental protection
Employee rights to
  decent work conditions
Transparency
Accountability
Dialogue
Collective benefits
Reduced harms
Fairness
Going beyond regulatory
  compliance

The short story here is that the modern global manager is operating in a vise, with the pressures of financial analysts and stockholders and the countervailing pressures of other stakeholders threatening to crush him or her at any moment.

Risks for Poor Decisions Are Higher than Ever

Or at least they seem to be. Word gets out much faster with electronic communications systems available everywhere. Competitors know a lot more about your business and aren't far behind in taking advantage of wrong decisions and delays in meeting commitments. Media reports get to corporate critics and shape public opinion much more quickly than in the past. Accountability—and blame—are reaching both up and down the corporate structure. Pressure on managers is up, and job security is down.

Short-Termism Is Rewarded Here Too

Achieving "the number" for projected earnings targets or growth in market share is the primary goal for corporate leaders because the consequences of not achieving "the number" can be dire. Financial analysts may downgrade the stock, and investors will sell if they can find a more attractive investment. Managers who own stock worry about the value of their portfolios, and employees fear job layoffs and budget cutbacks. Corporate directors are beginning to ask unnerving questions about the quality of executive leadership and may "clean house" if the top management team does not produce as expected. It is naïve to think that executives will be able to forego achieving "the number" for very long when such consequences are clearly detrimental to their interests.

There's a Crisis of Confidence in Management Integrity

The crisis of confidence in business integrity reflects very personally on managers themselves. After the high-tech bubble that raised stock prices to an all-time high in the late 1990s, the twenty-first century opened to a long series of enormous business failures and scandals resulting from fraud, conflicts of interest and self-dealing, over-the-top "innovation" in financial instruments and tax dodges, and top management team arrogance—all nurtured by ineffective corporate governance. Jeff Skilling, Andy Fastow, Bernie Ebbers, Dennis Kozlowski, and members of the Rigas family are names permanently associated with white-collar crime and unethical dealings. Enron, Arthur Andersen, WorldCom, Tyco, HealthSouth, Ahold, Adelphia, and Parmalat are just a few of the companies that lost economic value, reputation, and, in the case of Arthur Andersen, its very existence due to ethical failures. And the consequences to their many stakeholders have been grave—from job losses and demise of employee retirement funds to suppliers left with bills outstanding to brown-outs and political crisis in California and elsewhere.

Investors seeking high returns at reasonable risk found instead a years-long pattern of falling stock prices and market turbulence. The public policy arena has given investors little more than patchwork band-aids like the Sarbanes-Oxley Act of 2002 in the United States.[4] Meanwhile, Wall Street brokerage and investment banking firms, including Merrill Lynch, GoldmanSachs, Citibank, and J.P.MorganChase, were charged with manipulating stock market valuation by coaxing or coercing false research reports and by essentially bribing top executives with unduly favorable investment opportunities, loan terms, and so on. They agreed to pay $1.4 billion to settle the charges and "get this behind them."

In this climate, investors are frightened and angry, and many are demanding dramatic changes in corporate governance and public policy oversight. Furthermore, managers who have been glorified as great wealth-creators are now doing hard time in prison! How can confidence be restored in the integrity of top management and the market system? How can managers avoid the terrible personal consequences of a giant misstep?

How to Manage/Juggle Relationships for One's Own Career?

Adding to the stress of the manager caught in the vise is worry about how to manage internal relationships to keep one's job, earn bonuses and stock options, and get promoted. Fitting into the corporate culture may require compromises with one's personal values, and temptations abound to keep quiet and "go along to get along."

How can businesses and managers convince people that they will do the right thing? It is essential to build trust, and to do so as rapidly as possible. Building trust means convincing stakeholders that you consider their welfare and take responsibility for the consequences of your decisions. It means acting on bigger and more lasting concerns than profits at any cost. More stockholders need to step up to the plate, as some institutional and individual investors are now doing, and agree that this is also in their long-term best interests. It also means enforcing higher standards of individual executive conduct to eliminate self-dealing.

Managerial discretion, influence, and autonomy are bound to shrink if individual executive and business behaviors continue to focus on immediate self-interest and short-term financial performance at the expense of other legitimate stakeholder objectives, including the long-term objectives of environmental sustainability and a life of dignity and opportunity for everyone. The short-term focus is too subject to the opportunism, fraud, and exploitation that destroy trust or prevent it from forming in the first place. Focusing on sustainable business value, on the other hand—the way of global business citizenship—is the way to create trust in a turbulent world and thus to enhance managers' positive influence.

The performance vise is not going to disappear, of course. But there will be more room to develop adequate and ethical responses to the range of pressures that managers face if stakeholders have greater confidence in executive integrity and business responsibility.

Capitalism Itself Is Threatened

There is an even greater danger, however, than losses to individual managers and companies. Indeed, the greatest threat to capitalism itself may be apathy by business leaders in dealing with legitimate stakeholder needs and expectations. The enemies of capitalism are also the enemies of satisfying

Figure 2.2 **Managerial Influence**

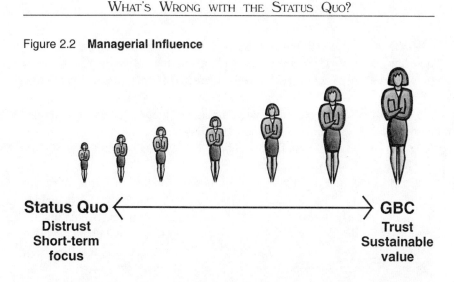

Status Quo ⟵⟶ **GBC**

Distrust	Trust
Short-term	Sustainable
focus	value

organizational performance and of a life well-lived. Fundamental to sustainable capitalism are socioeconomic questions about the nature of the capitalist institution and sociopolitical questions about who gets what and who controls business behavior. To these questions we now turn.

The Ideal Is of Wealth, Autonomy, and a Good Life for Anyone

Capitalism thrives in a great many circumstances. It is an adaptive system of innovation, production, distribution, and wealth creation, able to tolerate wide variations in political regime, socioeconomic and demographic profiles, natural resources, cultural patterns, and ethical values. It is egalitarian in the sense that its rewards are not limited to an aristocracy or a chosen few, but are available to *anyone* who can generate surplus value and leverage that value to grow a business.

The Reality Is a Widening Gulf Between Rich and Poor

A fundamental criticism that business has to address is who benefits and who suffers from global business activities. The current reality of global capitalism often appears to be skewed toward widening gaps in wealth, dependent upon exploitation of the poor and the earth's resources. Its leaders too often exhibit a head-in-the-sand approach to human rights and environmental abuses. These are the very problems that could ultimately bring capitalism down by providing evidence that plays into the hands of charismatic extremists of many persuasions or by forcing imposition of controls that reduce the freedom essential for successful long-term capitalism.

Today a great gulf divides those who believe that capitalism offers the best hope for humanity and those who believe that capitalism is the most powerful barrier to achieving human welfare and enlightenment. On the side of democratic-capitalist enterprise are those who make a moral argument—not a purely self-centered one—based upon the "greatest good for the greatest number" (utilitarianism) and individual human rights. Adam Smith argued long ago that the free pursuit of self-interest eventually yields the highest level of collective economic welfare.

On the other side, as Tom Friedman has so vividly illustrated, there are people who believe that capitalist societies are by definition shallow, exploitative, and morally bankrupt.[5] Some of those others are incensed that intense poverty in the developing world supports first-world wealth. Others are filled with fear that their way of life is being destroyed, and this fear has been turning to rage. Global business is not seen by them as a provider of all things good and desirable, but as a vessel of Satan that rips apart traditional beliefs and ways of life as emphatically as a Boeing 767 rips apart a skyscraper. And some know that capitalism and its attendant values will erode their personal power bases and deprive them of the wealth, power, and privilege they enjoy at the cost of others' dependence and suffering. Business leaders cannot ignore these deeply held beliefs and power structures if they want capitalism to thrive.

Capitalism Requires Stable Environments and a Rule of Law

Global businesses benefit from stable political and social environments. Political stability can be achieved for awhile via dictatorship, military control, or foreign intervention, but these modes are not inherently stable and eventually spawn revolution, sabotage, terrorism, and other threats to social order. As capitalism spreads, moral values and citizenship behaviors play a significant role in creating needed stability.

The rights and privileges of citizenship attach to duties, and these duties also must be claimed by businesses. This language of rights and duties is the language of ethics as well as citizenship. It is a language that connects disparate human activities into an interdependent global web of cause and effect. Aristotle, writing of citizenship long ago, developed three essential duties of the citizen: participating in the political process, paying taxes, and defending against enemies of the state and its people. Business citizenship, similarly, involves active participation in defense against threats to capitalism as well as assertive rethinking of how to bring the capitalist dream to all the world's peoples.

Sustainable Capitalism Requires a Base of Human Rights and a Healthy Natural Environment

Capitalism operates best in fulfilling its promise of providing the highest level of human welfare when it fosters human freedom, opportunity, and dignity within a strong community. At least, that's what its supporters and beneficiaries think. Economists know that capitalism works best when individuals can act freely and with full information within a system that protects individual property and other rights. Individual liberty and economic welfare work together.[6]

There's a lot to be said for capitalism's ability to raise living standards, nurture innovation, demand better and broader education, and open up opportunities for individuals. As religions scholar Huston Smith tells it, the ideals of capitalism are simple and Semitic: things of the world are so good, everybody should have more of them![7] This is the ultimate capitalist ethic. It is not an ethic of greed or of winner-take-all in every market, but *an ethic of widespread economic welfare.*

In order for this to happen, humans need to be free and able to choose, and there must be a rule of law where all have equal access. It is not an accident (though neither is it inevitable) that capitalism thrives in democracies; it is not an accident that so many of the world's peoples long to participate in the American, Canadian, or European economy.

So—if the issue is that the "haves" keep the "have nots" from having, then an overt and rapid transformation of the world's economies that is coupled with compassionate and citizen-like corporate behaviors in all local arenas might go a long way toward convincing people worldwide that capitalists are not the merciless exploiters, rather that capitalism is the path to more and better material goods, that democracy and personal liberty are the necessary companions of capitalist satisfaction, and that religious values need not be threatened by universal political and economic freedom.

Governments Are Too Weak to Provide What Capitalism Needs

Another major question that managers must ponder is this: What will they have to do in order to get the freedom to operate? A first cut at answering this question is "obey the laws wherever you do business" because of national sovereignty. But more is required than legal compliance to meet stakeholder expectations today.

National sovereignty has a long and important history in global organization, and a nation's legal requirements play a significant role in shaping how companies do business. Many examples can be found to show that minimum

27

legal requirements have improved the operations of markets and the behaviors of firms. However, just doing what the law requires and allows is not enough to meet ethical expectations for at least three reasons.

One reason is that, even in the most democratic and responsive countries, the law-making process is typically slow and subject to many competing interests and differing cultural norms. Legal requirements are often compromises to limit the costs of complying with new rules rather than guidelines for optimal business performance. Legal standards and regulatory requirements can differ considerably, so that a company operating in many jurisdictions faces a confusing array of local rules.

Another reason is that capital and information now flow so freely across borders that national sovereignty can no longer be much of a force in shaping business operations. If a company doesn't like one nation's legal or regulatory requirements, it can usually find another place to incorporate or operate. Local laws can even become less protective of human beings and the environment, in a perverse "race to the bottom" when developing nations are competing for *any* share of the economic benefits of the developed world.

A third reason is that too often national sovereignty has provided cover for dictators, thieves, and local warlords to have their way with a traumatized population. The United Nations has occasionally intervened—as in Somalia, Rwanda, Bosnia, and Liberia—to override national sovereignty rights with concern for the welfare of citizens and minority populations.[8] But more often, national sovereignty has prevailed even in the face of mass starvation, tribal vendettas, and "ethnic cleansing" *aka* genocide. When the government is corrupt, or powerless, or over-powerful, the law will be ineffective in achieving the stable environment in which capitalist enterprise thrives.

It is clear that compliance with local law does not serve as sufficient guidance for multinational enterprises. And, in the absence of a supranational government, and with declining power available to national governments, business itself has to take on a self-governing aspect. There is a long history of industry self-regulation, with varying degrees of enforcement, visibility, and accountability, so this is not a new phenomenon.[9] In the global environment, as in other complex and turbulent environments, self-regulation is coming to be accepted as the best way to create a stable business environment and to ensure that all parties play by the same rules. As Virginia Haufler observes in her study of industry self-regulation, there are several factors that seem to yield greater efforts to self-regulate:

> a high risk of government regulation at the national or international level; relatively low economic competition but high asset specificity; high probability of transnational activist pressure; reputation as a key asset of the

company or industry involved; and high levels of information exchange, learning, and consensus within the industry.[10]

Business self-regulation is indeed a way of asserting "a public role for the private sector," the title of Haufler's book. The concept of global business citizenship, as we shall see shortly, articulates a political and social rationale for business self-regulation and shows how businesses can be full participants in achieving a better life for all the world's citizens.

Business Will Have to Fill in the Gaps

Business can begin to assume its citizenship role by moving away from the slick, superficial "we're just here to make a buck" image it often cultivates. Business needs to claim its true identity, to redefine itself as the powerful institutional force it already *is*. Then it can undertake the mighty task of proving to the world's peoples that "capitalism is best, it leads to greater happiness, it respects human rights, and it ultimately makes justice possible." Consequently, every business organization is a member of a powerful transformative global institution, and every manager therefore has certain responsibilities with respect to the world's well-being.

The conflicts between owner-stakeholder value and other-stakeholder value and between business and ethics are false dichotomies.[11] Today's global economic environment has less room for the externalization of costs onto innocent third parties and increasingly supports the activism and influence of a multitude of stakeholders. There is strong evidence that a link exists between poor financial performance and irresponsible management practice.[12] Stakeholder expectations regarding business's responsibilities for the "triple bottom line"[13]—financial, social, and environmental—are increasingly focused on every firm's contributions to sustainable development and long-term value creation.

Capitalism Requires Public Support

The developed world is being called upon to live up to its ideals. Business must either stop standing in the way or become a much more active supporter of positive change. The "we don't do politics" response just won't work as a defense against self-regulation, ethical conduct, and involvement in citizenship; we know far too much now about business's deep and abiding involvement in political matters that interest and concern them.

We believe that our business leaders are much better than this, much more capable of guiding the world toward a better future by doing what they do best—conducting normal business operations. But there's a catch: The aim of business organizations is not to make as much money as possible, but *to make as much money as they can within the limitations of ethical conduct, guaranteed human rights, environmental protection, and other legitimate expressions of individual and collective interest.*

Business leaders must play a role because of their brainpower, control of resources, and global reach. Global business citizenship has a dual purpose: to make the world safe for capitalism, and to make capitalism safe for the world, its people, and the natural environment. This means *promoting choice*—allowing people to reap the appropriate rewards from their work; allowing people the freedom to develop as much as they choose to; allowing people to live in dignity, no matter what their particular circumstances.

The Promise of Global Business Citizenship

The predominant realities of the manager's status quo—increasing interdependence and higher risks of making poor decisions—take on a new urgency in light of threats to the very existence of capitalist freedom to operate. There isn't much that can reduce the momentum of increasing interdependence, except for disaster scenarios that need to be avoided. But the good news is that the risks of poor decision making can be reduced.

Global business citizenship provides a template for grasping the big picture of business's role in creating a desirable future for the organization and all its stakeholders. And it illuminates the vectors that begin in complex problems and lead to systematic solutions. That is, GBC offers both a theoretical lens and a practical toolbox to managers trying to grapple with the difficult problems of citizenship and ethical conduct in an unsettled world.

A bit of good news about the status quo: We see the beginning of such activities in industries that rely on developing nations for their natural resources or their semi-skilled labor. Market leaders in apparel, sports shoes, and several other consumer goods areas have begun to forge coalitions with human rights organizations to monitor suppliers and enforce codes of conduct designed to protect workers from abuse and exploitation.[14] We will learn about some of these efforts in upcoming chapters.

There is also considerable attention throughout business communities to global codes of business conduct. The United Nations Universal Declaration of Human Rights and the Rio Declaration have become more than dusty documents of idealistic rhetoric. The United Nations Global Compact, launched in late 1999, is gathering at least the rhetorical support of hundreds of global firms. The Global Reporting Initiative (GRI) is enrolling more firms each year to report publicly about their social and environmental performance in addition to their economic performance. Even the Millennium Development Goals—a hugely ambitious set of objectives for ending world poverty and environmental degradation (see Exhibit 2.2)—have the attention of world business leaders participating in the International Business Leaders Forum (IBLF), sponsored by the Prince of Wales. How can businesses make a difference? Here are the domains of action suggested by IBLF participants:

> Most companies have some impact on development and can make a contribution in the following spheres of influence:
>
> • Their core business activities—in the workplace, the marketplace, and along the supply chain;
> • Their social investment and philanthropy activities; and
> • Their engagement in public policy dialogue and advocacy activities.[15]

This, too, is how global business citizenship works—in normal business operations, in stakeholder relations and charitable giving, in interactions with government, and in attempts to influence public policy.

Conclusion

The principles of global business citizenship are addressed to the millions of managers who would prefer to work for long-term gains and a real chance at meaningful success. In order to be sustainable, the global business institution and its member-companies must and should identify and implement policies to promote ethical conduct, to ensure basic human rights, to protect the environment, and to move toward social justice and collective well-being, wherever businesses operate.

This has to be done with due consideration for cultural differences and with ultimate respect for common humanity. Global business citizenship helps managers resolve these issues, and it allows for the irrevocable reconciliation of ethics and business.

Fundamental to sustainable capitalism are socioeconomic questions about the nature of the capitalist institution, sociopolitical questions about who gets what, who has power and who should have it, and philosophical questions about what defines "the good life." GBC can be a vessel that holds what is good and true about capitalism, as well as what is good and right for human beings and the earth. It is necessary because capitalism cannot thrive and spread its many benefits around the globe if its advocates and practitioners do not satisfy the multiple legitimate claims of stakeholder groups, especially in support of human rights and sustainable development.

Exhibit 2.2

The Millennium Development Goals

As the 21st century began, the United Nations adopted a set of objectives to dramatically improve the quality of life worldwide by the year 2015. Signatory nations committed to provide annual contributions of 0.17 percent of GNP toward meeting these objectives. Based on the fundamental values of freedom, equality, solidarity, tolerance, respect for nature, and shared responsibility, the Millennium Development Goals are as follows:

1. *Eradicate extreme poverty and hunger*
   - Reduce by half the proportion of people living on less than a dollar a day.
   - Reduce by half the proportion of people who suffer from hunger.

2. *Achieve universal primary education*
   - Ensure that all boys and girls complete a full course of primary schooling.

3. *Promote gender equality and empower women*
   - Eliminate gender disparity in primary and secondary education preferably by 2005, and at all levels by 2015.

4. *Reduce child mortality*
   - Reduce by two thirds the mortality rate among children under five.

5. *Improve maternal health*
   - Reduce by three quarters the maternal mortality ratio.

6. *Combat HIV/AIDS, malaria and other diseases*
   - Halt and begin to reverse the spread of HIV/AIDS.
   - Halt and begin to reverse the incidence of malaria and other major diseases.

7. *Ensure environmental sustainability*
   - Integrate the principles of sustainable development into country policies and programmes; reverse loss of environmental resources.
   - Reduce by half the proportion of people without sustainable access to safe drinking water.
   - Achieve significant improvement in the lives of at least 100 million slum dwellers, by 2020.

8. *Develop a global partnership for development*
   - Develop further an open trading and financial system that is rule-based, predictable and non-discriminatory. Includes a commitment to good governance, development and poverty reduction—nationally and internationally.

(continued)

- Address the least developed countries' special needs. This includes tariff- and quota-free access for their exports; enhanced debt relief for heavily indebted poor countries; cancellation of official bilateral debt; and more generous official development assistance for countries committed to poverty reduction.
- Address the special needs of landlocked and small island developing States.
- Deal comprehensively with developing countries' debt problems through national and international measures to make debt sustainable in the long term.
- In cooperation with the developing countries, develop decent and productive work for youth.
- In cooperation with pharmaceutical companies, provide access to affordable essential drugs in developing countries.
- In cooperation with the private sector, make available the benefits of new technologies—especially information and communications technologies.

Source: http://www.un.org/millenniumgoals/ (accessed January 23, 2005).

The need for leaders in global business citizenship, although building for decades, has never been more apparent or more urgent. Global business citizens recognize that the most serious threats to capitalism are failures of liberty, human rights, and civil justice, as well as environmental degradation. It seems clear that peace and prosperity can never be established in a world where liberty is the privilege of a few and justice is available only to some. A new ethic must emerge, one that builds upon the obvious interconnections and similarities among the world's peoples and that harnesses the drive and innovativeness of capitalism.

Global business citizens can lead in these and their own initiatives by learning how to orient their business operations to support freedom and justice, and by serving as exemplars within their industries. Stay tuned for the theory of global business citizenship.

➤ 3 ◄

The Lens of Global
Business Citizenship

Citizenship is a very big idea. For many centuries, philosophers, government leaders, and ordinary people have thought about what citizenship means, what it should accomplish, how it works, and to whom it applies. Corporations often claim to be "good citizens," and stakeholders typically want them to act as good citizens. But what does this mean, especially now in the global economy?

Our task in this chapter is to show you how the concept of citizenship for individual persons can be translated to citizenship for business organizations, and how the local and national arenas of citizenship can be expanded to incorporate new global realities.

A global business citizen is much like an individual in terms of expectations at home and when traveling, working, and living in other countries. The ultimate aim of a *theory* of business citizenship, grounded in political theory, is to illuminate the structural and moral ties among business organizations, human beings, and social institutions, and to offer guidance on the rights and responsibilities accruing to business organizations in the global environment. In practical terms, a good theory makes it more likely that business practice will be effectively guided by citizenship principles.

The Concept of Citizenship

In simple terms, citizenship relates to the particular status of membership in a political unit. For example, one is a citizen of Buenos Aires, Argentina, or the nation of South Africa, or Cook County, Illinois, or the European Union.

Citizenship typically involves certain protections that are based upon rights guaranteed by the political and legal constitutions of the polity. Most such

---

Exhibit 3.1

What Is a Global Business Citizen?

A **global business citizen** is a business enterprise (including its managers) that responsibly exercises its rights and implements its duties to individuals, stakeholders, and societies within and across national and cultural borders.

---

rights involve freedom from interference and freedom from harm. For example, in the United States the Constitution has a Bill of Rights that specifies rights of the citizens to freedom of speech, freedom of assembly, and the right against self-incrimination, among others.

Citizens are likely also to have duties. Israeli citizens, for example, are obliged to serve in the military, and in most polities, citizens have a duty to pay taxes. At the local level, rules about when rights and duties apply to the citizen are determined by the polity. For example, in the United States you have the right to vote at age 18, and the duty to register for military service at age 18, but you have the right to representation at trial at any age.

There is considerable debate and justifiable concern over the question of whether businesses—or any other organizations—can be "citizens" in the same way that people are. First there's the issue of rights and who—or what—has them. Should corporations in constitutional democracies have the same rights to, say, free speech as individuals do? Do corporations deserve the same rights of noninterference, for example, or freedom from harm? Isn't there something different, and special, about the status of human citizens?

Then there's the question of duties. If citizens have a duty to pay taxes, shouldn't corporations, if citizens, also pay taxes? Should they be able to shelter their income in tax-free zones abroad in order to avoid paying taxes at home? Most importantly, there's the issue of political participation and power: is it fair that large corporations so greatly exceed the ability of human citizens to influence the direction of government? On the other hand, isn't it fair that corporations should have a voice in the public policies that affect them?

We do not mean to discount these questions by calling them legalistic, but indeed they are, and can be resolved only by legal statutes, judicial decisions, and cultural norms. In our globalized economy, though, *national* laws are insufficient, and international laws are in their infancy. So, we want to call attention to a way around this problem in the absence of a coherent international legal framework: the idea of business organizations as *secondary citizens.*

It very often serves human purposes to treat organizations as ongoing entities with independent goals and legal rights. However, there's no reason to suppose that organizations actually *are* independent of human purposes or citizenly duties, much less equal to humans in status. Organizations are always created and maintained to meet community purposes. If those purposes are not being met, the organization can be restructured or disbanded. The community sets the rules for corporate creation and governance. In this sense, organizations don't have the same claim to a "right to life" as the human person does. Therefore, organizations are not entitled to the same rights to noninterference and freedom from harm (although society may decide to grant *some* such rights to organizations).

Furthermore, citizenship typically means more than just a political standing. It also reflects the citizen's identity that is bound up with the nature and history of the community. Boundaries and rules of membership are highly significant, and the obligation to consider one's own community as important becomes justifiable and perhaps even required. Citizens of the community typically have a duty to participate in making rules about membership and in carrying them out in order to preserve the distinctive culture of the community. There is every reason to think of business organizations as citizens in this sense.

So, how can businesses be citizens? First, by being subordinate in value to human citizens, and second, by upholding the identity and values of the communities in which they operate.

Making the Leap from Individual to Business Citizenship

Because citizenship is ordinarily a status of *persons in a place,* we need to examine two shifts in the level of analysis to arrive at GBC. That is, we need to be able to move conceptually:

1. from the individual person to the business organization as citizen, and
2. from the local polity to a global setting.

Table 3.1 illustrates the four states of citizenship that exist when one considers individual persons and organizations as units of analysis, and local scope or global scope as levels of analysis.[1] (If you're not familiar with the theoretical device of typology construction, check out Exhibit 3.2 first.)

Reading across Table 3.1, we see that individual persons can be local citizens of a polity, and/or global citizens of the planet. Similarly, organizations can be "corporate citizens" tied to a particular culture or polity, or they can be "global citizens," acting responsibly within and across polities.

Exhibit 3.2

Building Theory: The Idea of Typologies

Simply put, theories are efforts to explain:

1. what happens or what exists (descriptive theory),
2. what will happen if something else happens (instrumental or causal theory), or
3. why something happens the way it does (explanatory theory).

In science, theory can be based on logic (deductive theory) or on observation (inductive theory). What we're going to do in this chapter is to lay out a deductive, descriptive theory of business citizenship, based on a set of typologies.

A typology is a way of categorizing some class of phenomena according to some relevant variable. The simplest typology employs two extreme values of a single variable, as in "There are two kinds of people in the world. . . ." The usual implication is that everybody can be categorized this way, and you're either one or the other, but not both. That is, the categories are *exhaustive* and *mutually exclusive*.

A two-by-two (or 2×2) typology cross-hatches the extremes of two variables. Here's an example of a very simple 2×2, meant to reason about the relationship between, say, whether an act is legal or not, and whether it is ethical or not, and what could be expected under the various combinations:

	Legal	Illegal
Ethical		
Unethical		

Now we have established the structure of our typology, and the next step is to logically name the categories represented by the cells in the remainder of the table. There are four cells, and thus four categories: legal and ethical, illegal but ethical, unethical but legal, and illegal and unethical.

We now have a set of categories that represent all the logical combinations of the extremes of legality and ethics, and we can use this set as a single variable in other typologies. For example, we might want to make a typology that classifies behaviors by their ethicality/legality and their profitability, resulting in an 8-cell typology.

In this chapter, we construct typologies based on ideas about citizenship, global strategy, levels of analysis, and degree of moral certainty. Not all of our typology categories are meant to be mutually exclusive and exhaustive; some are inclusive of the cell before but go beyond, sort of like saying, "Rain is nice, but sunshine is nice and warm too." Categories, whether mutually exclusive or additive or simply descriptive, help the theorist to sort out the issues with respect to the categories.

And so, using a series of typologies, we end up with a theory about why companies can be citizens and how they can think about putting citizenship behaviors into practice.

Table 3.1

Four States of Citizenship

Unit of analysis	Level of Analysis	
	Local scope	Global scope
The individual	CELL 1 Local citizen A person can be a citizen of a city, province, or nation	CELL 3 Global citizen A person can be a "citizen of the world"
The business organization	CELL 2 Corporate citizen A company can be a citizen of a local community or nation	CELL 4 Global business citizen A company can be a "citizen of the world"

Sources: Logsdon and Wood, 2002; Wood and Logsdon, 2002.

The Local Citizen

Cell 1 represents the ordinary meaning of citizen as a person who holds a legal relationship to and often a national or cultural identity with a specific "local" polity such as a town or city, a state or province, a nation, or a supra-national/regional grouping like the European Union.

Citizenship is defined by the rules of that polity, which normally specify what relationship exists between the interests of persons and the polity as well as the rights and duties that accompany citizenship. Of course, individuals typically are citizens of a variety of polities at various levels of government (town, state, country, region), and some are even privileged to have dual national citizenship.

Political theorists have argued for centuries about whether the government exists to serve citizens, or citizens hold their status to serve government. In modern times, the former position typically carries more weight. Governments are seen as entities that guarantee the baseline conditions for acceptable human life in communities. Citizens are typically granted a bundle of civil and political rights (voting, due process, individual liberties), and they are expected to fulfill duties such as those Aristotle named so long ago: paying taxes, participating in political affairs, and helping to defend the government from its enemies through military or other service.

The Corporate Citizen

Despite the concerns raised earlier, it is not a leap of faith to think of business organizations as citizens of local communities or of nations, as in Cell 2. This is the fundamental perspective underlying most current ideas about "corporate citizenship." A corporate citizen is a business organization that is a responsible player in its local environment. Its community activities emphasize voluntarism and charity, not rights and duties, and the organization's social identity tends to reflect the local culture.

The duties of citizenship need not be spelled out exactly in order to exist. That is, both individual and corporate citizens may be expected to fulfill some citizenship role without having that role specified precisely. The idea is to give back *something* relevant and significant in support of a long-term viable relationship between government and its citizens.

Your firm probably has some community outreach initiatives that are intended to improve the quality of life of human citizens that include the workforce, customers, and other stakeholders. The employees probably volunteer in community projects, and your company may make financial contributions to the local schools or nonprofit arts organizations. In these ways your company demonstrates its willingness to give back to the community in which it operates. There's no requirement that your company make charitable contributions or sponsor the kids' soccer club, but there are a wealth of opportunities to interact and assist in ways that make sense for the company and its employees.

The Global Citizen

Cell 3 refers to the history of ideas concerning individuals as "citizens of the world." The global citizen is a person who holds a relationship to all peoples, regardless of polity, based on ideas of common humanity, interdependence, and universalism, and grounded in a few key rules or laws concerning universal rights and duties of persons to each other. When one begins to travel outside his/her own community, this awareness tends to develop or is strengthened.

By the late twentieth century, technological advances in communications and transportation had made it possible for billions of people around the globe to observe the same events contemporaneously, watch the same entertainment, eat the same food, experience the same disasters, and to some extent develop a shared understanding of their common humanity.[2] An understanding of the commonalities among peoples of different cultures rather than a focus on differences between them gives one the sense of belonging to a larger human community, and provincial thinking fades.

James W. Nickel observes that the United Nations Declaration of Human Rights gave the world a common language of rights that has shaped national and international relations for decades:

> Shaky governments facing severe problems often try to preserve their power by jailing, torturing, and murdering those who oppose their rule. When cases of this sort come to our attention, we are now likely to describe them as violations of human rights—instead of simply saying that they are unjust, immoral, or barbaric.[3]

In addition, having a common language of rights and a concept of universal "citizenship" gives credence and power to non-governmental mechanisms of social control that can override the politics of national sovereignty. In particular, cross-national market pressures of consumption and investment, along with global media attention and risks to reputation, have come to the fore as viable social control mechanisms in the hands of global stakeholders concerned with human rights violations in sovereign nations.

The Global Business Citizen

Finally, in Cell 4, a Global Business Citizen is not just Swiss, or Chinese, or American—it is a company that thinks globally and acts locally. Here, business organizations are also considered citizens of the world, with corresponding rights and responsibilities. To repeat the definition:

> A global business citizen is a business enterprise (including its managers) that responsibly exercises its rights and implements its duties to individuals, stakeholders, and societies within and across national and cultural borders.

The point of Table 3.1 is to illustrate that the idea of global citizenship for business organizations requires two major transformations: from person to organization, and from local to global arena. As we'll see, each of these transformations involves problems and opportunities as we strive to understand just what global business citizenship is and what it means for managers.

Three Approaches to Citizenship

What type of citizen is your company? Is it a law-abiding, mind-your-own-business kind of firm? Is it a rah-rah local good citizen, always jumping in to help out and to boost the community? Is it an enterprise with a strong set of values and operating principles that apply everywhere it does business?

When a company says it is a "good citizen," what does that mean? Political theory offers a variety of meanings and types of citizenship, but we have boiled them down to three currently relevant approaches to citizenship: the minimalist theory of civic association, the communitarian model, and the universal principles perspective. These are useful in sorting out practical and ideological differences in relationships among persons, organizations, communities, and polities. Two of these approaches lack the elements essential to global business citizenship and cannot in the long run yield a capitalism that is sustainable. To illustrate the differences among these three approaches, we'll use an example of how a business might define and respond to a pollution problem within each of these perspectives.

Minimalist Citizenship: A Status of Convenience

The minimalist theory of civic association values individual liberty and the pursuit of self-interest above all. In the minimalist's dream world, there are no restraints on his or her behavior. In the real world, however, the minimalist acknowledges that some restraints are necessary to keep others from infringing on one's right to liberty.[4]

Thus, civic associations form when residents of a common jurisdiction recognize and agree to certain rules that regulate their conduct. Social units (like governments) exist because they are essential for individual survival, but social bonds are seen as weak. Compliance with laws is seen as contributing to achievement of personal goals, and citizenship is viewed as a status of convenience as long as it serves citizens' self-interests and liberty.

Civic association is not to be confused with community, which has the special meaning of a shared enterprise. The moral relationship among citizens in a civic association requires the right to justice and equal treatment under law. These rights could be put into effect as basic legal rights such as the right to protection from robbers, the right to legal representation, and so on. Rights evolve and are extended to more groups only as the association discovers intolerable problems that are not dealt with effectively under the more constricted system of rights. This essentially libertarian view of citizenship requires equal treatment in terms of "negative rights"—that is, the right of citizens to pursue their own interests without interference. This approach permits citizen participation in rule-making but has no penalties for citizens who do not participate.

Minimalism has a direct counterpart in the stockholder view of the firm. Contracts—among persons who freely enter into them with full knowledge—form the assumed structure of business transactions in the minimalist perspective. The firm itself is not a real entity but is merely a "nexus of contracts"

41

among suppliers of various inputs whose rights are negotiated as part of their contracts with the firm. In this view, shareholders provide capital and acquire property ownership. Management's role is to coordinate the negotiating process among the various input providers, acting as agents for the shareholder-principals. Shareholders are vulnerable because their delegation of power to agent-managers leaves them with high monitoring and control costs and a subsequent higher risk that managers will succumb to temptation and act in their own interest instead of in the interest of the shareholders. Corporation law, in this view, exists largely to protect the shareholders from managerial opportunism, but only as a supplement to market forces, that is, as a correction to the rare market failure.

Managers operating with the minimalist perspective seek the lowest cost of production in order to maximize profit. They would prefer not to spend money to control pollution, but rather dump it into the air, water, or land. If other members of the polity sue because the waste is a nuisance or make a convincing case that their rights are being violated, managers will either install the minimum pollution control equipment or they will relocate. There is no loyalty or attachment to the civic association for a minimalist person or company.

Simply put, in a minimalist world, a business organization is merely a shell within which individual sales, employment, and investment contracts are negotiated and fulfilled. If and only if the principals (in capitalist organizations, the shareholders) perceive it to be in their self-interest, they may direct the organization to act in particular citizen-like ways such as contributing to charity or participating in a community event. The language of citizenship might even be used, but the motivation is not to provide a collective good or to contribute to society's well-being, but only to achieve a private end.[5] *The organization itself cannot "be" a citizen, analogous to individual persons, in the minimalist approach.*

Communitarian Citizenship: One for All

Communitarian reasoning embeds citizens in a particular social context, rather than viewing them as essentially autonomous, detached decision makers and actors as the other two models do. One's personal identity is bound up with the nature and history of one's community, culture, or country. Boundaries and rules of membership become highly significant, and the obligation to consider one's own community as more important than other communities becomes justifiable and perhaps even required.

Citizens of the community have a duty to participate in making rules about membership and conduct and in carrying them out in order to preserve the

Exhibit 3.3

"Good Corporate Citizens"

A great many companies consider themselves to be good corporate citizens. You might think that this means that they are responsible and law-abiding, but in fact it generally means that they are charitable and do "good deeds." The "corporate citizenship" category in *Industry Week*'s annual "100 Best-Managed Companies" is measured as percent of pretax earnings given to nonprofits. In *Fortune*'s annual "most admired" list, the corporate citizenship category measures the company's community involvement and sometimes that of its employees separately.

Certainly it is admirable, and likely a sign of good management, for a company to engage in philanthropy and community volunteer activities. However, these things won't make a company into a global business citizen.

It's like the idea of "random acts of kindness," which finds so much favor with so many people. But why should kindness be random instead of routine? Similarly, why should a company's community responsibility be voluntary? If we as individuals have a duty to be kind, is it a stretch to say that business organizations have a duty to be responsible?

distinctive culture of the community. According to the communitarian view, rights have been overemphasized in some nations, such as the United States, to the detriment of collective well-being, but the citizens' duties to the community are just as important as rights, if not more.[6] In addition, communitarians recognize that guaranteeing rights is costly and time-consuming, and thus more stringent requirements for citizenship can make sense in political-economic terms. A communitarian society typically limits membership to "our" people, however defined.

The business organization in the communitarian view is not an empty shell, or a mere "nexus of contracts," but is a tangible and functioning member of a community, distinguishable from the individuals who own and work for the organization. Business organizations are entities that emerge to help the community and are expected to act in the community's interest as a duty of membership. And, indeed, the business organization *wants* to act in the community's interest because the community gives meaning to what the organization is and does.

In some ways this view is compatible with early definitions of corporate social responsibility—the idea that businesses should be responsible for how the benefits and harms of their actions are distributed. In addition, the communitarian view is consistent with the concept of "corporate citizenship" when it is focused exclusively on the concerns and welfare of specific communities.

A communitarian firm's response to pollution would take into account its community's understandings and norms about collective well-being. Such a firm would likely exercise willingly a duty not to harm the community. However, a communitarian approach to pollution control would be limited to its own specific community and would not include other communities where it does business but is not a member. Thus, a communitarian company-citizen might well keep local waters clean in its home community by putting its wastewater in the streams or sewers of other communities.

Citizenship Based on Universal Principles

The universal principles perspective, a third prevalent view of citizenship, is based on the moral assumption of rights as necessary for the achievement of human agency—defined as the freedom to pursue one's interests. Citizens with this view see the primary role of government as securing and protecting these conditions of human agency, not just for oneself, but for every individual. Not only must the state protect negative rights of non-interference—those guarantees of human liberty such as protection of the right to free speech and assembly, and the right to vote—but also it must identify and protect positive rights that must be provided in order to achieve autonomous human action, such as the right to education and the right to health care. A critical issue in this perspective is the possibility and process of arriving at a set of common values and related rights and duties that can be supported across cultural boundaries, and perhaps political ones as well.

Individuals and societies delegate to business organizations much of their ability to achieve their diverse wants and needs, and they must therefore also give organizations a degree of freedom from direct and constant control. Privately owned organizations are given many important tasks needed by the society, such as job creation, economic growth, research and development, and provision of consumer goods. Organizations do not have rights and privileges identical to those of individual persons, but they do have limited rights and associated duties so that they can achieve these goals. The rights and privileges granted to business citizens are those needed to permit the organization to act appropriately as agents of people and societies. Ethical values and mechanisms of social control, such as honesty, trust, and rule of law, are ways of structuring relationships and exchanges so that uncertainty is reduced and efficiency can be enhanced. The global business citizen integrates these basic ethical values and mechanisms of social control into its internal ways of making decisions and uses them as guidance everywhere they operate.

A universalist firm would likely enact a duty to all people and all communities to minimize pollution wherever its harms are experienced. Such a firm would not dispose of its wastes in an unsafe manner in any community. It would recognize the legitimate need for efficient government regulation to protect humans and the environment from externalities and other market failures. Recycling, reclamation, and redesign to minimize waste in the first place would be preferred ways of addressing pollution problems even if local regulations do not require this degree of pollution control.

Comparing Views of Citizenship

It is interesting that although the minimalist position and the universal principles view seem to be far apart in perspective, they are united in their support of human autonomy and certain rights for citizens. They differ in the means acceptable to reach this desirable end. The minimalist view tends toward a "least government" approach, while the universal principles view is more willing to accept the validity of government action to ensure rights. In contrast to both, the communitarian position does not emphasize individual liberty above all, preferring to balance concerns for liberty with concerns for the collective well-being. In addition, a communitarian society might have more or less government, depending on what the community believes is needed to enforce rights and duties in its particular context.

Business organizations are viewed very differently in the three approaches to citizenship. Businesses in the minimalist view are just shells within which various actors (investors, employees, customers, suppliers) engage in contracts to pursue their own interests. The organization itself cannot be a citizen in this view. By contrast, firms in the communitarian perspective *are* citizens in the sense of having an identification with their home community and supporting its well-being. "Corporate citizen" is an appropriate term for a firm operating on communitarian assumptions. Finally, a firm that operates according to a universal principles view of citizenship is one that can claim the name of "global business citizen," from cell 4 back in Table 3.1. Such a company "thinks globally and acts locally" by having basic ethical values that apply everywhere it operates, and by implementing those values in a manner consistent with and respectful of legitimate local cultural differences.

So—what kind of "good citizen" is your company? Is it a profit-seeking minimalist citizen, putting up with government and community only because they serve the firm's own purposes? Is it a local community star, identifying and fully integrated with a region but not so concerned about "those others" who live elsewhere? Is it a global company that is trying to wrestle in good faith with the challenges of multiculturalism and globalization? Is your firm a global business citizen?

45

The Process of Global Business Citizenship

Multinational enterprises are not bound by the rules of a single community, but are challenged to deal with differences among community norms, rules, and performance expectations. The traditional view is that corporations should conform to local practice by always following local laws and customs— "when in Rome. . . ." An alternative view has emerged over the past quarter-century that companies should apply uniform policies across their worldwide operations. Both of these approaches have weaknesses, but together they contain the seeds of an optimal hybrid strategy.

What does it mean in the modern world to argue that businesses are members of *society* and are thus subject to societally based social controls? Is this a viable idea in a world where virtually all the factors of production move freely among nations and cultures?

Consider, for example, the *Wall Street Journal* article explaining why, amid the international boom of mega-mergers, it was not surprising for Daimler Benz AG and Chrysler Corporation to merge:

> In the culture that leaders of global businesses inhabit, where shared values of open markets, hard money and standardized technology increasingly take precedence over old-fashioned nationalism, such transnational combinations are logical, and they are becoming more commonplace every day. . . . More and more, national boundaries, cultural variations and accidents of geography such as the Atlantic Ocean aren't stopping business leaders who see a chance to expand their reach as trade barriers fall, communication becomes cheap and consumer tastes for everything from cola to cellular phones converge.[7]

Business citizenship defines a business organization's relationship to nation-states, to other organizations, and to human beings. It is thus an *ethical* enterprise. But in this diverse world, which ethics—whose ethics—should prevail? GBC addresses this question by acknowledging varying degrees of ethical certainty about what is the right thing to do. A global business citizen accepts a limited number of basic universal principles, such as, "it is wrong to harm innocent persons." However, in conducting business activities, this organization realizes that although application of the fundamental principles is straightforward in many cases, there are situations where local norms appear to be in conflict with those principles, or application of the principles will cause unintended negative consequences. There are even situations where the local manager cannot tell whether local customs conform to or conflict with company norms, or whether the comparison is even relevant. In these cases, the degree of ethical certainty is much lower.

Table 3.2

Implementing Business Citizenship: Strategic Approaches

| | Approach to Strategy | |
Degree of Ethical Certainty	Multi-Domestic	Globally Integrated
High: The company accepts a limited number of basic universal rules or principles.	(Ethical relativism)	**Code of conduct**
Moderate : Local norms are consistent with, or vary acceptably from, basic principles.	**Local implementation**	(Ethical imperialism)
Low: Local norms appear to conflict with, or are incompletely governed by, principles.	**Analysis and experimentation**	**Organizational and systemic learning**

Source: Adapted from Logsdon and Wood, 2002.

In international business, a company will struggle to decide between a multi-domestic strategy, which tailors its strategy to local conditions, and a globally integrated strategy, which strives to achieve a unified strategy across all units. The analysis in Table 3.2 illustrates that one or the other of these strategies alone is inadequate to address global business issues across all levels of ethical certainty.

When a matrix of strategy and ethical certainty is constructed, as seen in Table 3.2, some striking results emerge. First, a multi-domestic strategy cannot logically rely on universal principles.[8] This is the "when in Rome" philosophy that values compliance with local norms above all. Operating in different ways in different cultures constitutes *ethical relativism*, which can too easily allow a company to violate ordinary standards of ethics, especially where a local government is lax, repressive, or corrupt. An example of ethical relativism would be allowing for racial discrimination in plants located in South Africa when apartheid was legally required, while professing and practicing equal opportunity employment in the United States and Canada. The problem, of course, is that managers trying to use a relativist approach can find themselves condoning practices that are morally abhorrent to them and unacceptable to their companies.

A second "aha!" is that a globally integrated approach simply will not work when it comes to the local variations of human practice and belief. A globally integrated approach requires that identical principles and practices occur everywhere a company does business, and that is nothing more than

Figure 3.1   **The Process of Global Business Citizenship**

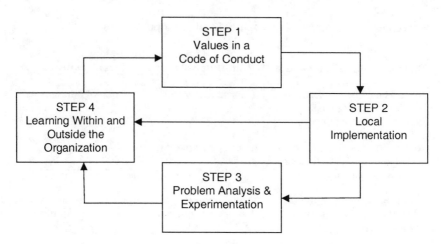

ethical imperialism, that is, "my way or the highway." This is dysfunctional because it fails to recognize and respect legitimate differences in practice that do not violate principles.

However, a hybrid approach to strategy and ethics in global business operates in different ways at different levels of ethical certainty. We have eliminated the ethical relativism and ethical imperialism cells of Table 3.2, leaving the four remaining cells to constitute the process of implementing global business citizenship.

Guidelines for Implementing GBC

Figure 3.1 shows a 4-step process model for implementing global business citizenship, based on the analysis shown in Table 3.2.

Step 1. Values in a Code of Conduct

As a first step toward global business citizenship, the company accepts a small set of basic principles that govern its conduct wherever it operates. At this step, a globally integrated approach is not only appropriate but desired; a high degree of ethical certainty governs the choice of principles included, and these are the principles the company stands for and lives by.

We propose that every company begin the trek to global business citizenship by formulating a values statement, using principles that reflect a universally acceptable and reasonably complete set of human values. These principles of good conduct should be based on core values drawn from the convergence of the world's major philosophical and religious traditions that apply regardless of common practice or local belief. The norms identified in the United Nations Universal Declaration of Human Rights might serve as a good source of such principles because of their pervasive moral authority and widespread acceptance. This exercise is especially beneficial for surfacing and clarifying ethical values and their underlying hypernorms for companies that have not been articulate about these in the past, whether or not they have been acting upon such values.

A code of conduct serves both as a statement of basic ethical principles and as an operational guide to behavior. Thus, the code should provide specific guidance for situations that employees will typically encounter. A useful code of conduct will cover normal business functions and operations, as well as any situations that are specific to the firm or its industry. For example, a company that makes extensive use of subcontractors would include guidance on how to monitor workplace practices on site to prevent violation of a principle against inhumane labor conditions in the manufacture of its products. More on this step in chapter 4.

Step 2. Local Implementation

Imagine a firm that has a strong value for respecting workers' private lives, but then implements this value by imposing home-country religious holidays in all locations. Christmas and Easter holidays would not mean much in Israel; Yom Kippur and Passover holidays might stir labor unrest in Pakistan or be forbidden in Iran. Eid ul-Adha (Muslim), Gantan-sai (Shinto), Janam Ashtami (Hindu), Maunajiyaras (Jain), and Nichiren Daishonin (Buddhist) are all sacred holidays, but they fall during different times of the year and are observed only by practitioners of that religion.[9]

Managers must implement the global code of ethical conduct in all the various locations where a company does business. They may have learned how to handle the variety of religious holidays, but this is an easy problem compared to many others. What are managers to do, if they don't want to be ethical imperialists and force an unpalatable solution on the local workforce? The GBC process suggests that as long as the big principles are not violated, there is plenty of room—and reason—for local variations in implementing a company's code of conduct.

In some cases, there will be no conflicts or gaps between the guidelines of the code and local customs, cultural norms, or national standards. In such cases, the company can readily apply its code without modification.

But many situations in international business are of moderate ethical certainty. This means that it's not necessarily clear whether the company's big principles and the locale's customs and norms are compatible, but at least they do not seem to be incompatible. One can allow and even plan for variations in implementation of the code of conduct without violation of the big principles. To stick with the holiday example, companies doing business in predominantly Christian regions could, perhaps, have a few fixed holidays and a few floaters, to accommodate workers of various religious traditions. The alternative, ethical imperialism, exists when organizations fail to respect or to value the existence of local cultures, and exhibit naïve or coercive disrespect of legitimate variations in how ethics are lived out in different locations.

Of course, managers must be conscientious in making these judgments. They must be aware of the problems that may arise by arbitrarily applying the company code in cases where customs or local standards are in conflict with it. Or, there may be unintended consequences from implementing the company code that will create either problems for stakeholders or ethical dilemmas for the company that were simply not addressed in the code itself. Engaging in stakeholder dialogue and being open to feedback about code implementation is essential to uncovering such problems. How else would the managers discover that the operations of their organizations were in conflict with local norms if they didn't talk to the locals?

When it comes to the attention of the organization that conflicts exist, managers must take the next step in the GBC process.

Step 3. Problem Analysis and Experimentation

Ethical uncertainty reigns when cultural norms are incomplete, nonexistent, or appear to be in conflict with those principles that are contained in the code of conduct. When this is the case, the organization must make two important steps in its journey toward citizenship.

First, the company must analyze cases in which local customs or norms seem to be at variance with company standards. These cases may include situations where local custom diverges substantially from the company code, and local managers will need to examine whether these differences should be resolved in favor of the code or not. Second, after thoughtful stakeholder engagement and careful analysis, the organization needs to design experiments to test ways to implement the code in conformance with big principles and with respect for local culture.

Analyzing ethical and cultural conflicts is little different from analyzing production or financial or distribution problems. The task is to identify the problem, take it apart into its various pieces, and search for similarities and differences that suggest solutions. As with other problems, a manager tries to ask good questions and learn from the experts. Stakeholders can provide important information about local practices, customs, and norms, and such input will help the manager to analyze conflicts or gaps. It is especially useful in the problem analysis stage to have an in-depth understanding of the principles underlying the company code.

Experimentation involves searching for creative and practical solutions to values conflicts. One wants to honor the spirit of the code by adapting practice where feasible, and sometimes nothing but trial and error will do. Managers may be up against a conflict they've never experienced or were completely unaware of. Being willing to experiment in good faith, working all the while with affected stakeholders, is key to implementing a global code of conduct in diverse settings.

In cases where the application of the company code will have unintended negative consequences for one or more stakeholders, the manager needs to carefully consider the nature of these consequences and whether they can be mitigated. Because headquarters personnel are not necessarily aware of negative consequences arising in some local cultures, you, as manager, may need to recommend changes in the company code itself.

Let's take an example such as setting a fair wage. Managers may not be aware when first entering a new country that wage practices vary dramatically from the home country, although such information should be routinely included in the demographics of site location decisions. No matter—they quickly discover from local peers, government officials, and workers themselves what the norms and expectations are regarding compensation. Through continuing stakeholder engagement, the managers can discern whether or not local customs are in conflict with company norms. If so, it may be that managers can find through experimentation a reasonable way to incorporate local customs and still be consistent with company standards. In other cases, the manager may resolve conflict by supporting the company's code and will need to communicate clearly and respectfully to locals the reasons why this decision has been made. Principles with universal acceptance can be most helpful and persuasive in articulating these reasons.

Let's say that the company code specifies that compensation will be adequate to sustain a minimum lifestyle and will not be discriminatory on the basis of age, sex, religion, or ethnicity. Operating in a heavily unionized area would likely call for acceptance of a legitimate bargaining representative and formal contract negotiations. Operating in a country that bans trade unions might require a different approach to setting wages—comparing job requirements, investigating the quality of life of ordinary workers, and gathering information from government agencies as well as from local community leaders. In a developing country, the firm might even consult with NGOs that assist the poor with health care, food supplements, water, electricity, or education—just to find out what life is like for workers.

Then there's the issue of discriminatory wages. In many of the world's developing nations it is considered equitable to pay women quite a bit less than men, even though they may be doing the same jobs. In various countries, longstanding ethnic, religious, or racial tensions have created "permanent underclasses" of workers who can legally be given lower wages for comparable work. In such circumstances, a GBC company is careful to check out the history and practices of a new locale, compare the cultural norms to its code, and seek ways of meeting its fundamental principles while respecting local cultural differences where possible.

Needless to say, managers would need to verify their information and sources to avoid being taken advantage of by sharp locals who see an opportunity to gain unfairly via bogus wage claims! We explore the crucial techniques of stakeholder engagement further in chapters 5 and 6.

Step 4. Learning Within and Outside the Organization

This essential last step in the GBC implementation process is the one that turns trial and error into practical systematic knowledge. No company wants its managers to keep making the same mistakes over and over. Eventually, with good data and a company-wide effort to shape and share it, managers can learn to differentiate situations and then apply solutions accordingly. Chapters 7 and 8 address the organizational change processes that can be used to help companies learn how to learn.

Local implementation (Step 2) as well as analysis and experimentation (Step 3) will best serve the human enterprise and the organization's purposes when the multinational enterprise (MNE) institutes feedback loops and learns systematically from all its experiences. Systematic learning involves grasping the structural and normative similarities and differences among the various situations the MNE encounters in its many locations, extracting the essence of these experiences, and providing models or exemplars of what works and what doesn't work in terms of adapting and experimenting with implementation.

After systematizing what it has learned from implementation and experiments, a GBC company will institutionalize those policies, practices, and behaviors that best serve the interests of people and the firm wherever it operates. A database, training modules, and other means of incorporating learning throughout the organization are characteristic of this mature phase of global citizenship behavior. For example, Levi Strauss & Co., Inc., after a decade of experiments in implementing its supplier code of conduct and

---

Exhibit 3.4

GBC Simplified

1. A company should select a small set of big principles to guide its decisions and activities.
2. The principles should be applied wherever the company operates, with sensitive appreciation for differing local customs that are not in conflict with the fundamental principles.
3. In cases where implementation of the basic principles will cause unintended harms or conflicts with local norms, managers can experiment creatively with locally effective ways of implementing code principles.
4. The entire organization can learn from implementation and experimentation, and these lessons should be shared with organizations experiencing similar problems.

---

country terms of engagement, finally began to compile a systematic database that will help all the company's managers identify problems and issues and apply workable, tested solutions to them. Names, dates, places, and cases all find their way into the database, so no manager need be blindsided by the shenanigans of a known cheater or a subcontractor who likes to skate on the wrong side of labor law.

Ultimately the GBC process is cyclical. As a company learns how to implement its code, and how to understand its local stakeholders, there will be instances where the code turns out to be wrong, or unworkable. Cycling back around, then, the good-citizen company learns how to critique its own values and processes and to change its guidelines when it becomes apparent that certain aspects of the code of conduct cannot reasonably be implemented or should not stand as guiding principles.

There's one more aspect to GBC learning, and that is sharing knowledge with other companies so that the entire business sector—and other types of organizations too—can learn. In several upcoming chapters, we'll explore some of the ways in which businesses are beginning to share their experiences and attempts at being good global citizens.

Conclusion

Most companies and their managers *want* to operate responsibly, and there's a lot of innovation and good ideas and experimentation out there already. What we are proposing is that managers learn how to serve as the role models they can be by standing for something bigger than their organizations, something bigger than profit, and by systematizing their knowledge as it emerges.

Global business citizenship provides the conceptual and operational vehicle for bringing the conscience of capitalism into the twenty-first century. By accepting the mantle of global citizenship, individual managers will take their places belonging to humanity, rather than only to a local polity. Acknowledging the universal rights and duties of both individuals and business organizations and accepting their dependence on a thriving natural environment, managers are in the best position to implement global business citizenship. Indeed, *only* managers can do this.

> 4 <

Principles, Codes, and Policies

The Guidance System for Global Business Citizenship

Many wonders of this world—from high-tech missiles to automobiles—operate according to built-in guidance systems that set parameters for action, respond to external events, and help the operator make appropriate choices. People too, and their organizations, have guidance systems, built on values, learning, and experience. A good way to think about *values and principles*—those underlying preferences and big ideas that guide our actions and to which we refer when evaluating outcomes—is as a guidance system for human beings and for their organizations. Global business citizens require particular kinds of guidance systems that ensure alignment between "talk" and "walk."

Organizational Guidance Systems

A corporate guidance system can be as simple as the founder's few dictates or as complex as the vast management control and information systems network that characterize most large firms. Corporations based in developed economies are likely to have a mission, a vision, a values statement, a code of conduct, and a set of policies with respect to the code. At least since the ethics meltdowns of the late 1990s and early 2000s, executives have struggled with finding ways to establish clear standards and to tie them consistently to corporate structure and process as well as to relevant legal requirements. A recent study of companies in 22 nations, for example, reported that "in 1999,

78% of boards of directors were involved in establishing ethics standards compared with 41% in 1991 and 21% in 1987."[1]

When it comes to organizational ethics guidance, terminology matters less than content. Managers may think there's no code of conduct in their company, but they may have a detailed employee handbook—or a rules and regulations booklet, or a policies and procedures manual, or a statement about legal compliance and conflicts of interest—that serves the same purpose under a different name. Whatever the title, what matters is that organizational members have guidance on how to handle the commonplace and the difficult dilemmas and ethical situations they may face in the workplace.

Some companies do not depend on complex rule books for guidance, referring instead to a simple statement of values or principles. Johnson & Johnson's familiar credo, for example, is a short page of priorities that appears in company conference rooms and managers' wallets. The credo is the primary point of reference when any questions arise as to whose interests the company should serve or how they should act. Guidance by value statements is more typical of smaller companies. The Mudd Group, for example, an Iowa-based automotive advertising agency, tries to do business according to its three core principles—respect people, make money, have fun—without systematizing these values into a detailed rule book.[2]

For large U.S.-based companies, the rules of the ethics game changed in 1991, with the adoption of new U.S. Sentencing Commission Guidelines to apply in cases when corporate employees are convicted of crimes. The guidelines allowed companies to shield themselves from significant liability *if* they had a code of conduct, regular training, processes for reporting legal violations, due diligence in hiring, and other compliance-related policies and practices. The sentencing guidelines were updated in 2004 to include ethics practices as well as legal compliance. Furthermore, the Sarbanes-Oxley Act of 2002, passed in the wake of the Enron/Arthur Andersen meltdown, imposed stringent ethics and accounting requirements on all firms listed on American stock exchanges, no matter where they are based. And, the European Union (EU) has been moving toward similar policies to govern EU-based companies.

Although terminology as well as legal standards vary in practice, there's one idea here that can distinguish GBC companies from non-GBC companies. The key difference appears in Step 1 of the GBC process, which involves *accepting a small but reasonably comprehensive set of universal principles* and incorporating them into codes and policies that make sense for and reflect the core values of the organization and its stakeholders.

"Small" is the easy part of this criterion. It's the "reasonably comprehensive" and "universal" parts that are difficult. The Mudd Group's principles,

Exhibit 4.1

**Johnson & Johnson
Our Credo**

We believe our first responsibility is to the doctors, nurses and patients,
to mothers and fathers and all others who use our products and services.
In meeting their needs everything we do must be of high quality.
We must constantly strive to reduce our costs in order to
maintain reasonable prices.
Customers' orders must be serviced promptly and accurately.
Our suppliers and distributors must have an
opportunity to make a fair profit.
We are responsible to our employees, the men and women
who work with us throughout the world.
Everyone must be considered as an individual.

We must respect their dignity and recognize their merit.
They must have a sense of security in their jobs.
Compensation must be fair and adequate, and
working conditions clean, orderly and safe.
We must be mindful of ways to help our employees
fulfill their family responsibilities.
Employees must feel free to make suggestions and complaints.
There must be equal opportunity for employment,
development and advancement for those qualified.
We must provide competent management, and their
actions must be just and ethical.

We are responsible to the communities in which we live and
work and to the world community as well.
We must be good citizens—support good works and charities
and bear our fair share of taxes.
We must encourage civic improvements and better health and education.
We must maintain in good order the property we are privileged to use,
protecting the environment and natural resources.

Our final responsibility is to our stockholders.
Business must make a sound profit.
We must experiment with new ideas.
Research must be carried on, innovative programs
developed and mistakes paid for.
New equipment must be purchased, new facilities
provided and new products launched.
Reserves must be created to provide for adverse times.
When we operate according to these principles,
the stockholders should realize a fair return.

Source: http://www.jnj.com/our_company/our_credo/ (accessed January 31,
2005). Used with permission.

Table 4.1

Comparing Organizational Guidance Systems

	GBC companies	Non-GBC companies
Mission	Articulates the company's reason for existing and the meaning of its work, *consistent with universal principles*	Articulates the company's reason for existing and the meaning of its work
Vision	Articulates what the company aspires to be and what its future should look like, *consistent with universal principles*	Articulates what the company aspires to be and what its future should look like
Values	Articulates what is most important to the company, *consistent with universal principles*	Articulates what is most important to the company
Code of conduct	Identifies areas of vulnerability and offers general guidance to employees, *consistent with universal principles*	Identifies areas of vulnerability and offers general guidance to employees
Policies	Within the framework of the code, offers specific guidance to employees in areas of vulnerability, *consistent with universal principles*	Within the framework of the code, offers specific guidance to employees in areas of vulnerability

for example, are a small enough set, and they provide good guidance for a small company. But where's the environment? Where's the idea of not causing undue harm? Where is legal compliance? Where is honesty, loyalty, trustworthiness? And can "having fun" really be thought of as a universal value in business? In Table 4.1 we hammer home this point. GBC and non-GBC companies alike can have well-developed, articulate, functional, and meaningful missions, visions, values, codes, and policies. *What differentiates a GBC company, though, is that the principles upon which all these statements are based are a small, reasonably comprehensive set of universal principles.*

Okay, perhaps you're thinking, principles are all well and good, but what about the differences between what we say and what we do? So let's bypass these tricky ideas of "reasonably comprehensive" and "universal" principles for the moment and take up this question of words versus actions.

WorldCom had a perfectly fine mission, vision, and values statement. It had a code of conduct and a very extensive set of corporate policies. Before the company crashed into Chapter 11 bankruptcy, though, executives made what they called a one-time exception to ordinary accounting and reporting procedures in order to "fix" results to conform to Wall Street expectations. The slippery slope of deception came to be normal procedure; as time went on, it became routine practice to "fix the numbers to meet expectations" every quarter; more people became involved; and the problems got more serious and increasingly unresolveable.[3] Later it became clear that the CEO, the CFO, the accounting chief, and numerous other senior executives had been engaged in a fraud that eventually totaled $11 billion.

What's wrong with this picture? Simply put, WorldCom senior executives lived by a set of values and principles emphasizing corporate growth and shareholder value—so that the code of conduct and its policies were just so much printed paper when push came to shove and quarterly projections weren't going to be met. *WorldCom was not governed by a small set of reasonably comprehensive, universally acceptable principles.*

Even the best managers in the most ethical companies need to take this message to heart. The problem is, a code of conduct and specific policies that are not grounded in strong, comprehensive, universal principles are going to fail when employees meet head-on with the world's many and diverse cultures and the inevitable financial pressures of globalization.

GBC Requires a Small Set of Comprehensive, Universal Principles

Principles are the underlying statements that support a theory or belief system or world view.[4] Principles may express values ("human life is sacred"), or understandings about how and why things are ("I think, therefore I am"), or beliefs about what is true ("that act is good which creates the greatest good for the greatest number").

The set of principles governing a GBC company and informing its mission, vision, values, code, and policies has three essential attributes that are worth reiterating:

1. The principles are *comprehensive* in the sense that no major domain of ethical conduct and responsibility is left out.
2. The principles are *universal,* not in the sense that every person on earth accepts them, but in the sense that most cultures would consider them to be valid, though perhaps not preferred, sources of guidance.
3. The set of principles is *small* to enhance clarity and lessen confusion. And after all, the set of *possible* universal principles is necessarily small.

It doesn't really matter whether principles are expressed in mission, vision, or values statements. Companies have different practices here, and it isn't a problem. What matters, though, is that the principles accommodate a broad range of ethics in a way that can be generalized to all the company's sites and enacted by all the company's employees.

Take as an example General Motors, one of the world's largest and best-known companies. GM's Board of Directors has a mission statement, which focuses on shareholder interests, with stakeholder obligations as an add-on:

> The General Motors Board of Directors represents the owners' interest in perpetuating a successful business, including optimizing long-term financial returns. The Board is responsible for determining that the Corporation is managed in such a way to ensure this result. This is an active, not a passive, responsibility. The Board has the responsibility to ensure that in good times, as well as difficult ones, Management is capably executing its responsibilities. The Board's responsibility is to regularly monitor the effectiveness of Management policies and decisions including the execution of its strategies.
>
> In addition to fulfilling its obligations for increased stockholder value, the Board has responsibility to GM's customers, employees, suppliers and to the communities where it operates—all of whom are essential to a successful business. All of these responsibilities, however, are founded upon the successful perpetuation of the business.[5]

GM's ambitious vision is found in a website section called "GMability," which apparently refers to the company's social responsibility stance, although the vision itself does not:

> GM's vision is to be the world leader in transportation products and related services. We will earn our customers' enthusiasm through continuous improvement driven by the integrity, teamwork and innovation of GM people. Becoming the best is an unending journey, a constantly changing destination. But that's where we're determined to drive—one car, one truck, one customer at a time.[6]

Values are the preferences we hold that determine in large measure how we give priority to certain things or actions or beliefs over others. Values establish a hierarchy of worth and tell us which things or behaviors are worth our time and effort. Of GM's six core values, two are directly ethical in nature, and four are focused on traditional business processes, as seen in Exhibit 4.2.

At GM—the company that brought us the ultimate gas guzzler, the Hummer—customer enthusiasm is the Number One value priority. It follows that GM's budgeting and planning would emphasize product design, quality production, customer service, and marketing. What happens at GM when the desire for customer enthusiasm clashes with the values for integrity, respect,

```
Exhibit 4.2

General Motors' Core Values

   1. Customer enthusiasm
   2. Integrity
   3. Teamwork
   4. Innovation
   5. Continuous improvement
   6. Individual respect and responsibility
   _____

     Source: http://www.gm.com/company/gmability/sustainability/reports/04/
   300_company/311_vis_vis.htm(accessed November 27, 2004).
```

or responsibility? The core values statement itself doesn't give us any guidance here.

Finally, GM's code of conduct is entitled "Winning with Integrity." It contains extensive and more or less standard guidelines for employee conduct in areas of personal integrity, fair treatment and respect, diversity, health and safety, conflicts of interest, integrity of information and property, gifts, entertainment and gratuities, fair competition, insider trading, government bribery, the Foreign Corrupt Practices Act, export controls, and integrity toward the environment.[7] We won't examine GM's implementing policies here, but the code of conduct is extensive enough to serve as a policy statement itself.

Are GM's values—and presumably the principles based on them—comprehensive and universal? The four business process values—customer enthusiasm, teamwork, innovation, and continuous improvement—are neither comprehensive nor universal, and they don't have to be. These values represent GM's core competencies and strategic advantage; they *shouldn't* be applicable to all companies.

The values of interest for GBC, though, are different. Integrity plus individual respect and responsibility are ethical values that could be considered universal, as we shall see shortly. But are they comprehensive? Would these values keep GM from polluting the earth, shifting production rapidly and thoughtlessly to the cheapest labor sites, or interfering with legitimate government processes?

Universal Principles and Ethical Relativism

Questions such as these lead us back to the really tough problem—this idea of universal principles. Where do they come from? How do we know when we have found the right ones? Do principles change, and, if so, how can they be "universal"? And worst of all, with so many cultures in the world, so many religious beliefs and philosophies, how could any principle ever be considered "universal"?

When dealing with cultures that differ considerably from our own, we may be struck by the superficial differences and assume that the fundamental social values also differ. This may seem shallow, but think back to your first experience of a different culture. Were you captivated by differences in hair style or skin color, by colorful clothing, by homes and furnishings outside your comfort zone? The first step is often to state that each culture creates its own values, and they should all be honored. This is an easy step to take, but it is a path to the quagmire of *cultural and ethical relativism.*

For example, casual observation of a Japanese business executive might suggest that family is a less important value than work dedication, because husbands often spend very long hours at work and then stay out late, drinking with fellow workers. While Japanese cultural norms may differ somewhat in terms of how worker loyalty is evaluated and how trusting male relationships are formed and maintained, compared to American or European norms, it is not obvious to the naïve observer that Japanese men put up with all this *because* they want to provide a good income to support their families.[8]

Ethical relativism is not just misleading; it is ultimately a trap that keeps us from making sound judgments about what is good and bad. All human cultures have fundamental values for life, family, relationships, loyalty, authority structures, and so much more. There are many problems with a relativist stance, but the main one is this: a relativist ultimately cannot take a stand on anything at all. Any behavior, no matter how repugnant or harmful or violent, has to be accepted by the observer if it is accepted within the culture being observed.

Push hard on ethical relativism, and we ultimately arrive at an "ethical" justification for horrors no rational person would want to accept. GBC companies do not want to go there, and so they will emphasize a small, relatively comprehensive set of universal values that can be implemented in a variety of culturally sensitive ways but that have limits as to how far they can be pushed. "When in Rome, do as the Romans do" might be good guidance for etiquette, but it is not good for matters of ethics.

What Are "Universal" Principles?

As the world grows figuratively smaller and literally more intertwined, the search is on for values and norms that can be respected and upheld by all the world's peoples. A great many social or religious groups attribute universality to *their way of thinking,* but such belief systems tend to exclude all others, as invalid, misguided, or even "evil." In global business, the search for universal principles shouldn't be seen as a chance for companies to claim "my way or the highway." Instead, the search expresses a need for a coherent nexus of standards that can accommodate cultural variations and still retain fundamental values such as integrity, trustworthiness, causing no harm, and aiding those in need.

Questions of social power and interpretation inevitably arise when we try to think of universal ethical principles. Whose values will prevail? To whom are certain values to be applied, and in what manner, and under which circumstances? Who counts as a human being? What value do non-humans have? And so on.

The problems may seem insurmountable, but the fact is, there are a number of efforts already underway to actually identify and define a small and reasonably comprehensive set of universal values. These efforts are occurring within the three major sources of ethical principles:

- religion
- reason and philosophy, and
- social consensus and political arrangement.

Let's take up each in turn.

Principles Originate in Religion

Many people believe that religions—serving as the root of cultural values—are so different across cultures that there is no basis for comparison and no way of thinking about "universal" ethical principles. Consider, however, the ethical rule that is embedded in Western religious and humanist philosophy as the Golden Rule. In modern English, the rule would be this:

"Treat others as you want to be treated."

Now take a look at the central texts of the world's major religions, and see if there is anything like the Golden Rule[9]:

Hinduism:	"This is the sum of duty: Do naught to others which would cause pain if done to you."
Buddhism:	"Hurt not others in ways that you yourself would find hurtful."

Table 4.2

Some Values Common to the World's Great Religions

- The world is our family: "All are the sons and daughters of God."
- Cause no harm: Be kind to others and hurt no one.
- Preserve the earth, keep the water clean, take only what you need.
- What we sow, we shall reap.
- Speak the truth and do not conceal it.
- Be guided by the spirit of the law more than its letter.
- Practice moderation in all things.
- Give to the poor, give from the heart, give without return.
- Be hospitable to strangers, for there really is no such thing.
- Wealth is a blessing that anyone can share.
- Avoid doing what you know to be wrong.
- Live in unity with all of humankind.

Source: Adapted from Moses 2001.

Confucianism:	Tsze-Kung asked, saying, "Is there one word which may serve as a rule of practice for all one's life?" The Master said: "Is not reciprocity such a word? What you do not want done to yourself, do not do to others."
Islam:	"No one of you is a believer until he desires for his brother that which he desires for himself."
Judaism:	"What is hateful to you, do not do to your fellow man. This is the entire Law; all the rest is commentary."
Christianity:	"Whatsoever you wish that men would do to you, do so to them, for this is the law and the prophets." And, "Love your neighbor as yourself."

Not so different after all? There's more. Aside from a universal rule about not causing harm and treating others as you want to be treated, most of the world's religions offer strict prohibitions against murder, rape, incest, lying, stealing, and a variety of other behaviors that are detrimental to the social order and to the interests of individuals.[10] There are positive values in common as well. Table 4.2 illustrates a number of other values and principles the world's great religions have in common.

These are only a few of the common elements that have been identified by scholars. The devil's in the details, of course—there are major variations in to whom and under what circumstances these principles apply—but nevertheless, the prohibited behaviors are recognized as so harmful that rules must be made about them, and the encouraged behaviors are seen as essential to a high-quality human life in association with others.

Superficial cultural and religious differences can easily obscure the fact that underneath it all, people living in different societies have the same concerns and worries, similar hopes and dreams, and the same need for broad rules that make possible a good life.

Principles Come from Reason and Philosophy

In science, principles are rules that cannot be positively proven but whose effects can be observed consistently—for example, the law of conservation of matter. Scientific principles are derived from continuous observation and are tested by experiments designed to prove them untrue.

In philosophy, principles are fundamental truths arrived at by the rigorous use of logic. Take, for example, Kant's criteria for principles of ethical conduct, derived from a lengthy and exhaustive exercise in logical analysis.[11] Kant concluded that, in order to be ethical, a reason for acting must be:

1. *universalizable*, that is, applicable by anyone and everyone in a similar situation, and
2. *reversible*, that is, the actor would be willing to have the rule used by someone else even if the resulting action was detrimental to him/her.

Kant extended this logic to demonstrate that human rights are desirable—because everyone wants what they have to offer, and inevitable—because it is ultimately recognized that no one has secure rights unless everyone does. Even more, Kant recognized the failings of human conduct and reasoned that, even though people often do not act on universal, reciprocal principles, we should all act *as if* we lived in a world governed by such principles, thus making it more likely that, over time, the principles will indeed prevail.

Both the scientific and the philosophical examples demonstrate that principles can be deduced from logic or stated as an overarching explanation for some common behavior. These deductions and statements serve as the basis for many current attempts to define and assure guidelines for ethical conduct.

Principles Arise from Social Consensus and Political Arrangement

Standards of business conduct have been under intense scrutiny since at least the early 1970s, when consumer safety, environmental protection, and equal opportunity concerns came to the forefront of public consciousness in the industrialized world. More recently, with the emergence of truly global corporations larger than many nations, multilateral collaborative efforts to establish standards of conduct have been undertaken.

Why?

65

Think about it. The spread of global capitalism may eventually float all boats, but its early outcomes have been quite mixed. Despite rising per capita gross national product in most developing nations, we don't know yet how the wealth is distributed and with what effects. And, disasters, disease epidemics, and other serious challenges have accompanied capitalism's expansion. Non-governmental organizations (NGOs) and global media have not been slow to highlight disasters such as Union Carbide's Bhopal explosion in 1984, Nike's reliance on sweatshops and child labor in the 1990s, and the exposure of Parmalat's and Ahold's financial houses of cards in 2003.

The initial post–World War II effort to design universal principles is contained in the United Nations Universal Declaration of Human Rights (UDHR), passed in 1948. The UDHR can be thought of as a stretch-goal document for national governments, but more recently multinational corporations (MNCs) have been called to task to do their part to uphold human rights, and, indeed, their leaders are responding.

In Table 4.3 are listed some of the major current efforts to develop worldwide standards of business conduct. Although substantial differences are apparent among these codes, and although each is purely voluntary, there is a surprising degree of consistency on the "big ideas" to which these codes subscribe:

- All people are entitled to basic human rights.
- All people are entitled to a measure of social justice.
- The natural environment must be protected and preserved.
- Economic opportunity must be extended to all the world's peoples.
- Multinational corporations are powerful players on the world scene, and thus have an obligation to minimize the harms they cause and act to create positive benefits for all their stakeholders.

As a specific example of the principles included in such efforts, consider the Global Compact, an initiative of United Nations Secretary-General Kofi Annan in 2000. The Compact is to be considered "not as a substitute for effective action by governments, but as an opportunity for firms to exercise leadership in their enlightened self-interest."[12] Key areas relate to human rights, labor, environmental protection, and anti-corruption, and its ten principles are compiled from the UDHR, the International Labor Organization's Fundamental Principles on Rights at Work, and the Rio Principles on Environment and Development[13]:

Human Rights

Principle 1:   Businesses should support and respect the protection of internationally proclaimed human rights; and

Table 4.3

Major Efforts to Develop Global Codes of Conduct

Asia Pacific Economic Cooperation Forum (APEC) Code of Business Conduct	http://www.apecsec.org.sg/apec html (for an overview of the code, see http://www.cauxroundtable.org/ APECForumBusinessCode of Conduct.html)
Caux Round Table Principles for Business	www.cauxroundtable.org/ principles.html
Global Sullivan Principles of Social Responsibility	www.globalsullivanprinciples.org/
OECD Guidelines for Multinational Enterprises	www.oecd.org/dataoecd/56/36/ 1922428.pdf
Social Accountability's SA 8000	www.cepaa.org/SA8000/ SA8000.htm
United Nations Global Compact	www.unglobalcompact.org

Principle 2: make sure that they are not complicit in human rights abuses.

Labor

Principle 3: Businesses should uphold the freedom of association and the effective recognition of the right to collective bargaining;

Principle 4: the elimination of all forms of forced and compulsory labor;

Principle 5: the effective abolition of child labor; and

Principle 6: the elimination of discrimination in respect of employment and occupation.

Environment

Principle 7: Businesses should support a precautionary approach to environmental challenges;

Principle 8: undertake initiatives to promote greater environmental responsibility; and

Principle 9: encourage the development and diffusion of environmentally friendly technologies.

Anti-Corruption

Principle 10: Businesses should work against all forms of corruption, including extortion and bribery.

Let's make this simple list of principles even simpler. What's being said here? Multinational corporations should:

- uphold human rights in principle and in action,
- support labor rights and humane, equitable working conditions,
- engage in active protection of the natural environment, and
- resist dishonesty in themselves and others.

Whether principles are based on religion, reason, social consensus, political acts, or on some combination, when you boil them down to their essence, it's not difficult to find a small set that can be applied universally: for example, respect human beings, protect the earth, cause no undue harm, give aid to the vulnerable, support honesty. Putting such values and principles into print may seem superfluous. But think what a difference it can make in corporate culture if the firm's guiding value is "increase shareholder wealth" or "cause no undue harm." Under the guidance of each, different things become possible and impossible, imaginable and unthinkable. And that is the central function of values and principles—to set the parameters for decision making and action.

Codes of Conduct: What's Covered?

The code of conduct or code of ethics may be as short as a pamphlet or as long as the Tokyo phone directory. Regardless, a GBC code will contain language that helps employees find answers to four essential questions:

- What are this company's core values and guiding principles?
- What must I do to be in compliance with law, regulation, and company rules?
- For normal business functions or very specific vulnerabilities, what guidance is available when the rules don't apply or are in conflict?
- What channels exist for reporting, communication, and problem resolution?

Core Values and Guiding Principles

Before a code is ever written, the company's top management team and board of directors, probably with the help of an external facilitator, need to decide upon and articulate the core values and guiding principles. Then, in the code, a succinct and prominent statement of core values and guiding principles helps to orient employees to the fundamentals upon which the code is based.

Consistency between the big values and principles and the specific rules and guidance of the code is essential. Imagine the disillusionment and even chaos that could result if a company's core values are respect, integrity, and ethical judgment, but its code of conduct is all about obeying local laws and doing what's in the company's short-term best interest! Thus, the code not only needs to restate the firm's values and principles, but it should also reflect those values and principles at every turn.

Compliance with Rules

Compliance in codes of conduct has to do with the behaviors that are firmly required or firmly forbidden. Employees should know that if they do (or don't do) these things, there will be consistent, fairly applied consequences.

Every country in which the firm does business will have laws and regulations with which employees must comply. This is ordinarily a non-controversial component of codes of conduct, although it may be difficult and complex to actually capture and interpret the details of local law.

But there may also be national or local laws and regulations that are routinely ignored or subverted for any number of reasons, and the code needs to advise employees on what to do in such circumstances. It may be that locals themselves ignore the laws, as in the case of Italian tax negotiations, where the government assumes that companies will grossly understate their profits and will issue a tax bill based on a much higher estimate. The final tax bill results from negotiations.[14] Or it may be that company employees are advised to follow a "higher" law. For example, during the apartheid regime of South Africa, very strict laws of racial separation forbade multinationals from promoting blacks or allowing them to live in "white" company compounds. As global pressure mounted on companies to challenge these policies, more and more firms began circumventing local law, appealing to a higher moral standard of non-discrimination.

Finally, regardless of a country's legal environment, a company may have firm rules of conduct that employees should know about. How employees are to comply with laws, regulations, and company rules needs to be spelled out in the code of conduct.

For example, U.S. multinationals must comply with the Foreign Corrupt Practices Act of 1977 (FCPA) which forbids payments to high-ranking foreign officials but permits "grease" payments to facilitate or speed up services that would have been delivered anyway. Companies may spell out exactly the circumstances in which money can and can't be paid to foreign officials, in compliance with the law. Or they might simply forbid bribery of any sort, choosing to override the FCPA with a higher standard of conduct.

Exhibit 4.3

An Extreme Example of Ethical Guidance

An extreme example of ethical guidance, as opposed to legal compliance, is found in Nordstrom's well-known advisory to employees: "Use your own best judgment."

Guidance Beyond Rules

Employees need guidance on what to do when the rules or laws don't apply, are inappropriate, or are in conflict. Such situations may involve the specific details of normal business functions or the vulnerabilities that are unique to the firm or its industry.

For example, a company that makes extensive use of subcontractors should provide guidance on monitoring workplace practices on site to prevent violation of a principle against inhumane labor conditions in the manufacture of its products. A company whose processing requires use of very large quantities of water would contain code language on the value of clean water and policies relevant to specific plant locations and water supply.

Channels of Communication

Finally, employees need to be aware of how to report problems they observe and how to seek additional guidance when the written code does not address their concerns. Channels of communication should be spelled out in the code of conduct, even if they are as simple and straightforward as "report any wrongdoing to your supervisor."

Of course, it could be the supervisor who is doing the wrong! So, a code of conduct should reflect the organizational structures and processes that are available to report problems or violations, resolve conflicts or confusions, and redress grievances. A confidential 24/7 hotline or helpline has become standard practice in most large U.S.-based firms, and the idea may be catching on around the world.

Table 4.4 lists typical categories that appear in business codes of conduct.

Codes of Conduct: Temptations and Dilemmas

The idea of temptations and dilemmas offers another way to think about the content of codes. Temptations are those situations where a person knows the

Table 4.4

Typical Categories Covered in Codes of Conduct

Accuracy of business records
Alcohol and substance abuse
Antitrust and competition
Competitive information
Compliance with laws, regulations, and company policies
Conflicts of interest
Customer relations
Employee privacy
Environmental compliance
Equal employment opportunity
Export control and import laws
Gifts, favors, and entertainment
Government investigations
Government procurements
Harassment
Health and safety in the workplace
Insider information and securities trading
Marketing, selling, and advertising
Outside business activities
Political activities
Product quality and safety
Protection of confidential information
Protection of intellectual property
Purchasing practices
Records management
Reporting violations
Retaliation
Supplier relations
Use of computer networks and information
Use of corporate assets

Source: Ethics Officers Association. "Creating an International Management System Guidelines Standard for Business Conduct." http://www.eoa.org/bcms.asp (accessed July 16, 2004).

right thing to do, but for some reason doesn't want to do it. Dilemmas, by contrast, are situations where the right answer is ambiguous or unknown. Codes of conduct and policy statements, at their best, cover a company's domain of temptations and provide for avenues to resolve dilemmas that are more difficult or complex.

When a company develops a code of conduct for the first time, leaders may not be fully aware of the specific situations that employees typically encounter. A useful approach to identify an expanded set of ethical vulner-abilities is to conduct an ethical risk assessment with both internal and external stakeholder dialogue. Depending on the firm's particular circum-stances, risk categories that may show up include legal compliance, conflicts of interests, stakeholder interests and harms, vulnerability to lawsuits, market vulnerabilities, or safety and environmental risks. In the paragraphs below we explain a bit more about some of these.

Temptations to Benefit Personally

Virtually every company has policies concerning conflict of interest, and for good reason. This is a very common type of ethical transgression in firms, where the individual has an opportunity to benefit at the expense of the work group or the entire organization. Typical conflicts of interest covered in codes include arranging contracts with businesses from which the employee or family members benefit, tending to personal business on the job, making personal use of company equipment or supplies, receiving gifts in exchange for particular purchasing arrangements, mingling personal and company funds and other assets, supervising friends and family members, or insider trading of the company's or any partner's stock based on nonpublic information. Non-compete clauses attempt to protect the company from employees' taking confidential information and working for competitors.

Company-specific conflicts of interest arise from the firm's particular products, employee base, location, competitive strategy, and so on. National defense contractors, for example, are often dealing with classified information, political overlays to normal business decisions, and a workforce that may have strong military links. In addition to following their own code guidelines, they must abide by the government's terms of engagement as well.

Industry-specific conflicts of interest are those arising from the nature of the business and the competitive environment. Intel Corporation, for example, prohibits its employees from trading in the stock of future partner companies, where the upcoming partnership will be material to the market value of the partner. With this guideline, Intel is acknowledging that its market dominance can mean significant stock price boosts for its small partners, even though such partnerships may not alter Intel's stock price at all.

Temptations to Benefit the Department, Division, or Company

These temptations will not necessarily benefit the individual, but are perceived to benefit the company somehow. Some examples include paying bribes to gain access to decision makers or to secure contracts or resources; gift-giving beyond company guidelines; obtaining and making use of confidential competitor information in bidding; hiding or falsifying information needed by partners to benefit one's own group; and hiring retiring government officials primarily to obtain their privileged information or access.

Stakeholder Harms

A code of conduct and company policies need to acknowledge the major interests of the company's stakeholders and the firm's responsibility not to cause undue harms to them. Such acknowledgment makes it easier for managers and other employees to be forthcoming with questions, concerns, and information, and to tackle problems before they get out of hand. We will revisit these important issues in the upcoming chapter on stakeholder engagement.

Many companies face temptations to hide, deny, or delay action on issues that are likely to affect some stakeholder group negatively. Sometimes the stalling results from fear or from failure to perceive the issue's importance; at other times it is criminal negligence or outright criminal intent. Most often, though, it's a matter of having to deal with too many things at once, and something important slips through the cracks. Codes can help to prevent such problems through clear statements of values that give managers a reason to act on what they know to be true.

For example, workers in tropical climates may not like wearing safety gear such as masks, gloves, and rubber aprons. The gear is hot, sweaty, and irritating. The plant manager knows well enough that the workers have to wear the gear to be protected from harmful substances in the workplace, but he may put off dealing with the problem if the company's code of conduct makes little or no mention of worker safety as a core value and then does not spell out the procedures to be followed and the consequences of ignoring them.

Novel or Unexpected Vulnerabilities

In a turbulent environment, new developments can quickly change the risk profile of a company, and this may require changes in the code of conduct and policy statements. Although codes should be relatively stable so as to provide consistent guidance, they will have to accommodate changing circumstances, technologies, labor conditions, and much more. Policies, of course, are subject to revision as the environment changes.

Technological developments certainly cause new risks. For example, Internet privacy concerns were simply not an issue for companies in the 1980s, because the Internet was at that time primarily an arcane tool for military programmers. Now, however, privacy issues have exploded, and companies find themselves needing to reassure customers, employees, and other stakeholders that web-based information is secure and not subject to misuse. A code statement of respect for privacy, backed up by specific policies governing information access and use, is now essential.

Unexpected vulnerabilities often arise when companies enter new parts of the world. Western firms rediscovered the critical importance of infrastructure—physical, social, and legal—when they began doing business in Russia and the countries of Eastern Europe in the early 1990s. With local governments in shambles or in deep transition, who was responsible for maintaining physical infrastructure? (No one.) How many years would it take to get phone lines installed? (Perhaps ten.) When was a deal finished? (When the money was really transferred.) How was property ownership determined? (Often by simple seizure of state-owned assets.) Why did workers go stony-faced when Western managers talked about the human resources department? (Because the department had been an arm of the Communist Party.)

Traditional tools such as political risk assessment can be useful here in uncovering vulnerabilities that should be included in the code of conduct and in policy statements. Beyond this, however, the code and policy should help managers understand the ambiguities and uncertainties they will face, and should provide avenues for reconciling them with good business practice. At first this may involve a simple statement that the in-country manager needs to communicate with headquarters experts for guidance about how to handle unexpected vulnerabilities. Later, as in-country managers learn what challenges they face, specific policies can be developed to address their needs.

What Does a GBC Code Look Like?

If one wants to determine whether a company is a global business citizen or not, the first place to look—but not by any means the last—is the company's code of conduct. Codes of conduct are becoming pervasive in large firms headquartered in developed nations, and there is no longer any distinction in merely having a code. Furthermore, codes can be designed for many reasons and be intended to fulfill various types of goals. For example, a code can be image-building to external parties without reflecting true corporate identity, as Enron's code so amply demonstrated. Finally, and most importantly, a code of conduct cannot by itself encourage or enforce ethical performance if the essential supporting policies, procedures, and consequences are damaged or missing in the organization or the society.[15]

The proof is in the pudding—the actual language of codes may be very similar or even identical, but how the code is presented, interpreted, incorporated into policy, and emphasized over the long term, and whether sanctions are known, consistently enforced, and fair, will make a huge difference in whether we are looking at a GBC company or not.

Nevertheless, we suggest just a few key attributes that are likely to be observed in the codes of GBC companies:

Table 4.5

Attributes of GBC Language in Codes of Conduct

Attribute	Components
Orientation	• A simple expression of universal values
	• Identification of key stakeholders, including those involuntarily affected
	• Sensitivity to cultural differences
	• Attitude of "extra-legal" compliance—going above and beyond the law
Implementation	• Clear identification of specific situations that are likely to arise in this industry
	• Guidance on what to do when the code is in question or when the culture demands adaptation
	• Support for employee ethical development
	• Support for structures, systems, and processes that facilitate ethical decision making
Accountability	• Emphasis on stakeholder engagement
	• Transparency of reporting
	• Independent assurance—verification of information, openness to monitoring

Source: Logsdon and Wood 2005.

- *Comprehensiveness*—the code and its policies cover a broad scope of issues and are applicable in every place where the company does business. It covers supply chain responsibilities as well as direct company actions, and takes special note of stakeholder interests and possible harms.
- *Language*—the code and policies contain *orientation language* that sets the stage for behavioral expectations in the company's values; *implementation language* that makes explicit how decisions should be made; and *accountability language* that promises employees and other stakeholders access to information they need to meet their interests.
- *User-friendliness*—the level of detail contained in codes and policies is less important than the ease of use. Regardless of length or detail, the code and policies should be readily accessible to everyone in the organization, easy to comprehend, and unambiguous. Users should know how to move to the next step, should they need clarification or more information.

It might be useful to say a bit more about the language of GBC codes. Table 4.5 lists a number of specific characteristics to look for in a company's orientation, implementation, and accountability language, and a few of these components are illustrated with text from the codes of global companies.[16]

75

Identification of Key Stakeholders

Most companies will acknowledge certain responsibilities to investors, employees, customers, and suppliers. A GBC company, however, will go beyond these core economic stakeholders and explicitly identify communities, host countries, and other stakeholders who may be involuntarily harmed by the company's actions. Shell, for example, spells out five core groups:

> Shell companies recognize five areas of responsibility: to shareholders, to customers, to employees, to those with whom they do business, and to society. . . . These five areas of responsibility are seen as inseparable. Therefore, it is the duty of management continuously to assess the priorities and discharge its responsibilities as best it can on the basis of that assessment.

ConocoPhillips includes a very general stakeholder acknowledgment without naming any particular stakeholders:

> We are ethical and trustworthy in our relationships with all stakeholders.

Novartis (at its website, www.novartis.com/corporatecitizen) makes a general statement and a specific list:

> We care about the expectations and concerns of our stakeholders. We recognize the interest of our shareholders, employees, customers, neighbors, the authorities, and the public at large in our societal behavior, and the health, safety, and environmental impacts of our business.

Guidance on Resolving Questions and Conflicts

Employees need to understand how to implement a code of conduct on the ground, day to day. It is important, then, that a GBC code contain language that clearly guides the employee through the decision and action process.

Shell, for example, makes a very general and easily located statement on bribery, but then makes it difficult for employees to find specific guidance. One must dig through several layers of the website with little or no mapping in order to find specific language on how to resolve questions and conflicts about bribery:

> The direct or indirect offer, payment, soliciting and acceptance of bribes in any form are unacceptable practices.

BP, while also having several layers of instructions on bribery, makes a clearer, more accessible, and more complete statement of how the employee should respond to a bribery situation:

BP will never offer, pay, solicit or accept bribes in any form, either directly or indirectly. This includes those transactions formerly known as facilitation payments. Any demand for or offer of a bribe in whatever form to any BP employee must be rejected and reported ,immediately to line management.

Designing for Buy-In

Developing a code is the first step in global business citizenship, but it's all for nothing unless there is buy-in. Buy-in doesn't happen all at once, and it doesn't happen because a code has been written or because consultants design a snazzy roll-out. Consider these examples:

- Manager Pryor receives his company's code of conduct from the CEO, who is leading an all-day workshop on ethics, compliance, and the code of conduct in practice.
- Manager Rao receives a copy of her company's code of conduct from the legal department with a note that says, "Please sign and return this receipt indicating your acceptance of these principles and policies and your willingness to abide by them."
- Manager Tsu receives his company's code in the mail, but unfortunately he does not understand English very well, so he puts it in a desk drawer and goes on with business as usual.

Which company do you think really means it? Which has the best chance for widespread buy-in?

Lead by Example

No matter what's written in the code, no matter what structures are in place, the firm's leaders with power and authority have to be viewed as acting well above any minimums required of their employees. There should never be a question of the CEO using a company plane for a family vacation, if the company forbids the private use of corporate assets. If conflicts of interest are spelled out, the CFO should never be making sweetheart deals with her cousin's accounting firm or hiring her spouse as a high-paid consultant. Executives have to be above reproach, modeling and reinforcing the behavior that the code demands of everyone.

Try Harder to Communicate

Companies have to work to communicate a code as if they really mean it. Johnson & Johnson never has a management training session without making reference to the values of the Credo.[17] BP offers analytical information on how its 24-hour helpline is being used, allowing managers to see that this medium of communication is valued and alerting them to the types of issues that typically arise. For multinationals, it is particularly important to acknowledge the many languages that employees may be using and to ensure that every employee has access to code guidelines in a language that s/he understands well.

Put the Structures in Place

How much change will be needed to make a code of conduct work? A great deal depends on what type of organization it is, what the leaders intend, and what kind of trust exists in the workplace already. We will revisit these issues in upcoming organizational change and implementation chapters. For now, let's briefly review the kinds of things that are needed to make a code of conduct work.[18]

Assignment of Responsibility

Putting a secretary or a mid-level staffer in charge of the firm's ethics program will not show the kind of commitment needed for buy-in. A high-level line manager, preferably the CEO or a direct report, should have responsibility for promoting ethical conduct. Large U.S. firms are often dedicating a high-level position as Ethics Officer, and the Sentencing Guidelines of 2004 virtually mandate this approach.[19] In addition, an ethics committee of the board of directors can add credibility, and may even participate in developing the code. A visible chain of command for reporting and decision making can ensure that all employees take ethics seriously.

Regular Training

Every employee of the company needs to have a personal and understandable introduction to the code of conduct and the enforcement structures. New employee orientation is an ideal spot to build in this initial contact with the code. Managers need more exposure and a chance to practice ethical decision making and compliance with guidelines, so regular training and refresher sessions should be built into the manager's annual routine. Managers also need practice in sorting through the challenges they think they might face in trying to live up to the code. And, as new issues and problems arise, training is needed to help employees at all levels grasp and wrestle with the company's changing ethical environment.

Communication Channels

What happens at the top is important, but ethical conduct is more than a top-down phenomenon. All employees need secure and trustworthy access to communication channels whereby they can report problems, ask questions, and seek guidance on tricky issues. Many large companies are making extensive use of helplines (formerly called hotlines), where employees can call 24/7 to leave anonymous or confidential messages. Other vehicles include newsletters and on-line chatrooms, ombudspersons to whom an employee can turn for personal advice on ethics issues, and up-the-line reporting and problem-solving.

Incentives

It may seem silly to talk about incentives in the same breath as doing the right thing. But think about it—if managers are exhorted to manage ethically, and their entire incentive and compensation system is built on direct and measurable contributions to profit, won't there be a great many temptations to slip over the ethics edge to boost this quarter's financial results? Indeed, this situation guarantees the "conflict of interest" risk identified earlier. Building ethics and compliance into management evaluation processes is an essential step for a GBC company. For example, 360-degree reviews can ask a manager's reports, peers, and superiors to comment on his/her ethical leadership along with other attributes to be evaluated. In addition, codes of conduct need to be aligned with corporate succession planning and performance management systems to ensure that criteria for salary, bonuses, and consideration for promotions are aligned with the company's core values and principles.

Enforcement

It goes without saying that a code of conduct and its policies must be enforced if the company is serious about ethics. Consequences for violations should be clearly communicated in advance. Punishments should fit the crimes, and there should be no favoritism or status-based exceptions. This does not mean that enforcement should be rigid or exactly the same in every situation. There will be times when humane considerations or cultural circumstances require variations, and these variations must be explained so that they are perceived as fair and reasonably consistent.

The Biggest Mistakes in Codes of Conduct

Getting it right—developing and implementing codes of conduct and policies that actually offer appropriate guidance—can be tricky. There are several traps that even the most sincere companies can fall into. Take a look at five of these pitfalls that GBC companies especially want to avoid.

"Founderitis"

An organization's life cycle stage can be an important factor in its ability to adopt and enforce a GBC code and policies. Companies that are still founder-led, or are one generation of management from the founder, are likely to reflect the founder's strong values, that may or may not contain a reasoned and comprehensive set of universal principles. The problem here is that what is required to make a start-up flourish may be quite different from what is needed to sustain a large multinational enterprise. "Do what it takes," for example, may be a practical value for a new and struggling company, if everyone understands the ethical limits of the statement. But in truth, and certainly for a more established and far-flung operation, this value is an ambiguous and faulty guide for action and all too easily leads employees to cheat, lie, hide, and deny, all in the name of "whatever it takes."

"Founderitis" can also be a mistake in reverse, often when growth firms go public. That is, a company founded on strong values may find itself pressured to dump those values when a new generation of management takes over. One thinks here of H.B. Fuller Corporation, whose board eventually rejected the strong social service values of its founding family, or even of Levi Strauss Corporation, which resisted similar demands and upheld its values even as competition forced changes in its practice. For a GBC company, the founder's values represent a data point for thoughtful analysis. They shouldn't be written in stone, but neither should they be summarily abandoned.

Selective Exclusion

Many companies have gotten the initial message about values and principles, but their choices reflect the views or desires of top management, or the strategic direction of the company, and do not offer a comprehensive set of universal standards. Oil company TotalFinaElf, for example, lists these as its core values: "professionalism, respect for employees, an ongoing concern for safety and environmental protection, and a commitment to contribute to the development of host communities." Without further elaboration, these values could be seen as admirable but incomplete. However, the company goes on to assert its commitment to the principles of the United Nations Universal Declaration of Human Rights, the Organization for Economic Cooperation and Development (OECD) guidelines for multinationals, and the International Labor Organization (ILO) standards concerning child labor.

By reference to these comprehensive statements of principles, TotalFinaElf avoids the trap of selective exclusion.

Compliance Orientation

A great many U.S. companies have developed codes intended to provide little more than legal and regulatory check-offs for managers. For a GBC company, this approach is insufficient. Legal compliance is certainly important, but it should not be the only, or perhaps even the primary, emphasis of a code of conduct. Rather, a code and its policies offer guidance on behavioral expectations beyond the law. Compliance alone will not help a company manage its stakeholder relationships effectively or keep it from being blindsided by developments in the larger environment. Furthermore, when the lawyers take charge of the company's response to challenges, important avenues of problem resolution, relationship-building, and information transmission are closed off.[20]

Bragging

You'd think a GBC company would really have something to brag about, and actually, this might be so! A danger here is that the image management folks take charge of code and policies, and then what was meant as a guidance system becomes instead a bundle of pretty posters, flashy brochures, and press releases. Understand, there's nothing wrong with letting the world know when things are going right. But, regardless of how many colors are used in their publication, the code and policies have to be accessible to those on the ground and usable in everyday decision making.

Another danger with bragging is that the media and many NGOs are all too ready to snap up a sound bite from a company website or press release and use it for their own purposes, regardless of the context, the company's intentions, or the actual outcomes. We saw in an earlier chapter that many executives are gun-shy of media attention, and understandably so. Adopting a code of conduct and implementing policies is serious business with plenty of room for experimentation, mistakes, and learning. GBC companies have to be careful, therefore, to maintain good relationships with NGOs and media who may misuse their code/policy information.

All Talk, No Action

We can't emphasize enough that a code of conduct and its accompanying policies are useless if they are not widely known throughout the firm, used in decision making, and enforced through incentive systems and sanctions. In upcoming chapters, we explore these implementation issues.

Conclusion

A GBC company will base its code on a small, reasonably comprehensive set of universal principles. Such principles can be discovered through religion, philosophy, or social and political agreement, and their adoption helps companies to avoid the severe risks of cultural and ethical relativism. A comprehensive code will spell out once again the company's core values and guiding principles, provide specific rules of law and company policy, offer guidance in situations that may be ambiguous or conflicting, and specify how employees can report incidents and seek clarification. The code's specific content will depend to a large extent on the company's exposures because of location, industry, nature of workforce, or inherent commitments. The language of a GBC code will contain specific statements of orientation, implementation, and accountability.

Buy-in, that crucial step of spreading ownership of and commitment to a code of conduct, requires that executives lead by example, communication channels be open and fluid, and the necessary structures be put into place—training, evaluation, incentive systems, and enforcement that is systematic and fair. Effective implementation of a code can be all too easily prevented by "founderitis," selective exclusion when choosing values and principles, a strict compliance orientation instead of a focus on employee judgment, bragging, and faking it by being all talk and no action.

A GBC company's code of conduct does not need to be complicated. It does, however, need to be value-based, clear, and sincere. A code of conduct is necessary but not sufficient to help a company behave ethically. Especially for large companies, where the top manager is not in direct contact with most employees, a code and its policy statements provide guidance, but the real challenges lie in making it work day in, day out, in all of the company's locations. Developing a workable code and accompanying policies is a significant achievement to be celebrated; the company now has a guidance system that serves as a foundation for both routine and extraordinary decision making. But there is more to be done.

➤ 5 ◄

The Principle of Accountability and Processes of Stakeholder Engagement

Accountability is built into the fiber of publicly held corporations. Every manager quickly learns how to be accountable to those a step or two up the hierarchy. Every CEO and CFO knows how to be accountable to capital providers and financial regulatory agencies or suffer stiff consequences. But global business citizenship requires a fresh look at the principle of accountability and the many ways to engage stakeholders for organizational success. Accountability provides the basis for stakeholder decision making, and, as such, is a fundamental responsibility of the organization to all stakeholders who are significantly impacted by its existence.

GBC accountability goes beyond conventional one-way communication outward to a continuous process of *engaging with and responding to stakeholders* in order to develop and maintain trust over the long-term:

> GBC accountability is the principle of acknowledging and responding to the legitimate interests of stakeholders and society by learning what information stakeholders need and want, and by communicating information about the economic, social, and environmental impacts of the organization's performance to those who have a right to know.

GBC accountability requires a "look, listen, and learn" approach to stakeholders. If the company is simply providing minimum information required by regulatory agencies or a stock exchange, its managers probably aren't learning how well the company is meeting stakeholder needs. Nor does the organization get feedback from stakeholders about how useful or appropriate reported information is to stakeholders, or what else *they* might need to know to make their own informed decisions. Stakeholder-focused dialogue and information systems attempt to determine who needs to know what, what needs to be done, and what progress has been made to address the expectations and objectives of multiple stakeholders.

Remember, addressing stakeholders' legitimate interests involves more than providing information. It also means interpreting stakeholder dialogue and making the necessary organizational changes in order to be trusted by stakeholders. In this chapter, we focus on who these stakeholders are and how to engage with them. Chapter 9 will develop ideas on how to measure impacts on stakeholders and report information to them.

Accountability: An Overview

The components of accountability for a GBC company include stakeholder engagement, organizational responsiveness, compliance, transparency, assurance, learning, and innovation. So how do these components enable GBC? Only through *stakeholder engagement* can the organization learn what is expected of it. *Responsiveness* is the essential illustration to stakeholders of the extent to which the organization has taken their expectations and concerns into account and to what extent it has incorporated stakeholders into its organizational and decision-making processes. *Compliance* demonstrates organizational commitment to good citizenship by abiding by local, regional, national, and international regulations and ethical norms. Through *transparency,* the organization reveals the impacts of its behaviors on its stakeholders and thereby builds trust in the intention to do right by them; it also reveals stakeholder-relevant internal processes such as governance mechanisms and worker safety procedures. By providing independent *verification and assurance* of the data it reports, the organization provides external validation to external parties, which enhances trust. When it institutionalizes *learning and innovation,* the organization translates the totality of accountability components into meaningful organizational change towards alignment of organizational behaviors with prevailing stakeholder expectations and societal well-being.

Global business citizenship *requires* accountability—exceeding levels heretofore practiced by contemporary business organizations. As the GBC model articulates, experiments to address Step 3 problems—those experiments being perhaps the riskiest of ventures to corporate reputation and maintenance of social capital—are not possible without ongoing dialogue and true two-way communication with stakeholders. Furthermore, GBC requires accountability to accomplish the linchpin of sustainable competitive advantage—continuous learning and innovation.

So if GBC companies are to be accountable, to whom is accountability owed? Shareholders and other investors and capital providers have a claim on financial performance and information regarding it. Employees, suppliers, customers, communities, and governments have all laid claim to various other aspects of company performance. Yet beyond these well-established stakeholders, companies are now being challenged with the demands and interests of a host of additional stakeholders, including economically or socially marginalized people (poor, handicapped, illiterate, non-English-speaking, non-Western, under-age) and future generations. Although NGOs often claim to speak for such groups, in fact they are not being considered in any systematic way in most companies' decision-making processes. Nevertheless, they are the stakeholders most likely to be involuntarily harmed by a company's actions, and thus companies do have a moral responsibility to include their needs and interests in planning and operations.

To be clear, GBC does not require companies to solve the problems of world poverty and ignorance. But if a company is taking the land that native peoples require to feed themselves, or is polluting the only water supply in a region, or is putting employees in danger with old technologies that are upgradeable, then GBC does require attention to these kinds of specific consequences as well as accountability to the affected stakeholders.

Each distinct group of stakeholders is part of the greater society whose interests focus on environmental issues, social issues, and standard of living issues. The extent to which the economic, social, and environmental expectations of society can be met is largely driven by, and in turn drives, the financial performance of business. The importance of accountability to all stakeholders is becoming increasingly apparent as business comes to understand how the responses of one constituency directly and indirectly influence organizational performance. In Exhibit 5.1, Ford's accountability statement appears as an illustration.

We have to point out that stakeholders sometimes have interests and demands that are not legitimate or not essential for the company to address or meet. For example, companies aren't required to reveal proprietary "secrets" unless the public is endangered and no other action will protect it. Managers don't always get it right, but then, neither do stakeholders. A rational accountability process will contain evaluative steps to assess whether stakeholders are demanding information the company can and should legitimately provide.

Exhibit 5.1

Ford's Statement of Accountability

We will be honest and open and model the highest standards of corporate integrity. We will achieve this by:

- Being responsive to stakeholders' concerns on the impact of our operations, products and services through public disclosure and regular reporting;
- Making accurate and forthright statements, competing ethically, avoiding conflicts of interest and having zero tolerance for the offer, payment, solicitation or acceptance of bribes.

Source: Ford Motor Company 2003, p. 12.

Figure 5.1 displays the accountability model of the Institute for Social and Ethical Accountability (ISEA), a nonprofit organization that has been involved in developing voluntary standards for accountability processes.

In the ISEA model, accountability is possible only if stakeholder engagement processes are embedded in corporations so that relevant performance data are routinely reported to those who need to know. GBC incorporates and builds on the ISEA model in order to implement the essential four steps of: (1) values embedded in a code of conduct, (2) local implementation, (3) analysis and experimentation, and (4) organizational learning.

Having introduced the principle of accountability essential to a GBC company, the remainder of this chapter focuses on the nature of stakeholder engagement and tools to make such engagement and dialogue successful and organizational responsiveness effective. We address the other specific components of accountability in later chapters: compliance, transparency, and assurance in chapter 9; and learning and innovation in chapter 11.

Stakeholder Engagement

Dealing with selected stakeholders is a commonplace function in all business organizations. And virtually all large firms have a formal spot on the organization chart for investor relations, customer relations, employee relations, and community relations, to name a few. What does the idea of "stakeholder engagement" offer that's really new?

True, many companies have these functions, but they are often silos, lonesome outposts of staff rather than line responsibility, where there is little

Figure 5.1 **ISEA's Accountability Model**

Source: http://www.accountability.org.uk/uploadstore/cms/docs/AA1000 %20Framework%201999.pdf page 27 (accessed January 6, 2005).

communication across these stakeholder functions, and little reporting upward to a senior executive in charge of reputation management. This "elephant" of separate stakeholder responsiveness practices leaves practitioners in these various functions touching different parts of the stakeholder set without full information and cooperation to do their jobs as effectively as they could.

Organizational stakeholders are valuable sources of strategic and operational learning. GBC companies find it necessary to achieve a high-level dialogue with those with whom the organization must interact in order to learn how best to solve ordinary operational problems, cross-cultural differences, and code implementation issues in a sustainable way. While the conventional business model is likely to focus on "managing stakeholder relations" for the firm's explicit benefit, the newer idea of stakeholder engagement emphasizes the nurturing of ongoing dialogue and the development of trust. Partners in a trusting relationship do not always demand quid pro quo, but are

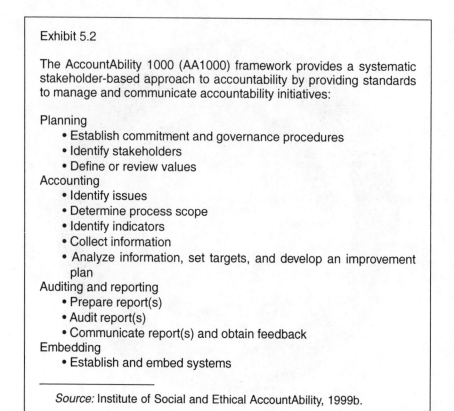

Exhibit 5.2

The AccountAbility 1000 (AA1000) framework provides a systematic stakeholder-based approach to accountability by providing standards to manage and communicate accountability initiatives:

Planning
- Establish commitment and governance procedures
- Identify stakeholders
- Define or review values

Accounting
- Identify issues
- Determine process scope
- Identify indicators
- Collect information
- Analyze information, set targets, and develop an improvement plan

Auditing and reporting
- Prepare report(s)
- Audit report(s)
- Communicate report(s) and obtain feedback

Embedding
- Establish and embed systems

Source: Institute of Social and Ethical AccountAbility, 1999b.

confident that, over time, the relationship will be mutually beneficial. The AA1000 process standard, developed by ISEA, has this to say[1]:

> [A]t the end of the day, stakeholders will develop trust in organizations, and will be willing to continue investing their time and effort only in those who are transparent, responsive, and who make decisions that take stakeholder needs into account.

Which Stakeholders Need to Be Engaged?

It's a deceptively simple but challenging question. A narrow definition of stakeholders focuses on individuals and groups that are directly relevant to the firm's core economic interests. These are easy enough to identify—customers, employees, investors, suppliers. Obviously a company's viability depends on staying engaged with these stakeholders, and indeed the "stakeholder relations" functions common in firms relate to just these groups.

Figure 5.2 **WBCSD Stakeholder Attributes and Engagement Objectives**

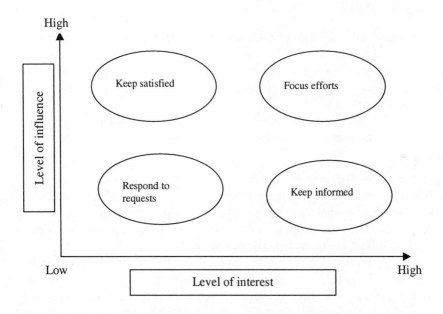

Source: World Business Council for Sustainable Development 2003, p. 17.

The World Business Council on Sustainable Development (WBCSD) developed a simple matrix to identify and categorize stakeholders by their level of influence on the organization and on their interest in the issues relevant to the organization, shown in Figure 5.2. This model can be a useful first step to decide how to proceed on an issue, depending on who is interested in it and who can influence the outcome. But something important is missing.

See if you can tell what it missing by looking at the following set of stakeholder characteristics, developed by Mitchell, Agle, and Wood.[2]

- *Power:* Does the stakeholder have the ability to influence the firm against its will?
- *Legitimacy:* Does the stakeholder have legitimate standing with respect to the firm, or does it have a legitimate issue or interest related to the firm?
- *Urgency:* Does the stakeholder have an urgent claim with high-magnitude consequences requiring immediate response?

The addition of legitimacy expands the manager's perspective on which stakeholders need to be engaged. Now consideration of the stakeholder set expands to include:

- Stakeholders who don't know about issues that are relevant to their welfare, for example, neighbors of the plant who are unaware of pollutants or potential hazards from the plant's operations. These stakeholders have interests in the firm's performance, but no knowledge that their interests are threatened.
- Stakeholders without a voice to express their interests, for example, poor workers in subcontractor sweatshops (absence of power or influence).

Legitimate stakeholders therefore can include those who lack awareness or knowledge of their interests and those who lack power because they are somehow marginalized. GBC companies choose to engage legitimate stakeholders regardless of their knowledge or power because of moral commitments (e.g., cause no harm) or because of their long-term perspective on the troubles that can arise from untended stakeholder needs.

Frankly not all stakeholders are cooperative, or accessible, or trustworthy. We must acknowledge the reality of cheaters, liars, thieves, con-artists, and the violence-prone. The GBC company will engage its legitimate stakeholders in counteracting these pests, and will keep on keeping on, trying to interact with all their important stakeholders in transparent and honest ways. And we need to consider the voiceless, and to judiciously scrutinize those who claim to represent them. For example, a company may be attacked by an activist group claiming that forced labor is used in the firm's supply chain. The firm might correctly claim that the activist group is not a legitimate voice for labor, or that it's attacking for its own selfish purposes, but the issue of forced labor may indeed be legitimate. The company would be wise to address the issue and to treat the activists with respect, even when they don't seem to deserve it. Even if the messenger is problematic, the message may be quite valid.

Figure 5.3 illustrates the relationships among these three attributes and the types of stakeholders that result described in Exhibit 5.3.

Mapping organizational stakeholders onto the stakeholder salience model is useful to plan how best to target stakeholder engagement initiatives, and to design the appropriate interventions for different groups. Logically those core stakeholders who exhibit all attributes—legitimacy, power, and urgency—should be identified first for appropriately significant engagement programs. But after that obvious step, what next? GBC companies can benefit strategically by carefully considering stakeholders whose issues would be urgent if their knowledge about firm impacts was complete. It could prove to be of significant advantage, for example, to a firm that created local good will by providing a solution to a future community transportation problem before

Figure 5.3   **Stakeholder Salience Model: Who Matters to Managers?**

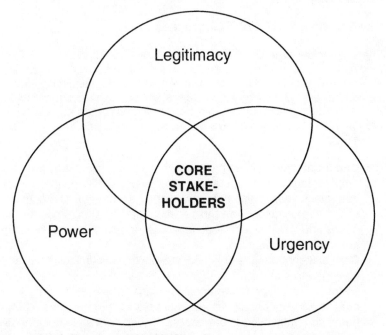

Source: Mitchell, Agle, and Wood 1997, p. 4.

the firm expanded its facilities. Of course, the stakeholder diagram will change with time and circumstance, so stakeholder mapping is an ongoing need.

We certainly acknowledge that in lean economic times, when companies are downsizing and squeezing out maximum efficiencies, it is difficult to think about how to use company resources for stakeholder engagement. Many companies simply do not believe they have the bandwidth for such a commitment. Managers go to the office each morning and step into a blender full of pressing tasks that shove out any attention to longer-term issues. The point of GBC, however, is that stakeholder engagement is not a luxury or an option. It is an essential component of business accountability. If you're going to be a player on the global field, you need to have the right equipment.

Once the stakeholder targets are identified, it is important to choose and persuade the "right people" both inside the organization and outside to participate. Engagements are far more likely to be successful if participants themselves legitimize the effort. It may be difficult to attract representatives for important groups if they are not well-organized, but it will best serve to ensure that the full range of views within a stakeholder group is reflected and that a legitimate outcome is possible by paying close attention to whom to include.

91

Exhibit 5.3

One Size Does Not Fit All Stakeholders

The stakeholder salience model developed by Mitchell, Agle, and Wood (shown in Figure 5.3) is a handy way to think about how managers are *likely* to respond to certain kinds of stakeholders. The question is, Which stakeholders are going to get managers' attention in what circumstances?

In the model, stakeholders with two or all three of the key attributes are the ones most likely to have management's ear. The four types are these:

- **Dominant** stakeholders have legitimacy and power. They are best represented by "the usual suspects" in stakeholder analysis: investors, employees, customers, suppliers, government, and communities. Organizations tend to be structured to accommodate the needs and interests of these stakeholders, and so the relationship are routine and ongoing.
- **Core** stakeholders are dominant stakeholders (with legitimacy and power) who also have an urgent issue that they want the firm to address. Because of their ongoing relationship with the firm, they are likely to voice their issues and to expect prompt action. Managers generally need to pay attention when core stakeholders develop urgent claims.
- **Dependent** stakeholders have legitimacy and urgent claims, but have no power to influence the firm. An example might be a local charity that gives the working poor access to health clinics. Such an organization could well be on management's stakeholder radar screen, but the balance of power is strictly one way.
- **Dangerous** stakeholders have urgent claims and power, but no legitimate standing. Terrorists—or freedom fighters, depending on your perspective—might qualify. It seems odd that managers would give such groups any recognition at all, but it is clear that most large multinational firms now train their executives on how to respond to kidnappings, bomb threats, sabotage, and other acts of violence against the company or its people.

Less likely to get and hold managers' attention are the stakeholders who possess only one of the key attributes:

- **Discretionary** stakeholders have legitimacy, but no power over the firm and no urgent claims on it. These are stakeholders the firm may choose to be in relationship with, and those relationships may

(continued)

be very beneficial, but there's nothing compelling about them. A company's contributions to a local symphony orchestra might be an example.

- **Latent** stakeholders possess power to influence the firm, but they have no legitimate standing and no particular reason to use their power. These stakeholders are most likely to surface when managers engage in "what if" brainstorming or scenario-building exercises. The firm may have some policies and procedures for dealing with them if and when the time comes, but they're not likely to be high on managers' priority lists.

- **"Mosquitoes"** are stakeholders who have urgent claims on a firm, but have neither legitimate standing nor power to influence the firm's behavior. Managers are very unlikely to pay attention to "mosquitoes" unless their claim is taken up by powerful, legitimate others.

And this brings us to a final point about the stakeholder salience model: It is dynamic. Some *types* of stakeholders are going to be relatively stable. There will always be employees, investors, customers, and suppliers. But their relative weights will shift over time and with issues. And, discretionary, latent, or merely irritating stakeholders may discover that the key to meeting their needs is to align with core or dominant stakeholders—and that can spell big trouble for managers who haven't been paying attention to their stakeholder networks.

How and Where Do We Engage Our Stakeholders?

What constitutes the appropriate venue, tool, and process for a stakeholder engagement initiative? It depends. When multiple parties representing multiple points of view address issues of complexity, the task may quickly overwhelm the best intentions. Several important factors influence the "how" of stakeholder engagement.

Which Stakeholders Will Be Included? And Does This Depend on the Issue or Goal?

When a single, homogeneous stakeholder group is to be engaged (say the employees of an organization are going to give input into quality of work life issues), the appropriate process might be a simple survey given in the workplace. On the other hand, when suppliers for a multinational corporation are to be engaged in workplace practices of the supply chain, involving many geographic areas and diverse cultures, a multi-stakeholder design should take

93

into account the increased complexity of the engagement and utilize tools that take culture, language, and other relevant factors into account.

How Are Cultural Differences Accommodated in Stakeholder Engagement?

Discussing the challenges faced by multi-stakeholder designs, Susskind et al. examine the alternatives of simultaneous translation (expensive, and sometimes an obstacle to joint problem-solving), distribution of (translated) written materials (may cause different stakeholders to come away with slightly different conclusions about outcomes), and face-to-face dialogue (difficult for some groups). They conclude that multi-stakeholder dialogues are built on the premise that dialogue and deliberation best encourage problem-solving, but that there can be difficulties in any format when the stakeholders are culturally diverse.[3]

How Diverse Are the Stakeholder Perspectives?

A labor union is an example of a relatively homogeneous group, sharing views on the issues that affect the typical worker: wages, health care, workplace safety, retirement, and the like. Alternatively, consumers for a petrochemical company would include individuals and industrial consumers, wholesalers, and retailers—a heterogeneous mixture of self-interests and political perspectives.

How Complex Are the Issues?

Take the example of environmental protection. Biodiversity, ecosystem balance, global warming, pollution, weather patterns, and so on make for an extraordinarily complex issue that no single company could possibly solve. Multisector collaboration, including multi-government action, is essential to coordinate the many and complex stakeholders involved in this issue. However, if the issue is a particular company's environmental footprint and what it can do to lessen impacts, then the issue can be measured, evaluated, and dealt with via more contained stakeholder engagement processes. Even simpler, if the issue is a company's recycling, then very specific measures can be taken to address the problem and, perhaps, it is only the employee stakeholder group that really needs to be involved.

What Are the Resource Constraints on Engagement?

Stakeholder engagement isn't costless. Even a simple survey involves data-collection and analysis that take time and money. Multi-stakeholder dialogues are more expensive, and an international platform increases the price tag exponentially. Obviously it is essential to prioritize engagement initiatives according to the power, urgency, and legitimacy (or the level of influence and interest) of the stakeholders involved and issues to be tackled. Limited funds can seriously hamper the quality of the process, making legitimate results difficult to achieve.

Basic Approaches to Stakeholder Engagement

True stakeholder engagement aims to give multiple viewpoints voice in a decision-making process. However, the degree to which stakeholders are actually engaged ranges broadly from simple data-gathering techniques, such as surveys or interviews, to major multi-stakeholder processes that focus on issues. The techniques cover a broad spectrum of structure and levels of engagement, from data-gathering to consensus-building and collaboration, and at the local, national, or global level.

At the most basic level, a firm gathers information from its stakeholders via written surveys or focus groups. Data-gathering of this sort is quick, easy, and cheap, but too often remains a one-way feed that benefits the firm without payoff for stakeholders. While such data-gathering can be easily accomplished at local and national levels, it does nothing to build trust between a firm and its stakeholders without careful attention to responsive feedback.

The British telecommunications firm, BT, reveals an array of basic stakeholder engagement practices in Exhibit 5.4.

More Complex Approaches to Stakeholder Engagement

Global business poses tough dilemmas that are best suited for a broad-based approach to problem-solving that involves multiple constituencies. ABB Ltd., headquartered in Zurich, began its stakeholder engagement process by talking with national and international NGOs, trade unions, central and local governments, academics, media, religious groups, and the business community in order to navigate the uneven ethical terrain in their multiple locations.[4] Some really tough questions arose:

- Can all suppliers really be expected to meet the same standards? How could ABB monitor compliance?
- If the local government won't protect human rights, what should ABB do?
- Gender discrimination is against ABB's policy, but what about locations where women are not permitted to work in factories?[5]

Exhibit 5.4

BT's Statement about Stakeholder Engagement

BT, a global leader in stakeholder engagement and investor relations, engages with different stakeholders in different ways. Here are some examples they provide.

Customers
- Consumer liaison panels
- Surveys on quality of service and future expectations
- Telecommunications advisory committees

Employees
- Annual employee survey
- Relationships with trade unions
- European Consultative Works Council

Suppliers
- Annual supplier satisfaction survey
- Ethical trading forums with key suppliers and industry colleagues

Shareholders
- Developed the Investors section of the annual report following consultation with analysts specifically interested in the social and environmental performance of the company

Community
- Survey of stakeholders revealed that education should be a top priority for social investment of the firm.

Source: http://www.btplc.com/Societyandenvironment/Socialand environmentreport/Stakeholderdialogue/Stakeholderengagement/ stakeholderengagement.htm (accessed September 14, 2004).

In 2001 ABB Ltd., a global power and automation technologies firm with suppliers around the globe, both published their first corporate social policy and addressed the moral dilemmas they faced by launching an ambitious stakeholder consultation that involved meetings between ABB managers/ workers and local representatives from thirty-four countries.[6] Their objective in these extensive exercises was to design and implement an organizational social policy. Discussions focused on two areas:

1. whether the social policy was sufficiently comprehensive and covered the important topics and issues, and
2. how to implement and monitor the social policy.

In two rounds of stakeholder dialogues (second round dialogues included
eleven countries of the initial thirty-four), the participants discussed the firm's
social policy statement consisting of thirteen principles, prioritized the focus
on the list of principles, and highlighted the firm's vulnerability relating to
each. Measurement of the firm's performance on social principles and lack
of consistent indicators were frequently voiced concerns. Finally, the participants noted the need for clearly articulated objectives and targets for each
principle, and the desirability of audited social reports.

In its 2004 Sustainability Review, ABB was able to report a great deal of
progress in implementing their social policy and stakeholder engagement
processes. Sustainability dialogues were now occurring in forty-eight countries, up from the initial thirty-four. Corporate-level dialogues in 2004 resulted in some structural organizational changes to facilitate integration of
social policies into operating procedures, a task force to examine women's
promotion issues, and a commitment to become a carbon dioxide-neutral
company. Country-level sustainability dialogues focused on a variety of specific issues, including the business case for sustainability in the United Kingdom, community involvement and workplace safety and health in the United
States, and ABB's partnership with the United Way in Canada.[7]

Stakeholder Engagement for Large-Scale
Social Problem-Solving

Business organizations may need to collaborate to address big issues by lev-
eraging the resources and capacities of multiple partners and to mutually
learn from their experiments, successes, and failures. Often business organizations partner with governments and NGOs to address significantly complex issues within the domain of the environment and sustainable
development. Some issues can be addressed solo, and often circumstances
or competitive environment dictate an individual approach. Figure 5.4 frames
a way of thinking about how and when organizations might choose or be
forced to act alone and when they would benefit from working with others.

Lone Ranger Strategies

Lone ranger approaches make sense when organizations and their stakeholders take distinct paths pursuing independent goals without strong mutual

Figure 5.4 **Model of Business Collaboration**

	Weak common interests	Strong common interests
Low interdependence in accomplishing goal	Lone rangers	Technical/professional associations
High interdependence in accomplishing goal	Antagonistic stakeholders (management vs. labor)	Collaboration/partnership

Source: Logsdon 1991, pp. 23–37.

interests or when partners simply don't exist. For example, in the 1980s, pharmaceutical company Merck developed a cure for river blindness and then sought partners to pay for and distribute the drug in remote parts of Africa and South America. However, no international groups or governments stepped forward, so Merck decided to go it alone. However, the lone ranger approach is sometimes based upon an inaccurate assessment when the parties fail to recognize their mutual interdependence or when they fail to understand the commonality of their goals. It is rarely the case that a lone ranger truly exists in a vacuum, without need of or reliance on other stakeholders.

Antagonistic Strategies

Antagonistic approaches to stakeholder relationships occur when problem-solving must be highly interdependent but the parties do not share common interests. For example, management and labor rely on one another heavily, but each party may have mutually exclusive interests when negotiating labor contracts. Collaboration between them would contribute to attainment of the overall goal, but alignment of their distinct interests is difficult. When stakeholders themselves are antagonistic to the firm, dialogue is essential. Without it, there is little hope of reaching mutually beneficial solutions when conflict is present. Consensus-building processes that result in joint decision making are indicated in these situations.

Technical/Professional Association Memberships

Memberships are appropriate for organizations where mutual interests with peers are significant, but their goals can be achieved independently.

Because competition among businesses is fierce within industries, organizations can pursue the achievement of common goals without sacrificing competitive advantage. The coalition of pharmaceutical companies toward the eradication of AIDS in South Africa through professional association action is an example of this model. The association is an important source of benchmarking best practices for organizations whose interests align, whose motives for collaboration are weak, or who are highly competitive.

Collaboration and Partnerships

Collaboration and partnerships make sense when an organization is highly interdependent with the stakeholders with whom it shares a high level of mutual interest. Every player is seeking roughly the same goals for roughly the same reasons, and each has particular skills and resources to apply to the common problem. So it follows naturally that the players should get together and develop fruitful ways of working together. Collaboration is the mechanism for problem-solving when seeking to address global problems that exceed the capability of any single firm, government, or international organization. The UN Global Compact reports hundreds of collaborations and partnerships to achieve the Compact's goals, and we will report on some of these in subsequent chapters.

Multi-Stakeholder Dialogues

In 1992 the UN hosted a conference in Brazil to address environmental and social problems of the world. One outcome of the summit was Agenda 21, a comprehensive plan for achieving a sustainable environment in the twenty-first century. The UN Commission on Sustainable Development (CSD) was created to monitor progress on the agreements reached at the conference. The CSD has developed specific mechanisms of stakeholder involvement in order to create a forum for groups in the UN to discuss progress on these issues. They hold multi-stakeholder dialogues annually on emerging sustainability issues, and conduct ongoing multi-stakeholder processes via the Internet.[8]

Example: DestiNet for Sustainable Tourism

One good illustration of multi-stakeholder problem-solving is reported by Ramboll, a Danish knowledge management firm, in partnership with Ecotrans e. V. (Germany), the European Union, and the European Environment Agency.

Exhibit 5.5

AA1000—Guidelines for Stakeholder Engagement

- Participating stakeholders help to identify other stakeholders.
- Stakeholders help to define the terms of engagement (how, when, where, what's on the agenda, who can speak, analytic processes, feedback mechanisms, etc.)
- Company representatives in charge of stakeholder information are considered trustworthy inside and outside the firm.
- Stakeholders are engaged in two-way dialogue.
- Stakeholders are not penalized or disciplined for expressing their views.
- "Venting" and "hygienic outbursts" are permitted and encouraged as a way to clear emotional blocks.
- Uninformed stakeholders are heard, and then education is attempted. When the firm's representatives are uninformed, they too seek to be educated.
- Actual decision making is based on dialogue among informed and reasonable participants.
- All parties are aware that if their views are acted upon, there will be consequences.
- There is a public disclosure and feedback process to allow participants and others to assess and comment on the engagement process.

Source: Adapted and extended from Institute for Social and Ethical AccountAbility, 1999a.

The partnership seeks to gain synergy from their individual efforts on environmental protection by jointly sponsoring and operating DestiNet (http://destinet.ewindows.eu.org), a portal that provides information on sustainable tourism. Tips on resource management and links to related websites are available on DestiNet.

The partners hope to optimize successes in developing and enhancing regulatory and voluntary actions that concern tourist destinations. Each partner has a focus and target for contribution to the initiative. For example, the European Environment Agency will ensure that the technologies employed meet the informational needs of users, perform continuous performance evaluation, and ensure that all contributors receive the technical assistance necessary to collaborate in the effort. Ramboll and Ecotrans coordinate efforts to ensure distribution of relevant and timely information, to encourage use of the portal, and to promote optimal website design.

The upshot is that partners and their stakeholders benefit from easy access to best practices and up-to-date scientific findings to support their various decision-making requirements.

Example: Biomedical Research for Tropical Diseases

Novartis, a Swiss pharmaceutical company, has partnered with the government of Singapore and the World Health Organization to develop biomedical research for tropical diseases and to make treatments available and affordable in developing countries, initially focusing on dengue fever and treatment-resistant tuberculosis. The Novartis Institute for Tropical Diseases was established in January 2003, funded jointly by the partners. Most researchers will be local scientists from Singapore, with state-of-the-art biomedical research tools provided.

Making Stakeholder Engagement Work

Stakeholders can be identified, mapped, assessed, and engaged. The principle of corporate accountability makes these actions necessary for GBC firms. Exhibit 5.5 summarizes guidelines for designing meaningful stakeholder engagement. These guidelines can be used to establish ground rules for stakeholder engagement programs and also to evaluate the appropriateness of existing programs.

Now we know which stakeholders to engage and what constitutes accountability to them. But . . . how do we keep them interested? In the next chapter we use cases to illustrate the principle of accountability and stakeholder engagement processes for a GBC company.

➤ 6 ◀

Cases in Implementing GBC Stakeholder Engagement

We have explored the meaning of stakeholder accountability and the processes of stakeholder engagement. Now it's time to turn our attention to a variety of cases of how companies have engaged their stakeholders. These are some of the crucial patterns that managers and companies exhibit when negotiating the tricky waters of culture conflicts, integrity management, cross-border variations in custom and law, and a host of other problems faced by multinationals in today's global environment.

In this chapter we begin with a framework for understanding GBC-oriented stakeholder engagement. The framework, shown in Table 6.1, combines the key patterns of stakeholder engagement and accountability with the four steps of the GBC process. Cases chosen from the Global Compact database, AccountAbility, and various other company sources are slotted into the framework to illustrate the relationships, and each case is presented and discussed. The cases discussed are a healthy variety—some are exemplary of GBC conduct, some are first attempts, and others raise questions about appropriate implementation techniques or about the alignment of identity, image, and reputation or mission, vision, values, strategy, structure, and process. Our research shows that companies find themselves in different places with regard to implementing GBC-based stakeholder engagement, and this is to be expected. There's a great deal to be learned from their experiences.

Implementing Stakeholder Engagement

Most companies are naturally attuned to investors and customers as key stakeholders. Organizations are structured to be responsive to their needs and wants, and managers are likely to spend a great deal of their time thinking about

Table 6.1

Stakeholder Engagement and Global Business Citizenship

| | GBC Steps | | | |
Stakeholder engagement	Code of Conduct	Local Adaptation	Conflicts and Experimentation	Systematic Learning
Supplier/ employee relations	Hewlett-Packard electronics ind. code		Calcados Azaléia, Brazil: employee childcare	
Community advisory panel			Holcim/Union Cement, Philippines: Community conflicts	
Public-private partnerships			Volvo, Sweden: methane vehicles	
Multi-sector collaboration		Vietnam Footwear: UN standards		AngloGold Ashanti and Danfoss: HIV in the workplace

Note: The GBC steps across the column headings are intended to represent a progression of actions toward becoming a global business citizen. The row headings, however, are not in progression but are discrete. Any or all of them could be present in a particular case.

those needs and wants. Of course, there's more to think about—particularly employees, suppliers, local communities, governments, and non-governmental organizations (NGOs).

"Stakeholder engagement," you'll recall, is much richer and deeper than "stakeholder management" or "managing stakeholder relations." Engagement involves establishing and sustaining a long-term trusting relationship based on good listening, good interpretation, and good-faith responses. For GBC companies, engagement means achieving high-level stakeholder dialogue and learning how best to solve ordinary operational problems, cross-cultural differences, and code implementation issues in a sustainable way.

Employee Stakeholder Engagement:
Calcados Azaléia S/A, Brazil

Managers don't have to look far to find key stakeholders and to benefit from engaging them in long-term good relationships—think first about *those who do the work.* Calcados Azaléia of Brazil did just that with its large and far-flung employee base.

Calcados Azaléia S/A is Brazil's largest—and the world's fifth largest—shoe manufacturer, with worldwide sales of its Azaléia, Dijean, Olympikus, and Asics brands. It takes a sizeable workforce—15,000 employees and another 4,000 contract workers—to make 150,000 pairs of shoes each day.

In 1991, the company surveyed its workers to discover their needs and interests and to make good on its pledge to exercise social responsibility. Health, housing, transportation, education, and safety concerns surfaced—none of them surprising in a developing economy and an industry relying on semi-skilled labor. Among the company's numerous responses to employee stakeholders' concerns and the chosen focus of its initial Global Compact entry was the *Centro de Educação Vocacional* (Center of Vocational Education), an after-school child care and educational program for employees' children aged 7–15.

Parents participating in the program pay only for the children's food and transportation. Children take classes, enjoy sports and other recreational activities, go on field trips, learn about different vocations and their training requirements, read, learn to use computers, and discuss topics of general importance. They receive dental, medical, and nutritional care and are encouraged to go on to high school.

Calcados Azaléia reports a high level of satisfaction among parents whose children attend the Center. Recruitment and retention benefits have been magnified by improved productivity among employees who no longer worry about what their children are doing after school. Children themselves benefit from the tutoring, enrichment, and guidance. The company claims long-term benefits as well:

> By educating local children, the company is also better preparing the next generation of potential Azaléia employees. Participating children acquire greater knowledge, broaden their vision, develop a better awareness of what is going on outside their town, learn how to thrive in today's world, as well as recognize the importance of their family, community and future.[1]

The payoffs seem likely to spread throughout the industry as Calcados Azaléia reaps recognition for its comprehensive programs for children of employees. The Center has been designated a model child care center in Brazil, and the company itself has earned "most admired" status among its peers.

Stakeholder engagement does make a difference, and it's not a bad idea to start learning first how to make the process work at home. Calcados Azaléia is only one of many companies worldwide that has chosen to treat its employees with the kind of respect that core stakeholders deserve.

Supplier Engagement: Hewlett-Packard

Those who supply resources, components, and services to the firm have historically been core stakeholders: the quality, value, timeliness, terms of payment, reliability, and other task-related attributes they bring to a relationship are important to a firm's ability to meet its own commitments to its customers. These days, suppliers play an even more critical—and perhaps unexpected—role for global business. They require expanded attention because of the emergence of supply chain ethics as a new management concern.

Outsourcing is now so commonplace among globalized companies that it hardly causes a ripple of attention anymore. Too often, though, problems are outsourced along with the cost-reduction opportunities. A firm may claim not to employ children, for example. But if that only means that the company has outsourced to contractors and subcontractors who do employ children, then the company is merely manipulating appearances to mask the truth. "One step removed" no longer means the same as "not responsible for."

The clothing industry has well-known exposure to many labor issues, including child labor, forced labor, excessive overtime, unsafe working conditions, and so on. Less visible but no less exposed is the computer industry, especially in the making of chips and hardware components. Hewlett-Packard (HP), in recognition of this problem, has developed and begun implementing a supplier code of conduct.

In 2002, HP rolled out its Supply Chain Social and Environmental Responsibility (SER) Policy, which included its Supplier Code of Conduct. HP's procurement expenses in 2003 were more than $52 billion, spread across thousands of suppliers, leaving the company with an extremely complex implementation task. And, as the company notes in its website discussion, suppliers have supply chains of their own, making compliance even more difficult. Where could the process of ensuring compliance begin?

HP chose to start with its 50 top suppliers, accounting for 70 percent of expenditures, plus another 100 "high priority" suppliers that were added in 2004. The near-term goal was to incorporate the Supplier Code into all product materials procurement contracts by the end of 2005.

Key features of HP's Supplier Code of Conduct follow:

Environment

Suppliers must have environmental policies that cover energy efficiency, hazardous materials, information and labeling, manufacturing, packaging and product recycling and reuse. The code incorporates our General

Specification for Environment (GSE), which specifies restrictions on materials that may be used in our products.

Health and safety

Suppliers must meet health and safety requirements that include evaluating and controlling exposure to chemical, biological and physical risks, machine safeguards, occupational injury reporting, training and workplace ergonomics.

Human rights and labor practices

Suppliers must treat employees fairly and in accordance with local laws. They must not use forced, bonded, involuntary prison or child labor. They must provide wages and benefits that meet or exceed legal requirements and respect the rights of workers to associate freely, in accordance with local laws and established practice.[2]

HP's Supplier Code has now gone through several iterations, and HP is taking steps to implement the code, to monitor supplier compliance, and to work with suppliers who are attempting to meet the standards. HP largely relies on supplier sign-offs and self-monitoring, but it also conducts site visits and audits, and works with suppliers to achieve compliance.

In 2003, because of HP's industry leadership in setting up the first supplier code, several NGOs asked HP to do more. Soon after, early in 2004, a blistering report was issued by the Catholic Agency for Overseas Development (CAFOD), a nonprofit agency based in the United Kingdom. The report cited extensive labor, health & safety, and environmental standards violations in the overseas factories of the largest computer manufacturers, including IBM, Dell, and Hewlett-Packard. What follows is a brief excerpt from CAFOD's report, titled "Clean Up Your Computer!" which called on computer users to lobby manufacturers for justice in global trade practices:

- Low pay—in China, workers are paid well below the minimum wage of £30 a month. They have to do illegal amounts of overtime to earn enough to live on.
- Insecurity—workers are kept on short-term contracts of 28 days. They can be hired and fired easily. They can't get social security benefits like food vouchers, maternity leave, holidays or pension.

- Humiliation and harassment—to get a job some workers go through intrusive tests and are forced to take a pregnancy test. Workers who are pregnant, belong to a Trade Union or are homosexual might be refused work. In one factory in China, workers who made a mistake must wear a red overcoat.[3]

Amid widespread circulation of this report, IBM's response was to stiffly assert that it complied fully with local laws and regulations, and Dell professed ignorance but thanked CAFOD for bringing the problems to its attention. Hewlett-Packard, however, decided that the time was ripe to push for industry-wide standards to promote human rights, health and safety, and environmental protection around the globe.

On October 21, 2004, a joint press release announced the Electronics Industry Code of Conduct, sponsored by HP, IBM, Dell, and several of their leading suppliers. The purpose of the code and its availability for adoption by others are noted in the press statement:

> The code, which was developed in collaboration with electronics manufacturing companies Celestica, Flextronics, Jabil, Sanmina SCI, and Solectron, paves the way for a standards-based approach for monitoring suppliers' performance across several areas of social responsibility, including labor and employment practices, health and safety, ethics, and protection of the environment.
>
> Prior to the release of this Code of Conduct, the companies used their own respective codes of conduct, and suppliers were subject to multiple, independent vendor audits based on different criteria. HP facilitated this collaboration for the adoption of a single, global Electronics Industry Code of Conduct. The code reflects the participating companies' commitment to leadership in the area of corporate social responsibility and will potentially reduce inefficiency and duplication, and make performance easier to audit and verify. . . .
>
> The code may be voluntarily adopted by any business in the electronics sector and subsequently applied by that business to its suppliers. The participating companies invite other companies to review and adopt the code, the text of which is available upon request and at each company's website. Businesses interested in adopting the code may contact HP: http://www.hp.com/hpinfo/globalcitizenship/environment/pdf/supcode.pdf.[4]

Only time will tell if the voluntary industry-wide supplier code of conduct will do the job of convincing suppliers that human rights and environmental protection are important. But it seems clear that HP, consistent with its long history of social responsibility initiatives, intends to carry this ball across the goal line.

Local Community Engagement: Holcim and Union Cement

Communities form the social and governmental contexts in which a company's various units operate. It can be tempting to take advantage of local communities by externalizing costs on them, especially when the government is weak or corrupt. But with a bit of care and attention, local communities can join the ranks of a firm's best allies.

The Holcim Group, a Swiss-based multinational company, learned this lesson from its 1998 acquisition of Alsons Cement in the Philippines. Cement is one of the leading export products of the Philippine economy, and Holcim is one of the world's leading producers of cement. With 48,000 employees and 2003 revenues of more than 12 billion Swiss Francs, Holcim's mission is "to be the world's most respected and attractive company in our industry—creating value for all our stakeholders."[5]

But the Philippines presents some difficult challenges for accomplishing such a mission. The economy is a combination of agriculture (sugar, bananas, coffee, tobacco, sugar cane) and heavy industry (cigarettes, steel, cement) that relies on exporting for growth. Freed from the corrupt regime of Ferdinand Marcos in 1986, the country has since been burdened with labor strife, political intrigue, riots and rebellions, separatist movements, terrorism, and violent religious conflicts.

Union Cement, the Philippines' largest cement maker, was formed by a merger of three cement companies in 2000, joined two years later by a fourth.[6] The company employs 1,400 people and produces nearly ten million metric tons of cement annually, much of it for export. One of the former companies, Alsons Cement, had a long-standing poor reputation in its communities for its history of social and environmental neglect. Holcim had acquired a controlling interest in Alsons prior to the formation of Union Cement, and as part of the cultural turnaround that mergers and acquisitions generally require, managers began to pay attention to community issues. In 1999, the Alsons community was devastated by flood, and the company describes its response:

> Alsons' employees volunteered assistance in food, medicine, infrastructure repair and emotional support for the victims, and in doing so opened the door to improved relations. As a result, a community relations committee was created, made up of the company management, unions, local community representatives, NGOs and government agencies. This

committee assesses and validates Alsons' proposals for community activities, which have themselves been identified through a local stakeholder engagement process. Projects are then carried out in collaboration with partner organizations.[7]

For many companies, community advisory panels (CAPs) are proving to be powerful vehicles of stakeholder engagement. In the case of Holcim/Alsons/Union, the CAP includes neighbors, managers, NGO representatives, and government officials. This broad representation of stakeholders has paid off in smoothing the path toward multisector collaborations to develop sustainable income capacity among workers' families, to send poor children to school via scholarships, to augment educational quality by "adopting" schools, to provide potable water for neighborhoods, to help build affordable housing, and much more.

Union Cement has an extensive social responsibility statement with the following as the kick-off message:

> Our Corporate Social Responsibility (CSR) policy articulates our commitment to working with all our stakeholders, building and maintaining relationships of mutual respect and trust, and contributing to improving the quality of life of our workforce, their families, and the communities around our operations.[8]

And it's not just so many words on the website; Union's programs and community involvements are real, ongoing, and valuable in unforeseen ways. Political, social, military, and religious strife continues in the Philippines with no sign of abating. According to the CSR coordinator and communications manager:

> At the Lugait plant, security concerns are high due to the presence of rebel groups in the area. But if you are responsible and open to discussion then your community can actually become your first line of defence. In fact, our security guard numbers have not increased but on the contrary they have reduced to about 20% over the last three years—primarily because we have improved our relationship with the community and we know that they will help "protect" us.[9]

Recall from the stakeholder salience model of chapter 5 that powerless or illegitimate stakeholders can move onto the managers' radar screen by forming coalitions with dominant stakeholders who already have legitimate standing and power to influence the firm. The good news of the Holcim/Union case is that companies can do the same, building stronger barriers against unexpected threats from the external environment.

Public-Private Partnerships: Volvo and Göteborg

Methane gas is a polluting emission of gasoline-burning vehicles. Ironically, however, when harnessed as a fuel instead of emitted as a waste, methane burns more efficiently than gasoline at very little cost in vehicle performance. Methane gas occurs naturally in coal beds, and it can be produced from organic waste, especially manure.

Architect William McDonough makes a compelling argument that the environmental impacts of business will not be dramatically improved until businesses begin to think about design issues from the ground up—not only in manufacturing processes and waste recycling, but in the design of products themselves. [10] AB Volvo Group, headquartered in Göteborg, Sweden, has initiated an experimental public-private partnership to buffer the enormous risks of radical design innovation in the use of methane-powered vehicles.

Natural gas, liquid or compressed, has been used sporadically as a vehicle fuel since the early 1900s, but Volvo was the first company to market a passenger car for methane gas use. Volvo introduced its first methane-burning vehicle, the Volvo 850 Bi-Fuel, in 1996. Remarkably, the car met California's stringent emissions standards for the year 2000.

Göteborg, a port city of a half million people in a nation of less than nine million, is a leader in experiments with "green procurement" and environmental impact reduction. Many buses, garbage trucks, light-duty trucks, ambulances, police cars, and passenger vehicles in the city's fleet are now equipped with methane/gasoline, electric hybrid, or hydrogen-powered engines, cutting greenhouse gas emissions by a significant amount.

Volvo describes its methane partnership with the Göteborg region as follows:

> Its goal is to improve air quality in the Göteborg area. By working cooperatively with partners such as the Business Region Göteborg, Fordons Gas, Göteborg Energi and Renova [the area's municipal waste management facility], the project has given rise to new products, new infrastructure and government incentives to promote the use of environmentally friendly methane-fueled vehicles. Examples of promotion of gas-driven vehicles are two hours free parking permission for environmentally friendly cars, taxi lanes with priority for environmental taxis at strategic places (Central train station etc) and company car tax reductions for environmentally friendly cars. The project has also initiated several activities to stimulate the tax system to help promote gas-driven vehicles nationally. [11]

Initial results are impressive. Volvo reports that

In January 2002, 67 buses, 48 trucks >3.5 tons, 21 trucks <3.5 tons and 664 passenger cars (=800 gas driven vehicles (Volvo and others)), were running in the Göteborg area. In 2001, 450,000m3 of methane was used per month, replacing 200,000 litres of petrol and 325,000 litres of diesel. Emission reduction/month has been:

620 tons C02(Carbon Dioxide)
5,150kg NOx(Nitrogen Oxides)
4,400kg CO(Carbon Monoxide)
−250kg HC(Hydro Carbons)
−130kg PM(Particulate Matter)[12]

In addition, methane-powered vehicles are cheaper to operate because of a preferential tax structure on both the fuel and the vehicles.

There's a global bandwagon effect already visible, driven in part by a 2003 European Union directive on alternative fuels. In October 2004, for example, Fiat announced that it was shipping 200 bi-fuel (methane and gasoline) vehicles to add to Göteborg's "green fleet." Mercedes-Benz, Volkswagen, and Opel have also introduced bi-fuel models. And the People's Republic of China is tracking with great interest the European Union's push into natural gas fuels despite its limited supply of these gases.

Public-private partnerships are favored modes of stakeholder engagement when the problems being addressed are broad and intransigent. Government partners have the great advantage of being able to offer incentives—tax, research funding, subsidy, export/import support, and so on—to encourage the sought-after behavior. Without the critical cooperation of the government, Volvo's initiative would have failed because of a lack of fueling stations for methane gas and therefore an inability of customers to adopt the technology, no matter how attractive it appeared otherwise. Business partners, like Volvo, can make very effective use of the powers of government to further their business ends while at the same time moving toward a public-interest goal.

Multi-Sector Collaboration: Vietnam Footwear Industry

Multi-sector collaborations involve players from business, government, and non-governmental organizations who agree to work together to address common issues. The strongest rationale for a multi-sector collaboration is that all parties recognize that they are each negatively affected by the same problem and that they cannot solve this problem without cooperating.[13]

Globalization has brought many who are concerned about humankind and the earth to the brink of despair. They watch the "race to the bottom" of labor costs, environmental rules, workplace health and safety, and myriad other regulatory and market constraints, and they wonder how it will ever be possible for the world's workers to live a life of dignity and satisfaction. By contrast, we have argued in this book that global businesses themselves are going to demand higher standards and stricter accountability, if only to stabilize the playing field for legitimate actors. Thus, global business citizenship will become the norm rather than the exception.

The Vietnam Footwear Industry Initiative tells a story of emergent GBC in a developing nation hungry for economic growth and riddled with abusive labor practices.

About 400,000 Vietnamese workers are employed in shoe manufacturing, which accounts for more than $1 billion U.S. dollars in export earnings for the country. In the midst of global celebration of the Asian Tigers' "economic miracle," criticism broke out about labor practices in developing countries. A primary target was Nike, global market leader in sports shoes, and the leading foreign employer in Vietnam, through its Taiwanese and Korean subcontractors. On March 27, 1997, Bob Herbert related this front-page story in the *New York Times*:

> On March 8, which happened to be International Women's Day, 56 women employed at a factory making Nike shoes in Dong Nai, Vietnam, were punished because they hadn't worn regulation shoes to work. Factory officials ordered the women outside and made them run around the factory in the hot sun. The women ran and ran and ran. One fainted, and then another. Still they ran. They would be taught a lesson. They had worn the wrong shoes to work. More women fainted. The ordeal didn't end until a dozen workers had collapsed.[14]

"Horrible!" proclaimed the Nike spokeswoman, but more reports of violence, abuse, and hazards in the Vietnamese shoe factories poured in. Women were beaten with shoes, denied water and rest breaks, and forced to work more than 600 hours overtime each year, all in violation of Vietnamese law.[15] A segment of the CBS television program, *48 Hours*, put faces and voices to the stories, spurring a U.S. banker of Vietnamese origin to ask Nike's cooperation in investigating complaints. He found below minimum wage payments, excessive forced overtime, sexual harassment, humiliation and verbal abuse, and corporal punishment to be common practices.[16]

Ernst & Young also conducted inspections for Nike in 1997, and reported not only labor abuses, but also dangerous exposure of shoe workers to toxic and carcinogenic chemicals. Shoes need glue; there's just no way around it. And the glue that best stands up to heat and humidity is solvent-based, using the cancer-causing chemical, toluene. Polyvinyl chloride (PVC) is a common input into the "man-made uppers" of many shoes, and it too is highly toxic. Without proper storage and handling procedures, workers breathe in the noxious chemicals day after day. According to the Ernst & Young report, "workers at the factory near Ho Chi Minh City were exposed to carcinogens that exceeded local legal standards by 177 times in parts of the plant and . . . 77 percent of the employees suffered from respiratory problems."[17]

Nike's overall initial response to criticism was to hunker down, belittle the negative reports, defend its labor practices, and increase advertising expenditures. Eventually, though, this strategy failed and the company was forced to take dramatic steps to begin to monitor and enforce subcontractor compliance with workplace standards.

Meanwhile, as Nike stonewalled, the British government's Department for International Development published a report in 1999 on the use of toxic chemicals in Vietnamese shoe manufacturing. The Prince of Wales International Business Leaders Forum (IBLF) was then asked by the British government to convene a collaborative effort to improve workplace health and safety. The resulting group focused heavily, though not exclusively, on the use, storage, handling, and disposal of toxic workplace chemicals such as toluene and PVC.[18]

The partnership, founded in 2000 and called the Vietnam Business Links Initiative (VBLI), boasts an impressive array of participants, now including Nike, as shown in Exhibit 6.1.

Although convened by the Prince of Wales IBLF, the VBLI has as a goal to be a Vietnamese-driven organization, focusing on education and changing practices to make workplaces safer and healthier.

Among other accomplishments, the VBLI and its member-partners have produced a comprehensive handbook for managing environmental toxics, have held dozens of training programs, and have distributed training content and materials widely throughout the industry. Research projects are underway, as well as factory-level pilot projects for making specific workplace improvements.

The program has hit its major snags, apparently, in monitoring, evaluating, and inspecting factory conditions. There are far too few inspectors available, and those who can inspect are not yet sufficiently trained in health and safety issues. Documentation at the factories being inspected is on the light side, so it is actually quite difficult for even trained inspectors to judge the quality of health and safety practices.[19]

Nevertheless, the VBLI is a visible and to some extent successful experiment in multi-sector collaboration to solve endemic problems in the

Exhibit 6.1

Partners in the Vietnam Business Links Initiative

Public Sector:
DFID (United Kingdom Department for International Development)
Mekong Project Development Facility
Ministry of Health
Ministry of Labour Invalids and Social Affairs
Ministry of Science Technology & Environment
National Institute of Labour Protection
National Institute of Occupational & Environmental Health

Private Sector:
Adidas-Salomon
Asco Vietnam Office (Pentland)–Berghaus, Brasher, Ellesse,
    KangaROOS, Kickers, Lacoste, Mitre, Red or Dead, Speedo, and
    Ted Baker brands
ERM (environmental consultancy services)
HUNEXCO (a jobber for name brand shoes)
Nike (Vietnam)
SGS Vietnam Ltd. (inspection, verification, testing, and certification)

Civil Society Sector:
ActionAid Vietnam
Friedrich Ebert Stiftung
IBLF (the Prince of Wales International Business Leaders Forum)
International Federation of Red Cross and Red Crescent Societies
Leather and Footwear Research Institute
Vietnam General Confederation of Labour
Vietnam Leather and Footwear Association
Vietnam National Leather and Footwear Association

Source: http://www.vcci.com.vn/sub/vbli/default.htm (accessed November 12, 2004).

developing world. And Nike, in addition to its participation in VBLI, has restructured its social responsibility efforts and is partnering independently with NGOs to monitor subcontractor behaviors with respect to worker health, safety, and rights on the job.

Business leaders are often heard calling for a "level playing field" that does not give unfair advantage to competitors who cheat, lie, steal, defraud investors, harm customers, dump wastes, or put workers in constant danger.

The VBLI is one among many examples of the fact that it is very often business itself that must push for and ultimately establish the level playing field it longs for.

Collaborating on the Hardest Stuff: AngloGold Ashanti and Danfoss Group

In 2004, the World Health Organization estimated that more than 38 million people worldwide were HIV-positive or already had full-blown AIDS. AIDS is the world's leading cause of death by infection, and in Sub-Saharan Africa, it is the leading cause of death for any reason.[20] Africa is one of several vast developing regions in the world that is rich in natural and human resources. However, the disarray of governments and social systems in the region permits the poverty, corruption, and violent chaos that breeds massive, intractable disease epidemics such as AIDS, Ebola, SARS, and many other conditions that are difficult or impossible to treat. The HIV/AIDS epidemic attacks young adults of prime working age, children, and even infants, threatening to destroy the economic and social future of the already-poor developing nations.

Now you might reasonably ask what all this has to do with AngloGold Ashanti, a gold mining partnership with roots in England, Ghana, and the United States, or with the Danfoss Group, one of Denmark's largest industrial companies. We chose these two cases to illustrate the ultimate in systematic learning via multi-sector collaborations to solve serious social problems. AngloGold Ashanti seems to have the collaboration tools down cold; Danfoss, however, struggles on its own to address a set of issues much larger than any single company can handle.

AngloGold Ashanti Ltd.

AngloGold Ashanti Ltd. was formed in April 2004 by a stock-swap merger of U.K.-based AngloGold Ltd., controlled by AngloAmerican Plc, and the Ashanti Goldfields Company Limited, partially owned and largely controlled by the Ghanaian government.

The Global Compact website contains a modest entry from AngloGold Ashanti called "Embedding Social Responsibility into the Fabric of Corporate Life." The entry wanders around, with very brief presentations of mine safety programs, seedling plantings, HIV/AIDS awareness, and micro-finance efforts. One would not realize from the caselet the real story that is in hiding. AngloGold Ashanti's 2003 "Report to Society" provides a more comprehensive examination of the company's community, charitable, environmental, and health-related initiatives, and the findings of the social report are backed up by both independent news sources and auditing/attestation. We have chosen here to overview the company's remarkable HIV/AIDS programs.

Gold mining is by nature a dirty, dangerous industry. One ton of extracted ore yields a mere 10.57 grams of gold, and the work involves drilling and dynamite deep underground. Infectious disease has made the industry much more dangerous, in unexpected ways.

AngloGold Ashanti, by way of its AngloGold corporate parentage, has a relatively long history of recognizing and nurturing the integral relationship among company, community, and workforce. Bobby Godsell, CEO of AngloGold shortly before the merger with Ashanti, explained it this way:

> We at AngloGold have built mines and the towns that nurture them since we started doing business in the 1940s. We understand the inter-relationship between communities and the mines they support and we understand how dependent we all are on the people who invest their lives and their future with us. That's why we have invested a substantial amount in the past ten years ensuring that everyone who works for us can read and write, why we've committed ourselves to effectively managing HIV and AIDS, eradicating tuberculosis and malaria and making our workplaces at least as safe as any other mining operation in the world.[21]

Built into the company's extensive labor policies are these two principles:

- The company assures access to affordable health care for employees and, where possible, for their families.
- We are committed to prompt and supportive action in response to any major health threats in the regions in which we operate.[22]

Sure, these are great values. Now, imagine discovering that almost 30 percent of the workforce is contaminated with the HIV virus, with major annual increases expected!

AngloGold Ashanti's response is still unfolding, but its breadth is visible in the 2003 outcomes noted in the Report to Society:

- Agreement on an HIV/AIDS policy with all recognized trade unions, guaranteeing non-discriminatory treatment, confidentiality, health and retirement benefits.
- A Peer Education course that has trained 351 peer educators in two years, including women working near the mines in the "entertainment" business, that is, as prostitutes.

- Training for supervisors, managers, and all new employees.
- An extensive but voluntary worker testing program for sexually transmitted diseases, including HIV/AIDS among others.
- Counseling for employees discovered to be infected with HIV.
- AngloGold Ashanti's "Anti-retroviral Therapy (ART) program, launched across the company's South Africa operations in April 2003, is currently treating 566 HIV-positive employees, as part of the company's Wellness Program."[23] ART drugs are given to infected employees free of charge, and participants are closely monitored for subsequent health effects. The roll-out program reached an estimated 18 percent of eligible workers.
- Implementation of an internal auditing system to track outcomes of the company's wellness programs, based on comprehensive risk assessment tools.
- A network of home-based healthcare supporters for those too ill to work, and a wellness program for infected workers while they continue on the job.
- Partnering to support hospice care for the terminally ill and orphanages for the children left behind.

So far, the company has held the line on the growth and spread of HIV infections among its employees. More people are being diagnosed and treated; more are being educated in prevention. Ambitious goals were set for 2004, including verification of program procedures and results by an external auditor, a 100% increase in ART enrollment, a 200% increase in voluntary testing and counseling participation, continuation and growth of all existing programs, evaluation and monitoring, and outreach to other agencies and organizations that could fruitfully join in the fight against HIV/AIDS.

Perhaps most remarkable is the extensive partnering and collaboration that AngloGold Ashanti has relied on. The company has partnered with local, regional, and national governments, both in the ten countries where it operates and around the world. NGOs involved in labor rights, health care, AIDS, and worker safety have been willing collaborators. The United Nations and the European Union are partners. Last but not least, even AngloGold Ashanti's competitors are beginning to take part in AIDS education and prevention programs. Their success sends a loud message to GBC companies engaged in massive efforts—you don't have to do it all yourself: "we have learnt that sometimes it's better to tap into the expertise of others to achieve common goals."[24]

In October 2004, the European Union awarded 40 million euros to a collaborative program to improve the safety and social-environmental impact of Ghana's gold mining industry.[25] And in November 2004, AngloGold Ashanti announced a $14 million grant from the Bill and Melinda Gates Foundation to its subsidiary, Aurum Health Research, to further its work on HIV/AIDS and tuberculosis prevention and control.[26]

Danfoss Group

In sharp contrast to the multilateral collaborations of AngloGold Ashanti, the Danfoss Group has tried to go it alone in battling workplace HIV/AIDS. Danfoss is one of Denmark's largest industrial companies, dealing in mechanical and electronic components manufacturing, including refrigeration and air conditioning units, heating and water systems, and motion controls. The vision:

> Danfoss will be a global leader within our core businesses, as a highly respected company, which improves quality of life by mastering advanced technologies in customer applications while creating value for all stakeholders.[27]

With funding from the founder's Fabrikant Mads Clausen Foundation, Danfoss began a 24-month educational campaign in July 2003. Their efforts included installing condom dispensers in factory restrooms, along with brochures and posters advocating AIDS awareness. Here's how the company describes its project:

> The efforts to improve work, welfare and health issues must be adjusted to local cultures and local issues. In South Africa the spreading of HIV/AIDS is a large problem because of lack of information. Danfoss in South Africa has therefore implemented an information campaign, offering employees training and information on HIV/AIDS within working time. The employees are also offered a free and anonymous HIV test to be done at a clinic outside the workplace. The employees with the lowest pay at the company are also paid a health insurance grant so that they receive necessary support in connection with illnesses.[28]

Danfoss has a history of socially responsible efforts. Nevertheless, the HIV/AIDS program seems more self-focused than anything else—it is the risks to the organization that are of most interest. Their project is small and targeted to their own employees and not to the surrounding communities. More importantly, they're out there on their own—no partners, no collaborative ventures. This may seem like telling your children to stay indoors because there's a forest fire just outside. You clearly want to protect those children, but your vision of the problems they face is far too narrow.

Stakeholders Matter

Stakeholder engagement isn't the easiest thing for companies and managers to put into practice. Stakeholders may not understand you; you and they may want very different things; stakeholders may not even be on your side at all. Nevertheless, making the effort to engage stakeholders in meaningful, ongoing dialogue is a worthy and necessary step along the path to global business citizenship.

Conclusion: Implementing Can Be Fun

This chapter has illustrated the steps of GBC and the processes of stakeholder engagement with a variety of cases. We examined Hewlett-Packard's supplier code of conduct, Calcados Azaléia's experiment with employee child care, Holcim's efforts to make amends with a scarred community, Volvo's public-private partnership to foster innovative methane-gas vehicles, the Vietnam footwear industry's attempts to meet global standards for workplace health and safety, and the very different experiences of AngloGold Ashanti and the Danfoss Group in combating HIV/AIDS in southern Africa.

These cases are just the tip of the iceberg. So many experiments are taking place, and so much is being learned about how global companies can live in mutually beneficial relationships with their stakeholders. There are many more examples of global companies that are making the effort, but we have run out of space to tell their stories.

In the interests of transparency, though, we have to tell you that you should not necessarily take what companies put up on websites at face value. It's only natural for a company to want to put its best foot forward, but those stories don't necessarily give you what you need to know as a manager who wants to put global business citizenship into practice yourself. We're talking implementation here, and you know that it's essential to put every specific situation into its larger context. That's just what we have tried to do with the stories in this chapter and several upcoming ones. And now, on to the next crucial set of tools for GBC—organizational change and development.

➤ 7 ◀

Building the Citizen Company: The Principles of Organizational Change

(Nice Theory, But Will It Work?)

Some business organizations are built from the ground up to be good citizens—and it pays. Take Novo Nordisk, the Danish health care company and world leader in diabetes care, which evaluates its performance based on the triple bottom line: environmental, social, and economic impact. Novo Nordisk reported a 23 percent increase in net profit for the first half of 2003, which included a 17 percent increase in sales and a 3 percent increase in operating profit. Their dividend per share has increased steadily from 1.15 (DKK) in 1997 to 3.60 (DKK) in 2002 with several stock splits during this time period. However, Novo Nordisk makes a distinction between financial and economic performance:

> Finance concerns the market valuation of transactions that pass through company books. Economics, on the other hand, is the means by which society uses human and natural resources in the pursuit of human welfare.[1]

Novo Nordisk is among a group of fifty unique companies that were selected as best-practice examples at reporting on the triple bottom line by SustainAbility, a U.K.-based think-tank and consultancy.[2] Novo Nordisk and the other companies that SustainAbility evaluated are attempting to look holistically at their business decisions, being mindful of profitability while also taking into account their broader social, environmental, and economic impacts. That is, these companies that are reporting on the triple bottom line have embraced the notion that their footprint on the environment and society is worth examining.

Not all companies have such a story to tell. Many—perhaps most—need to revisit, restructure, and redesign themselves to incorporate the principles and practices of GBC. So, this chapter offers a brief lesson in organizational development, which we will then use in subsequent examples of how global business citizenship is and can be operationalized.

In this chapter we examine ways leaders can transform an organization into one where GBC can be valued, well designed, and properly assessed. The goal is twofold: first, to help individual managers reconcile personal, corporate, and universal ethical standards with local norms and customs; and second, to help managers learn how to manage multiple and often competing stakeholder needs through the creation and wise use of change management strategies.

Using change management concepts from the field of organizational development, we show how individual change agents at any level, organizational teams, and senior leaders can gain support for their ideas about transforming their company's mission, strategy, and operational practices so that ethical principles and stakeholder needs are acknowledged, respected, and sustained within local cultural contexts. Global business citizenship, you'll recall, is a hybrid strategy, balancing between local adaptation and systematic application, and the tools of organizational development can help with the balancing act.

Definitions, Levels, Principles

There's a simple definition of organizational development (OD)—one that is visible at 50,000 feet:

> OD is the theory and practice of bringing planned change to organizations.

And here's an alternative "textbook" definition:

> Organization development is a system-wide and values-based collaborative process of applying behavioral science knowledge to the adaptive development, improvement, and reinforcement of such organizational features as the strategies, structures, processes, people, and cultures that lead to organizational effectiveness.[3]

It's all about change—acknowledging it, managing it, assessing it, learning from it. Change can just happen—natural disasters, shifts in the competitive environment, demographics. Or, change can be intentional; that is, an *intervention* can be initiated to help the organization cope with unexpected change or to institute a desired change. Here we focus on intentional change, using the OD language of "intervention," with the understanding that change agents can be found anywhere and everywhere in businesses.

Bringing OD back to earth requires thinking about change at multiple levels of analysis—individual, team, and organization.

Intervention with Individuals

First is the *individual level,* where the intervention is designed to foster the growth and development of particular organizational members. Typical tools include training courses, 360° feedback, personality assessment, career counseling, mentoring, internship programs, executive assimilation, and coaching.

Companies that conduct regular ethics and stakeholder management training at this level will help individual managers grapple with the problems that they will actually face when managing competing stakeholder expectations. Managers will learn to understand the ethical implications of taking care of one stakeholder group at the expense of another.

For example, consider Lockheed-Martin's "Dilbert" ethics game: in the game, managers tackle ethics problems small and large, and learn how to be a force for ethical compliance on the job. In another example, First Data Corporation routinely provides online training programs that offer typical scenarios about legal and ethical business situations and how managers can correctly respond. The basic idea of OD at this level is this:

> *Developing individual leaders and managers so they make wise, sound, and just business decisions when managing the company's assets.*

Intervention with Teams

Second is the *team level,* where the intervention is designed to create high-performing teams. In most organizations, an individual can come up with fabulous ideas for change, but it'll never happen if the individual tries to go it alone. A would-be change agent has to have a team, and ultimately must have executive support and sponsorship.

Tools for team development include team building exercises, intergroup development, process consultation, mission clarification, and strategy alignment. For example, in team-level ethics training, a procurement team might examine the process they use to make supplier choices and contract decisions, what constitutes an acceptable gift and an unacceptable bribe, and how they surmount the ordinary conflicts of interest that arise in the purchasing function. The basic idea of OD at this level is this:

Developing high performing teams that ensure the alignment of values, processes, and corporate mission and strategy within functional and cross-functional teams.

Intervention Across the Organization

Third is the *organization-wide level* where interventions are intended to assess whether the firm's policies, practices, and procedures are in support of its mission and strategy, and, if not, to bring the various parts of the firm into alignment. At this level, OD is aiming for a business transformation on a broad scale.

Typical tools include strategic planning, organizational performance assessments, and organizational design/restructuring. An organizational assessment, for example, might reveal that the company's compensation system is having unintended consequences; for example, in order to meet sales targets, employees are shipping products to clients with the understanding that the goods will be returned after a quarterly "close-out" date. At this level, the basic idea of OD is this:

Ensuring that there is alignment of values, processes, strategy, and mission across all functions and operating units.

How Does Change Occur? The CHANGE Model

No matter what level the change is designed to address, the "change agent" and his or her change team need a game plan. It might be a mid-level manager trying to send a wake-up call to a senior manager, or a senior manager trying to implement a major change from start to finish, or a line supervisor needing rank-and-file commitment to support a change. It could be an effort to support the formation of a new senior leadership team created during an organizational restructure. It could be the need to manage the integration of merged companies. Regardless of the level at which the change is to occur, the steps are the same.

OD experts have a way of thinking about change as an ongoing process with identifiable steps or stages. Outlined in Table 7.1 is a road map that incorporates six steps necessary for individual change agents to gain support for their ideas.[4]

The model we present here is based on the experience and thought leadership of several respected and highly experienced OD practitioners and change theorists, and has been adapted to suit the specific requirements of GBC transformation.[5]

123

Table 7.1

GBC C-H-A-N-G-E Method

1. *Conscious and curious:* conscious of random incidents and curious about their root cause.
   - Notice "isolated" events
   - Diagnose root cause
   - Monitor activity
   - Decide if action is needed

2. *Hear and heighten awareness:* Hear the need for change and heighten awareness by creating the case for change.
   - Create a change management team
   - Define the problem or opportunity
   - Conduct cost/benefit analysis
   - Assess organizational readiness for the change
   - Create a preliminary change strategy

3. *Accept and act:* Achieve acceptance for the change and take action to make it happen.
   - Create a vision for the preferred future
   - Ensure leadership buy-in
   - Develop leadership skills to drive the change
   - Communicate and translate the vision
   - Evaluate the current organization relative to preferred future
   - Design the desired state

4. *Navigate and negotiate:* Navigate the implementation and negotiate resistance.
   - Create a detailed project plan
   - Develop timelines and metrics to monitor progress
   - Reward significant accomplishments
   - Continually communicate with key stakeholders and employees

5. *Guide and generate:* Guide systemic change by generating alignment of related systems and processes.
   - Align systems, structures, processes, and policies
   - Explain employee behaviors needed to support the change
   - Develop performance standards
   - Place proper talent in key roles to sustain the change
   - Identify new projects to keep the vision vibrant
   - Celebrate the achievement of major milestones

6. *Evaluate and enhance:* Evaluate the learning and enhance the organization's sustainability.
   - Create a knowledge management process
   - Document best-practices
   - Enhance the organizational capability to lead change

Step 1: Conscious and Curious

In the beginning of most change processes, "there is a lack of widespread awareness that change is needed." Although there are "isolated events"

Exhibit 7.1

Conscious and Curious

Become conscious of random incidents and curious about the root cause

- Notice "isolated" events
- Diagnose root cause
- Monitor activity
- Decide if action is needed

---

occurring, they haven't been recognized yet as relating to a recurring business issue that needs to be addressed. Only the tip of the iceberg is starting to appear. For example, Dennis Gioia has written compellingly about his experience as Ford Motor Company's recall manager in the 1970s Pinto case.[6] There were isolated reports of Pintos catching fire in rear-end collisions mingled with hundreds of other types of problems, none suggesting a pattern to him. His curiosity moved to deep concern when he received full-color photos of the charred Pinto in which four teenagers lost their lives. He began to review the data, and eventually identified the design defect that ultimately drove the Pinto from the marketplace.

Summary. In this first step in the change process, observant employees begin to notice new "things/events" appearing on the radar screen. Is it a flock of geese, a dust cloud, the 4:32 from Chicago, or incoming enemy aircraft? Are they isolated events or related? Are the events early warning signals of "something," or are they anomalies? This step is about becoming aware and curious, and monitoring random incidents in order to decide what, if any, action is needed.

Step 2: Hear and Heighten Awareness

This is the "aha" moment when someone recognizes that there is a problem or an opportunity. In the case of BellSouth Corporation, a large telecommunications company headquartered in Atlanta, Georgia, such an "aha" moment occurred in the late 1990s when its president and CEO, Duane Ackerman, heard the concerns of a group of employees that the composition of the company's "director and above" employee population did not reflect the markets and consumers it served from a gender or ethnicity perspective. Ackerman believed in the business case for cultural diversity, and consumer data were showing the increasing purchasing power of ethnic groups. He was also known and respected for believing that incorporating cultural

---

Exhibit 7.2

Hear and Heighten Awareness

Hear the need for change and heighten awareness by creating the case for change

- Create a change management team
- Define the problem or opportunity
- Conduct cost/benefit analysis
- Assess organizational readiness for the change
- Create the case for change and a supporting strategy
- Create a preliminary change strategy

---

diversity was the right thing to do in terms of the company's values.[7] Thus employee voices were heard and a change management effort ensued.

Ackerman created a diversity council comprised of senior officers representing cross-functional parts of the business. The company's organizational development team initially facilitated the diversity council meetings and provided overall project management support for the council's activities.

The first order of business was creating the "case" for changing the leadership profile and making the company more diverse. The case for change at BellSouth was based on the need for the company to better align its leadership ranks with the demographics of the consumers they served. This was seen as a strategic business imperative for ensuring the satisfaction of existing customers as well as achieving revenue growth from a new consumer base.

Legal compliance was likely a part of the case for change at BellSouth as well. The company's legal team must have felt a spine-tingling chill in 1999 when employees at Coca-Cola Corporation filed a class-action discrimination lawsuit against the company. Coca-Cola, also headquartered in Atlanta, was revered by local business peers for its employee practices. The attack on Coca-Cola must have caused others to think that if it could happen to them, it could happen to anyone.

BellSouth's heritage was that of a community-minded, values-based company, and Ackerman no doubt felt an urgent need to protect this important aspect of the company. A good businessman, Ackerman knew that the telecommunications marketplace was changing, and so too must BellSouth. The impact of non-action was a potential loss of revenue and reputation. To that end, the diversity council created an action plan for getting a critical mass of employees to understand and support the need for the change.

Summary. The goal of this step is to understand the need for change and articulate the business case. One person's "aha"—even if it is the CEO's—will

---

Exhibit 7.3

Accept and Act

Achieve acceptance for the change and take action to make it happen

- Create a vision for the preferred future
- Ensure leadership buy-in
- Develop leadership skills to drive the change
- Communicate and translate the case for change
- Evaluate the current organization relative to preferred future
- Design the desired state

---

not by itself change much of anything. A case for change must be built so that a critical mass of leaders and employees can get on board. Building the case for change requires calibrating the need, articulating a sense of urgency, and being forthcoming about the likely impacts of the change and of doing nothing. This step is also about understanding if the organization has the capacity and willingness to change.

Step 3: Accept and Act

The initial actions BellSouth took toward becoming a more diverse company involved creating a vision for how the leadership profile would change. The diversity council conducted an analysis of the company's leadership profile and established targets over a five-year period for percentage changes in the "director and above" leadership ranks in terms of categories, for example, blacks, Hispanics, and women.

One of the most significant actions that the diversity council recommended, and that Ackerman supported, was the creation of a diversity function. The diversity office had responsibility for designing enterprise-wide training programs, analysis of company programs and policies to ensure support of and for diversity, as well as support for employee groups based on cultural heritage and sexual orientation. The leader of this diversity function reported directly to Ackerman and was appointed by the Board as an officer of the company.

However, changing the complexion of the leadership team and making BellSouth a more diverse company would no doubt require a cultural change and a mind-set change by leaders and employees. To make this work, BellSouth had to have leadership buy-in and a way of translating and communicating the vision of diversity that all employees could understand and accept. It's apparent that the company has had some success, and their efforts have not gone unnoticed:

> This combined commitment to the business bottom line, and the inclusion of the diverse backgrounds represented within the BellSouth team, has brought forth recognition and praise from business and minority communities. BellSouth has won the NAACP Corporate Image Award (awarded for exemplary business practices and public service); been named in *Fortune* magazine's "50 Best Companies for Asians, Blacks and Hispanics" for several consecutive years; was honored by *Hispanic Magazine* as one of the "Corporate 100: The One Hundred Companies Providing the Most Opportunities to Hispanics"; and garnered several awards from the national level community on its advocacy for diversity within corporate legal departments and law firms.[8]

Summary. The goal of this step is to gain employee and leadership support for the change effort and to help employees and management understand what it means to the business and to them personally. Creating a shared picture of the desired transformation will increase the probability of achieving it. The goal is to create a critical mass of committed people supporting the same desired vision. This critical mass provides the energy and the momentum that is needed for the heavy lifting of implementation.

Step 4: Navigate and Negotiate

The devil's in the details, and so it is with implementing a big idea. The steps for roll-out, however, are straightforward and logical:

- Make a plan, including specific action steps, budget, personnel, timeline, and desired outcomes.
- Decide what metrics and measurements are appropriate and how to obtain them.
- Monitor and assess progress, identify and overcome barriers, share successes and difficulties, and build momentum.
- Reward and recognize steps as they are accomplished.
- Communicate, communicate, and communicate!

Novartis is a company that knows about implementing change to align its corporate strategy with sustainable development. Novartis, based in Basel, Switzerland, was formed from the 1996 merger of pharma-chemical giants Ciba-Geigy and Sandoz. It is a pharmaceutical company that employs 72,900

Exhibit 7.4

Navigate and Negotiate

Navigate the implementation and negotiate resistance

- Create a detailed project plan
- Develop timelines and metrics to monitor progress
- Reward significant accomplishments
- Continually communicate with key stakeholders and employees

people and operates in 140 countries. The firm's financial performance in 2002 included a net income of CHF 7.3 billion (USD 4.7 billion) with sales of CHF 32.4 billion (USD 20.9 billion) predominantly from its cardiovascular and oncology businesses.[9] The U.S. headquarters for Novartis is located in New York, and there are business unit locations in eight U.S. states.

Novartis chairman and CEO Daniel Vasella formally and publicly committed the company to sustainable development in July of 2000 by signing the United Nations Global Compact.[10] As we began to learn in earlier chapters, the Global Compact encourages businesses to support basic human rights and non-corrupt transactions, whether or not required by law, and to accept labor and environmental standards in all their business practices to offset possible negative impacts of globalization.

To implement these principles, Novartis created a corporate citizenship policy that Vasella introduced in October of 2001, providing the following rationale:

> The Policy was developed in response to our commitment to the Global Compact, which was set forth by the Secretary General of the United Nations, Kofi Annan. Across geographies and throughout our organization we will, in all our business, social and environmental activities, strive to be in line with the principles of the Global Compact. We believe that adhering to values is especially important for large organizations in times of rapid change and globalization, as they provide guiding principles. In our business, we are using innovative new technologies to search for novel lifesaving medical treatments. In some cases, these developments raise ethical challenges, which must be carefully considered with the establishment of proper boundaries, but Novartis' ultimate goal is to contribute to helping patients in need.
>
> On a global level, Novartis is committed to sustainable development and its three principles of economic, social and environmental progress.

We want to be a leading corporate citizen, both technologically and economically, and achievement of that goal is closely linked to our ability to contribute to the benefits of people. Our policy on Corporate Citizenship outlines our pledge, and is both a strategic business initiative—and the right thing to do.

To operationalize the corporate citizenship policy, Novartis has focused on the process of aligning its vision and strategy with appropriate standards and measures. At the board level, the audit and compliance committee took on responsibility for providing guidance and overseeing the progress being made to implement the principles of the UN Global Compact. Operationally, a corporate citizenship steering committee has been created to evaluate business processes and create guidelines that ensure alignment with the Global Compact. An extensive training program has also been launched to help employees translate what the sustainability vision means to them and their daily work. And, in 2002 Novartis implemented a corporate citizenship reporting process for all business units (over 300 worldwide)

The social impact of their efforts thus far has mostly been driven by senior management and includes projects to help people who lack essential health services to gain access to drugs by working with NGOs in developing countries. For example, through the Global Alliance to Eliminate Leprosy, Novartis donates a multi-drug therapy that can cure the disease within six months to a year, depending on the disease stage of development. Novartis is also actively involved in research on tropical diseases. Through a collaboration with the Singapore Economic Development Board, Novartis is conducting research on poverty-related diseases like tuberculosis and dengue fever.

Although implementation is well under way, truly aligning the company's business practices with its vision of sustainability is still a work in progress at Novartis. The biggest challenges the company says it faces include: "the ability to continually refine the process of measuring, setting, and achieving targets for the human rights dimension of Novartis and third-party operations . . . the capability of line management to integrate corporate citizenship into the economic business model, and to settle tensions between competing objectives as they arise, and the credibility of the process as perceived by internal and external stakeholders as well as the broader society."[11]

Access to health care has become an expected human right, at least in the developed world, and this has moved shareholders from being resistant to expecting the company to support these types of initiatives. The next frontier is getting operational managers on board with how their areas of responsibility can be transformed to support sustainability in a way that allows them to tangibly see the economic and social impacts of their efforts.

Exhibit 7.5

Guide and Generate

Guide systemic change by generating alignment of related systems and processes

- Align systems, structures, processes, and policies
- Explain employee behaviors needed to support the change
- Develop performance standards
- Place proper talent in key roles to sustain the change
- Identify new projects to keep the vision vibrant
- Celebrate the achievement of major milestones

Summary. The implementation step is both exciting and tedious. It involves a straightforward application of project management techniques as well as a sensitivity to progress and a willingness to mark milestones. Continual communication is key to sustaining the energy and momentum of the critical mass of dedicated employees.

Step 5: Guide and Generate

The goal of this step is to make sure that the new idea becomes part of business as usual. Downstream and associated changes are made, ancillary processes and policies are aligned, to ensure systemic change. While formalizing the new state sounds routine, it can be anything but. At this point the change has happened but is still unstable; thus, people can get really bored and stop paying attention, or the "saboteurs" can come out of the woodwork to snatch failure from the jaws of success. Leaders and their teams need to shape norms, revise practices, and reinforce benefits to have the change take hold.

Lasting change may seem improbable at this point because of forces in the larger environment that push against transformation. For example, William George, former CEO of Medtronic, a multibillion dollar medical technology firm headquartered in Minneapolis,[12] has pointed out that the corporate financial scandals of the early twenty-first century resulted in large part from systemic forces such as relaxed accounting rules, lesser regulatory oversight, and extraordinary executive compensation plans geared to short-term profit rather than long-term sustainability. Leaders who really mean for a change to stick will have to push back against these forces. Microsoft, for example, ended its practice of granting executive stock options in 2003, thus de-emphasizing short-term gains as a measure of management success.[13] The

---

Exhibit 7.6

Evaluate and Enhance

Evaluate the learning and enhance the organization's sustainability

- Create a knowledge management process
- Document best-practices
- Enhance the organizational capability to lead change

---

public buzz surrounding this change was surely intended to set an example for other industry giants to follow and thus to change one of the systemic forces affecting all companies.

Summary. Monitoring and fine tuning is the goal of this step. It's about making sure the organization doesn't fall backward, that things actually happen. It requires thinking and acting systemically to ensure the alignment of behaviors, reward systems, and metrics.

Step 6: Evaluate and Enhance

One company that values learning is Levi Strauss. The company's Supplier Terms of Engagement, initiated in the late 1990s, was accompanied by substantial changes in the company's structure, procurement and partnering policies, and labor/human resource management practices. The aim was to keep the company "clean" on child labor and workplace rights issues, and also to foster positive change in the supplier environment. As they implemented the code and the new policies, company managers accumulated much knowledge and experience about country conditions, government and political factors, and religious and cultural customs. They learned which human rights organizations were viable partners and which were not. They acquired detailed knowledge of particular supplier practices and site concerns. But, until recently, this wealth of knowledge existed helter-skelter in various computer files or, even worse, only in the memories of managers.

Reflecting on years of experience in compliance management led the regional compliance directors to create a database, cross-referencing countries, suppliers, owners, practices, and so on. Any Levi Strauss manager anywhere in the world can access the information, understand what conditions to look for, learn from prior experiments, and submit new information. In addition, executives can use the database to look across categories, time periods, countries, or supply chains, to spot emerging trends and issues or to identify system-wide problems. This database, still under construction, represents knowledge management at its best—a condensation and presentation of what is known, what works and doesn't work, who helps and who hinders, so that everyone responsible for supplier compliance can learn from prior experience and contribute to future success.

Summary. Trite but true—change is eternal. This stage of the change management process is not so much the "last step" as it is the assurance that the firm is doing the best it can to recognize, understand, and manage the change that is inevitable. It requires a willingness to reflect on lessons learned as well as walking the talk of continuous improvement.

Why Do Some Change Efforts Fail?

If you think the GBC change steps sound easy, consider this:

- "Only 23 percent of all mergers and acquisitions make back their costs."[14]
- "Just 43 percent of quality-improvement efforts make satisfactory progress."[15]
- "Nine percent of all major software development applications in large organizations are worth the cost. 31 percent get cancelled before completion. 53 percent will result in cost overruns by 189 percent."[16]

Why such dismal statistics about change efforts? In a word: resistance. Rick Maurer provides an insightful explanation of the "resistance to change" phenomenon:

> Resistance is any force that slows or stops movement. It is not a negative force nor are there "resistors" out there just waiting to ruin our otherwise perfect intervention. People resist in response to something. Something that we . . . are doing evokes a reaction that we call resistance. The people resisting probably don't see it as resistance; they see it as survival. [17]

Maurer describes three types of resistance to change in organizations, illustrated in Figure 7.1.[18] The figure suggests that the three types—"I don't get it," "I don't like it," and "I don't like you"—can feed one another and shape-shift. This is truly one of the hardest parts of organizational change. People who are resistant have several strategies available and can cycle back to ones the change agent thought were settled already.

I Don't Get It!

New ideas tend to be fuzzy before the details are all worked out. This ambiguity can make people nervous—the state of confusion is pretty unpleasant,

Figure 7.1 **Maurer's Cycle of Resistance to Change**

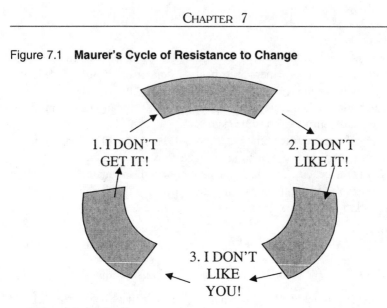

1. I DON'T GET IT!

2. I DON'T LIKE IT!

3. I DON'T LIKE YOU!

Source: Maurer 2002b.

and people are likely to stall for more time to think about or assess the new idea. To overcome this type of resistance, the facts and figures have to add up, the presentations have to be patiently constructed, the data and the logic have to correspond. Especially, check for these problems if you encounter the "I don't get it" form of resistance:

- Are the facts and evidence presented appropriately?
- Are your assumptions valid or reasonable?
- Is your logic tight and complete?
- Is the aim of the change desirable to many or most in the firm?
- Have you provided sufficient time for thought and questioning?
- Is there a relatively clear path from idea to implementation?

If this is all the resistance there is, count yourself lucky. Information and understanding are the easiest missing pieces to supply.

For example, say you're going to spearhead a change in your company's GBC policies from "local law governs" to a worldwide standard on minimum working age. Your area managers will want to know precisely what the new standard means for their operating procedures. Will they have to budget for age certification? Can they take the word of prospective employees or their parents? What will happen to underage workers? Likewise, the workforce is going to want to know what the new standard means. Will families lose much-needed income? Will their children be forced by economic necessity into more dangerous or unsavory workplaces? Is the company prepared to help families make the transition? Explaining clearly the reasoning behind the move and its implications for management and workers is the first step toward winning buy-in.

I Don't Like It!

Many people have a natural inclination to seek stability; there is comfort (however cold) in the "same old–same old." New ideas, by definition, mean that things are going to change, and this may be threatening to some people in the organization. To get this idea, think about a change you have experienced as frightening or threatening. Adrenaline pumps, pulse skyrockets, you're hyper-alert, and what about that blood pressure?

If you encounter this sort of resistance from staff or peers when you're making a change effort, take another look at the dynamics of the change, the particular people involved, and the threats that they may be experiencing. For example:

- Do people fear that the change will cost them their jobs or their financial security?
- Who will lose power, control, or autonomy because of the change?
- Will anyone lose status, face, or respect? Or does anyone fear such losses?
- Are some of your people afraid of failing? Will the change demand that they change their own ways of relating to work?
- Are your people overwhelmed already and thus reluctant to take on any new challenge, no matter how appealing or necessary? (There is such a thing as too much change!)

In our minimum-age example, it is certainly possible that portions of your company are profiting from child labor, either directly in company-owned sites or indirectly through contractor or subcontractor practices. This will now have to be halted, and area managers will have to figure out how to replace lost revenues from a reduced workforce. Laid-off underage workers and their families, likewise, are not going to be very happy at their suddenly reduced income. Workers' unhappiness can ricochet back to managers, of course, creating even more turmoil.

The emotional responses of those affected are perfectly understandable and need to be dealt with as part of the change process. Experiments are now proceeding with replacing workers' and families' lost income in a variety of ways, to try to overcome the negative emotional reaction to implementation of global labor standards.

I Don't Like YOU!

This is perhaps the most difficult of the resistance modes because it is often unexpected and does not respond well to logic or data. "I don't like you" is an intuitive emotional response that is typically based on lack of trust. People may think the idea is just great, and they may understand it perfectly well, but they will resist it because it's *your* idea, or because it represents something they do not respect or are afraid of. Or, if the truly resistant in the organization get no satisfaction from the other two strategies, they may pull out the big guns and argue that the proposed change is a stupid idea because *you* can't be trusted, whether or not this is actually true!

If you encounter this type of resistance, consider the following:

- Are you personally well-liked and well-respected?
- Are you representing someone, or something, that is *not* well-liked or respected?
- Is there a history here of backstabbing, surprise decisions, and unexpected harms?
- Are there certain employees who generally take a negative, personalized approach to their work, no matter what?
- Are there cultural, social, political, or religious differences among employees that make it difficult to earn respect and appreciation for your ideas?
- Do employees have significant disagreements over core values that affect their willingness to accept particular kinds of change?

In an upcoming chapter we're going to read the story of a company that implemented a minimum age for its workers worldwide, despite the fact that the founder himself had been employed since age 12! Although this company now has extensive policies and procedures designed to implement the minimum worker age, one could wonder about the wisdom of bragging on the website about the founder's early work experience. When it's "do as I say, not as I do," the end result can easily be disrespect for the change agent *and* his or her idea, even if the agent means well and the idea is a good one.

Resistance Strategies Are Moving Targets

There's more to be said about the distinctiveness—or lack thereof—of these three resistance types. People are complex. You may find, in fact, that your change effort is met with resistance that looks like one thing but is really something else, or with resistance that shifts types as objections are met.

For example, a new manager at a company we know had to implement a structural change that was not his idea. It involved shifting people and functions among departments and physical locations, and also meant a promotion out of the area for a beloved supervisor. Employees' first response was "I don't get it," and the manager focused on building the case for change. Fears and threats quickly emerged, however, and the focus of resistance shifted to "I don't like it." Finally, hostilities went public and the manager learned—through an anonymous threatening letter—about the overwhelming emotional reality of the change as resistance shifted to "I don't like you because you're making us change our working relationships and lose our favorite boss." It was never about logic, or data, or job insecurity. The truth is, it took this team a good bit of time to reach acceptance of the change. Time is—and was in this case—the great healer. Most people got on board, but not exclusively because of what the manager was able to do during the change process itself. Eventually, the new department structure began to exhibit its intended benefits, new relationships developed, and things settled down.

Change managers do have to be conscious and careful about moving through the steps of the change process, but don't fall into the trap of thinking that you're in charge of the universe or even your own little corner of it. Time, understanding of resistance, and compassion are necessary for managing change, but are by no means sufficient for control.

What if you miss a step, or forget to tend to a critical path of change management? In Table 7.2, we show what happens when any step is missed.

If you are not conscious of isolated or random events, you're sure to be blindsided by environmental changes. If you don't make a compelling case for change, your employees will be stuck in disbelief. If you miss out on the clear vision, everyone—including you—will be confused and the change will stall. If your action plan is weak or lacking, there will be a lot of false starts and probably no finishes. If you get all the way through initial implementation but are not successful at changing peripheral systems and processes, you will eventually hit a brick wall. And finally, if you overlook the learning and evaluation step, you'll find that you are re-creating the wheel every time a change is needed or desired, or every time a problem is encountered.

Conclusion

Whether you are working with individuals, teams, departments, divisions, or entire organizations, the concepts in this chapter will help you decide whether and how to proceed with your change effort. The CHANGE model offers guidance for managing each step of the process, and the ways in which people can resist change are now an open book to you.

Table 7.2

What If the Change Process Is Missing a Link?

Here's what you'll get:	Conscious and curious	Hear and heighten awareness	Accept and act	Navigate and negotiate	Guide and generate	Evaluate and enhance
Desirable and ongoing change	Aware of random incidents	Prepare a compelling case for change	Clear vision, leadership buy-in, design	Detailed plan, metrics, rewards	Align systems, explain, staff, celebrate	Learning, knowledge management, best practices
Blindsided	X	Prepare a compelling case for change	Clear vision, leadership buy-in, design	Detailed plan, metrics, rewards	Align systems, explain, staff, celebrate	Learning, knowledge management, best practices
Disbelief	Aware of random incidents	X	Clear vision, leadership buy-in, design	Detailed plan, metrics, rewards	Align systems, explain, staff, celebrate	Learning, knowledge management, best practices

138

	Aware of random incidents	Prepare a compelling case for change	Clear vision, leadership buy-in, design	Detailed plan, metrics, rewards	Align systems, explain, staff, celebrate	Learning, knowledge management, best practices
Confusion	Aware of random incidents	Prepare a compelling case for change	X	Detailed plan, metrics, rewards	Align systems, explain, staff, celebrate	Learning, knowledge management, best practices
False starts	Aware of random incidents	Prepare a compelling case for change	Clear vision, leadership buy-in, design	X	Align systems, explain, staff, celebrate	Learning, knowledge management, best practices
Brickwall	Aware of random incidents	Prepare a compelling case for change	Clear vision, leadership buy-in, design	Detailed plan, metrics, rewards	X	Learning, knowledge management, best practices
Re-creating the wheel	Aware of random incidents	Prepare a compelling case for change	Clear vision, leadership buy-in, design	Detailed plan, metrics, rewards	Align systems, explain, staff, celebrate	X

Of course, you might follow all these steps and still fail to implement a change; the tools of change management don't guarantee success. However, they *do* raise the odds of succeeding, and they give you and your team a lot to work with in implementing a lasting process for global business citizenship. In the next chapter, we examine several cases of organizational change, ranging from the simple to the profound, to see how these changes can be implemented with GBC in mind.

➤ 8 ◄

Organizational Change
the GBC Way
Cases in Implementation

On any list of core management tasks, implementation surely ranks in the top handful. Mission, vision, values, codes of conduct, and policy statements are only so many words on paper until they are put into practice, tested, and found worthy. Implementation is always a matter of managing change, even when the necessary changes are small and the process takes a very short time.

In this chapter and the next two, we continue our consideration of Step 2 and Step 3 implementation of a GBC company's principles, values, code, and policies. We do this here by briefly reviewing the change process model of chapter 7 and then showing how it can be used to map the various stages and payoffs of GBC implementation.

As we shall see in the cases, routine implementation (Step 2) and problem analysis and experimentation (Step 3) are not as separable as they may seem on the surface. The nature of the problem typically depends on where you place your eyes; in people's minds, a complex difficult problem may look simple, and relatively easy problems can look very hard indeed. Furthermore, the best solution to a problem may be a quick fix, but it can depend instead on choices quite outside the capability of cost-benefit analysis or other typical management tools.

The payoff of GBC implementation, aside from any strictly financial or marketing benefits, will be some combination of better vision and a broader view, more safety in avoiding quicksand and broadsides, the efficiency of easier decision-making, and sustainability via actions that are more ethical and logical.

What's Different About GBC Implementation?

Most managers will be familiar with some version of a corporate implementation process that has steps like this:

Set direction:	Mission–vision–values–code–policy
Develop strategy:	Direction-goal-setting-tactics-budgeting
Align:	Structure and process, mission and strategy, goals, and resources
Motivate:	Compensation–incentives–rewards
Evaluate:	Monitoring–adjusting–assessing

The point of implementation is to align strategy with structure, actions with intentions, results with rewards, so that the company and its employees are on the same track, and that track is headed in the right direction. Implementation begins with top management commitment to goals, continues on through a variety of learning processes as the management team adjusts practice and perspective, and culminates in the institutionalization of goals and strategies into the company's standard operating procedures.[1]

Executives spend their days—and often nights and weekends—keeping the organization operating in very complex and demanding internal and external environments. On any given day, executives are thinking about big picture questions like what new products to offer over the next five years, how to increase sales, which new markets to enter, where the most cost-effective production facilities should be located, how to deal with high-cost operations, and what to say to investors and analysts at next quarter's guidance call.

In addition, management has all the routine issues to deal with: gathering information into accurate and useful reports, invoicing receivables, paying bills, supervising staff, setting operational goals, motivating and rewarding, communicating, daily firefighting, and so on. According to management experts, managers spend most of their time in meetings, on the phone, reviewing or constructing reports, and talking with co-workers or customers. Although challenging, these tasks are certainly not front-page news, and the problems encountered do not ordinarily require escalation to top management or the board of directors. They are the nuts and bolts of day-to-day implementation.

What's different about implementation for managers in a GBC company?

A Broader View

First, the global business citizenship framework broadens the manager's attention span in terms of stakeholders, impacts, and time. As we explore in this chapter, this new breadth has some interesting consequences for the question of what makes a problem easier or harder to solve. Expanded breadth alone is not always such a great thing if you become mired in complexity and are unable to move through a problem toward a solution. On the other hand, being able to grasp the larger picture can reveal allies in unexpected corners or solutions outside the box.

Avoiding Quicksand

Second, the GBC process can help managers avoid getting stuck in the quicksand of escalating issues. A routine problem can become a crisis in an instant when a critical variable changes; an ordinary process can turn to disaster via the incremental slippery slope of carelessness or inattention or "just this once" rationalizing. Implementing GBC steers a company away from a great many of these quagmires and can prevent the company from being blindsided by unexpected attacks and crises.

Easier Decision Making

Third, the GBC orientation can actually make decision making easier and less complex. Actions that involve violations of core principles are not acceptable options, no matter how cost-effective they might be in achieving some of the company's goals. GBC implementation removes many of the temptations that can plague managers and makes it easier to handle certain trade-offs. For example, a GBC company might hesitate only a little to make a serious long-term investment in customer service that will lower next quarter's earnings results.

Logically Grounded in Ethics

Fourth, GBC implementation is grounded in ethical principles and represents a logical, coherent outgrowth of the company's mission, vision, and values. GBC is never an add-on, dangling precariously from a thin corporate branch. It is a way of designing and running companies sustainably.

What Makes a Problem Easier or Harder?

Easy problems are by definition easy to solve, but they can be hard to find.

Let's imagine: The situation is routine and well understood, and has reasonably certain outcomes, though it can still be a lot of work to accomplish. Decisions at the local level are in alignment with the company's mission, vision, values, and strategy. Stakeholders appear to be appropriately identified and their needs and interests are understood and accounted for. Stakeholders are not in conflict about appropriate outcomes. Costs and benefits are in acceptable balance, and risks are low.

Not much of a problem, right?

Well, let's investigate further. Remember those cross-cultural business problems laid out in chapter 1? Here's the first one:

> Marlene arrives in Haiti where her company contracts with a local supplier who subcontracts with small manufacturers. She meets with the supplier's senior executives and requests a final schedule of the previously arranged tours of production facilities. She is told that unfortunately, because of local flooding, the facilities are undergoing renovation and cannot be toured at present, and she is then urged to approve the anticipated three-year supply contract quickly, before competitors move in to appropriate the supplier.

First, let's say that Marlene works for a company that says it is all about profit and only about profit. Investors are the relevant stakeholders, and their interests are supreme. Under this condition, the situation may seem relatively simple to resolve. No inspection? No problem—we've seen the product already, and we are OK with the quality and the price. The inspection is part of the contract, but no one really cares whether it happens or not, so it's routine and uncomplicated to ignore it. So Marlene signs up and, if she needs to, explains the inspection discrepancy upward as a minor operating blip.

Meanwhile, in a probable scenario, the supplier settles in contentedly for three more years of importing poor young girls from the countryside, threatening them, and charging them more than their low wages allow them to pay for housing and to buy supplies and food at the company store. Human Rights Watch learns the story and sends out a worldwide alert, which is picked up by activists around the globe and turns into a public relations nightmare for Marlene's company.

Next, let's say Marlene works for a GBC company, intending to be profitable within the boundaries of its core values and principles. If implementation of GBC mission, vision, and so forth has already occurred and the GBC principles are institutionalized, supplier inspections are done not just to ascertain product quality, but also to check on labor conditions and environmental practices. Marlene's task here may also be easy. No inspection, no contract. Period, full stop. Then it's up to the supplier to renegotiate or reschedule the required inspection, and it's up to Marlene to report back to her manager that the supplier appears not to be in compliance and will be delayed in signing.

But let's say that Marlene's company is just beginning the GBC implementation roll-out, so she has some guidance in the code of conduct and policy statements, but there's no on-the-ground experience. How should she proceed?

Well, because the situation places the company at risk of violating a core principle, she knows she can't sign the contract right now. Should she go back to her boss and explain about the flood? Should she ask to waive the inspection requirement this one time? A lot depends on history, knowledge, and Marlene's understanding of how GBC implementation works in her company. Some ideas for Marlene:

- Check back through the pre-implementation planning process to see if there is any specific guidance she doesn't yet know about.
- If this is a new situation for the company, suggest that her boss convene a project team or task force to work out an implementation procedure, and offer to help.
- Find out who in the company "owns" the process of supplier compliance—Purchasing? Headquarters? Legal? Ask them to take responsibility and provide guidance. Ask them to be part of the new team.
- Check out alternative suppliers if this one seems really suspicious.
- Take the initiative—so what if the boss isn't paying attention right now—to work out a process for decision making, with the boss's knowledge and approval, of course.
- Talk directly with the supplier to try to work out an inspection schedule.
- Offer a short-term contract rather than the three-year version, or add a contingency that inspection must occur within so many months or the contract is voided before the first payment is made.

When there are conflicts in values or practices, or "empty spaces" in knowledge or experience, implementing GBC means that the company must place its trust in those managers who have to actually resolve the problems. Marlene's creativity needs to be defensible, of course, so that she is less vulnerable to attack should there be any corporate "enforcers" who are annoyed or upset by her actions. By the same token, her creative response needs to be defended and rewarded, thus sending a message to managers throughout the company: "We trust you to make it work." The beauty of new ideas is that they can transform processes and systems, and this is the basis for GBC's fourth step, discussed in chapter 11—systematic learning. Marlene's problem in Haiti could become a pilot project for the company to develop future standard operating procedures on GBC implementation.

Merging the GBC Process and the Change Process: Examples from Global Compact Cases

The Global Compact is a voluntary program spearheaded by United Nations Secretary-General Kofi Annan, beginning with his challenge to business leaders in a 1999 address to the World Economic Forum. Annan urged that the world's multinational corporations join together in support of nine principles concerning human rights, working conditions, and environmental protection, and the initiative got underway in 2000. In 2004, a tenth principle on corruption was added, following a lengthy process of stakeholder engagement on the principles themselves and whether they were sufficiently comprehensive to serve as universal guidelines.

The ultimate goal of the Global Compact is "a more sustainable and inclusive global economy."[2] The Compact serves multiple intermediate purposes:

- It is a sign-on opportunity—a public indicator that a company has agreed to strive for full implementation of the ten principles, first introduced in chapter 4 and revisited below in Table 8.1.
- It "offers facilitation and engagement through several mechanisms: Policy Dialogues, Learning, Local Structures and Projects."
- Its website provides a convenient and interactive mode of communication where companies can report their experiences and efforts, whether failed or successful or too new to evaluate, with opportunities for questions and feedback from anyone viewing the site.
- Periodic meetings are convened to bring together thought-leaders from academia, business, government, and the nonprofit sector to discuss and make progress on key issues that Global Compact companies face.
- "The Global Compact is not a regulatory instrument—it does not 'police,' enforce or measure the behavior or actions of companies. Rather, the Global Compact relies on public accountability, transparency and the enlightened self-interest of companies, labour and civil society to initiate and share substantive action in pursuing the principles upon which the Global Compact is based."

The cases we have chosen from the Global Compact website are all examples of GBC-like actions that illustrate various processes of organizational change. In chapter 7 we developed a change process model, repeated here in short form in Table 8.2, to succinctly describe the steps that need to be accomplished in any instance of organizational change.

In Table 8.3 we locate the six cases described in this chapter in a matrix that combines steps in the organizational change process with steps in the GBC process. This gives us a way to better understand the meaning of the various actions reported by companies and to glean some systematic learning from the vast array of experiences in implementation. There won't be a case for each cell of the table; here we merely intend to illustrate the relationships between GBC steps and organizational change processes.

Table 8.1

The Global Compact Principles

Human rights

Principle 1:   Businesses should support and respect the protection of internationally proclaimed human rights.

Principle 2:   Make sure that they are not complicit in human rights abuses.

Labor

Principle 3:   Businesses should uphold the freedom of association and the effective recognition of the right to collective bargaining.

Principle 4:   The elimination of all forms of forced and compulsory labor.

Principle 5:   The effective abolition of child labor.

Principle 6:   The elimination of discrimination in respect of employment and occupation.

Environment

Principle 7:   Businesses should support a precautionary approach to environmental challenges.

Principle 8:   Undertake initiatives to promote greater environmental responsibility.

Principle 9:   Encourage the development and diffusion of environmentally friendly technologies.

Anti-corruption

Principle 10:   Businesses should work against all forms of corruption, including extortion and bribery.

Source: "The Ten Principles." http://www.unglobalcompact.org/Portal/Default.asp (accessed August 17, 2004).

Table 8.2

The GBC C-H-A-N-G-E Method

1. Conscious and curious	Be conscious of random incidents and curious about their root cause.
2. Hear and heighten awareness	Hear the need for change and heighten awareness by creating the case for change.
3. Accept and act	Achieve acceptance for the change and take action to make it happen.
4. Navigate and negotiate	Navigate the implementation and negotiate resistance.
5. Guide and generate	Guide systemic change by generating alignment of related systems and processes.
6. Evaluate and enhance	Evaluate the learning and enhance the organization's sustainability.

Table 8.3

Change Processes and GBC: Illustrative Cases

	Global Business Citizenship Process			
Change process	Step 1: *Develop a code of conduct*	Step 2: *Implement locally*	Step 3: *Resolve conflicts, conflicts, experiment*	Step 4: *Systematic learning*
1. *Conscious and and curious: environmental scanning*				
2. *Hear and heighten awareness: the case for change*		EDF in Mali (solar panels for a village)		
3. *Accept and act: make it happen*			Hindustan Sanitaryware (low-water flush toilets)	
4. *Navigate implementation, negotiate resistance*		BouyguesTelecom (office waste recycling)		
5. *Guide and generate alignment*		Bernard Michaud (EU/ISO honey standards)	Aarhus in Burkina Faso (slave/child labor in shea nuts)	
6. *Evaluate and enhance sustainability through learning*				William E. Connor & Associates (an underage worker)

148

Exhibit 8.1

Three types of organizational change	Four beneficial attributes of GBC
Developmental change: improvement of what is	*Better Vision:* a broader, more comprehensive view
Transitional change: implementation of a known new state	*More Safety:* avoiding quicksand and broadsides
Transformational change: emergence of a new state, unknown until it takes shape, out of the remains of the chaotic death of the old state	*Greater Efficiency:* easier, less complicated decisions

Higher Sustainability: more ethical and logical actions |

In the discussion that follows, we also introduce the concepts of developmental, transitional, or transformational change, and we examine which of four beneficial GBC attributes, discussed earlier, are likely to be factors in each case. Brief definitions of these concepts appear in Exhibit 8.1.

EDF: Normal Business Practice

Even when privately owned, electrical power has some attributes of a public good, and so it is quite common for power-generating utilities to participate actively in the lives and well-being of their communities. EDF, a French-owned electricity conglomerate, is no exception. The project they describe on the Global Compact website appears in Exhibit 8.2.

Solar panels in Mali? Isn't this just a normal business decision that happens to have some important social consequences?

Yes and no. EDF is indeed a large supplier of electric power and, like most large suppliers, is experimenting with alternative energy sources. But there is little profit to be earned in poor countries like Mali. If the aim is to improve economic development and standards of living, joint ventures are the way to go.

Yeelen Kura, which means "new light," is a decentralized services company that is a joint project of EDF, the Dutch firm Nuon, local Malinese entrepreneurs, and several NGOs. In a recent presentation to the World Bank, representatives of EDF and Yeelen Kura spoke of the successes and challenges of their efforts to bring power to poor rural areas such as Mali:

149

Exhibit 8.2

Électricité de France: EDF in Mali

In Mali, within the scope of the ACCESS programme, two projects have been implemented to facilitate the access to electricity in rural areas. Two hundred families are now customers of Yeelen Kura, a local company set up in early 2001 with the help of EDF to provide power to 20 remote villages of the cotton-growing area in the southern part of the country. Power will be provided by means of solar panels (potential installed capacity 334 kWc) or a micro-network. The total potential number of customers of this company employing 33 people, all from the region, is estimated at 6,500. A small business zone has been launched in Tambacara (one of the four villages) at the beginning of 2004.

In November 2000, another decentralised electrification project of the same type was implemented farther westwards, in the Senegal River area: 400 families, living in four villages, now have access to electricity provided by another local company operating about fifty solar panel kits and four micro-networks supplied by diesel sets.

In both cases (Yeelen Kura and Senegal River), these projects are meant to generate a profitable and durable economic activity. They are sustainable from the point of view of:

- Social equity because access to energy is given to some of the world's poorest populations, vaccines and medicines can be preserved by means of refrigeration and alphabetisation and school work are facilitated by electric lighting.
- Protection of the environment because the priority is given to the use of renewable energies and even when using small generating sets associated with low-consumption bulbs, less carbon dioxide is released than with candles, kerosene lamps and paraffin burners.
- Economy because the projects are balanced economically over the long term and jobs are created within the local service company.

Source: www.unglobalcompact.org (accessed September 17, 2004), with additional information provided at www.edf.com.

In particular, they focused on equipment finance, lack of access to credit, legal impediments, and technical and personnel problems. They commented on how the World Bank can help improve the situation. [The speakers] noted that the World Bank could be instrumental in promoting the institutional and legal frameworks needed to allow small and medium enterprises to grow in these countries.[3]

Analysis. EDF is clearly aware of its larger environment and is eager to participate in providing the energy requirements of developing countries. It has a well-articulated case for change in terms of solar-powered generators in Mali. The solar panel projects represent developmental change, adding new locations for existing services.

However, as the plea to the World Bank indicates, EDF seems to be unclear about its own vision and buy-in; its action plan requires interventions from other organizations not yet in place; there is no apparent alignment of the Mali project with the company's mission and vision except at the most basic "we are an energy supplier" level; and we have no hint of how the project will be evaluated or how it will contribute to EDF's long-term sustainability. In GBC terms, it's a good start at local implementation, but what's the policy or principle?

Hindustan Sanitaryware: Design for Water Conservation

It often happens that a company can hone its citizenship skills by turning its own distinctive competencies in the direction of solving a social problem. The Hindustan Sanitaryware and Industries, Ltd., for example, has pioneered the design and manufacture of water-saving toilets in India, where clean water is in scarce supply. Not at all a charitable add-on, the project is central to the company's identity and mission. [4]

Part of the family-led Somany Group, Hindustan Sanitaryware earns about half of its revenue from the manufacture of glass bottles for food, wine, soft drinks, and medications. The other half comes from the manufacture and sale of bathroom equipment, including the company's own brands as well as several European brands under exclusive marketing tie-ups. It is the Indian market leader in both its lines, and it enjoys a significant presence in India's export markets.

In Exhibit 8.3, the company describes the challenges of clean water in India and its own contributions to water conservation.

Analysis. Hindustan Sanitaryware is ISO-compliant and no doubt has its eye on increasing its visibility in lucrative export markets. There are marketing points to be gained also with Western multinational enterprises (MNEs) siting facilities in India; Hindustan can rightly boast, "We cost a little more, but we're worth it." Interestingly, Hindustan Sanitaryware's efforts to lobby the Indian government to impose 6.0-liter flushing standards is a classic example of how companies can make strategic use of regulation and public policy while also advancing the public's health and quality of life.

Key points for GBC implementation here include the company's use of a high-level product development team led by the chairman—is there any better way to encourage design change? And it is certainly on the right track to use its manufacturing and marketing expertise to tackle a serious social

Exhibit 8.3

Hindustan Sanitaryware and Industries Ltd.

2003 was declared The International Year of Freshwater. Mr. Kofi Annan pronounced that ". . . lack of access to water—for drinking, hygiene . . . inflicts enormous hardships . . ." In India, 60% of the households do not have an in-house drinking water source, 64% lack basic sanitation, and the groundwater table levels have been plummeting dangerously in all the metros.

Water conservation has been an active focus area of the company since many decades. Long before the others woke up, the company actively pressed the Bureau of Indian Standards to progressively lower the 15 litre norm per WC flush (set since 1957) to 12.5 and then to 10.0 litres (in 1984). Now it is cajoling the BIS to lower it to 6.0 litres. Why is this important? Because it may seem trivial, but it is estimated that a family of 4 can save over 20,000 litres per annum if they switch from a 10 litre flush WC to a 6 litre flush WC. Most countries have a 6 litre standard, except Singapore at 4.2 litres; and they also have dual flush. In India potable water is used in the toilets. One-third of a household's water consumption is in the toilet.

So, the crux of the problem was to design and make water saving WCs. Recognizing the gravity of the problem, the Company even instituted a fully-empowered Product Development Committee to make WCs flush with less and less water. The team consisted of persons from Design, Marketing, Production, etc., and was personally chaired by the company's Chairman himself.

Now all the WCs (excepting a miniscule number in the double syphonic designs) made by the company flush with at most 6.0 litres of water. It has models at 5.0 litres (its Constellation model) and 3.5 litres (Super Constellation model). In case of the latter, a family will save 35000 litres of water annually. It was the 1st in the country to launch 5 litre wall-mounted models. The company was the first to introduce Dual Flush and to pursue its acceptance by the BIS. It recently launched an ECO Flush 4 litre-flushing Squatting Pan. It also collaborated on the 0.300 litre vacuum-assisted model for a European customer, and has now introduced a Waterless urinal.

It is estimated that these reductions in flushing quantities cumulatively saved the nation over two billion litres of water from the company's products alone, leaving aside the additional savings triggered by the competition's response of also making water-saving WCs.

Source: www.unglobalcompact.org (accessed September 16, 2004).

problem. It is clear, however, that the company's mission and vision are not targeted to improving the quality of life in India or elsewhere, but emphasize sales and earnings growth. If this can be achieved through design innovation that permits higher-end products and larger markets, great. From both the GBC and the change process standpoints, Hindustan has put a good spin on its engineering competence and does take a broader view on solving a big social problem, but there is little or no integration of its product lines and marketing strategies with a larger vision for the company or with structures and processes that would support social problem-solving absent the glowing market opportunities. The change is transitional and evolutionary.

Bouygues Telecom: Office Waste Sorting

The Bouygues Group of France is a diversified company employing 124,000 across 80 countries; its 2003 sales amounted to 21.8 billion Euros. [5] The company began in Parisian construction and has expanded worldwide into telecom, media, utilities and roadway building, and a variety of services. In addition to its record of growth and productivity, Bouygues promotes "social investment" by engaging in extensive charitable giving and community partnerships in education, health care, sports, and the arts. Most of the company's operations have been ISO quality certified, and attention has turned recently to safety and environmental certification. Subsidiaries are free to design their own social and environmental programs according to their specific needs and impacts.

Bouygues Telecom decided in 2003 to develop and implement a procedure for reducing, sorting, and recycling wastes. It may be that the impetus for this project was the arrival in July 2002 of strict national regulations (passed ten years earlier) governing waste disposal; among other things, French landfills were forbidden to accept anything but "ultimate waste" which could not be reused or further processed. Whatever the motivation, Bouygues reported its process on the Global Compact website, as shown in Exhibit 8.4.

Analysis. This is an example of a relatively easy problem that can be solved incrementally—a classic case of developmental change. Nothing drastic is needed, no organizational transformations. But that doesn't mean that no effort is involved. The Bouygues process moved from description of the problem to policy formulation; from investigation of regulatory, risk, and cost factors to identification of three reasonable options; from experimentation with those options to satisfaction surveys and selection of the best option. *Voilà*—less waste, more recycling.

From a GBC standpoint, the company is certainly not beyond Step 2, local implementation. There is no indication that the office waste recycling plan will be extended into other Bouygues Group subsidiaries or in parts of the world with less stringent waste control regulations. In change management terms, however, the company is fairly advanced, having navigated the action plan successfully. Of course, it's much easier to do a developmental change because it's less complex and not so likely to be resisted, particularly

Exhibit 8.4

Bouygues Telecom: Reduce Office Wastes

After a comprehensive review of the environmental impacts of its activity, Bouygues Telecom decided in June 2003 to introduce a structured and responsible policy designed to:

- ensure that waste is collected and recycled,
- prevent nuisance and pollution in connection with its activity,
- reduce consumption of energy, paper and packaging so as to preserve natural resources.

Each of the identified impacts has been reviewed in the light of:

- regulatory requirements,
- related risks (environmental, financial, human, brand image, etc.),
- the feasibility and cost of implementing the envisaged solutions.

An action plan involving 12 priority projects has been drawn up and will be fully effective by the end of 2004. Actions are divided into two categories:

- those related to Bouygues Telecom's core business,
- those of a cultural nature involving all employees, for example: waste sorting in offices.

At the end of 2003, Bouygues Telecom decided to introduce waste sorting at all its sites. This involves separating paper from other types of waste so that it can be recycled.

A pilot scheme was launched at four sites in mid-June 2003, enabling 1,400 staff to test three different solutions. A satisfaction survey was then carried out, eliciting constructive comments and guiding the choice of the most appropriate solution.

The waste-sorting scheme has been in effect company-wide since mid-November 2003. The scheme's launch was backed up by an extensive communication campaign on each site and on the company intranet. At the same time, posters were distributed to raise awareness among staff about how to reduce paper consumption in offices.

Source: www.unglobalcompact.org (accessed September 19, 2004).

with the kind of stakeholder involvement Bouygues achieved in this instance. We do not know, though, if the company will move ahead to integrate the new waste management system with other company policies and practices or whether there will be any systematic learning that will aid the parent company in its long-term sustainability.

Bernard Michaud: Quality Control in Beekeeping

The Bernard Michaud Company has produced high-quality honey and related products from its base in the French Pyrenees for more than 100 years.[6] Founder Yves Michaud learned how to isolate monofloral honeys and developed technologies for extracting honey via rotary motion and filtration instead of older pressing methods. The founder's children and grandchildren have continued his zest for beekeeping and its products. The signature brand, Lune de Miel (Honeymoon), originated in 1959 and came to be associated with the company's innovativeness in apiculture, laboratory analysis, and marketing, also earning ISO 9002 quality certification.

The European Union (EU) has set very rigorous standards for beekeeping and honey products, and Bernard Michaud has been involved in setting as well as implementing those standards. The company is a member of the International Honey Commission, an industry group working to establish worldwide standards for honey purity and quality as well as for apiculture practices. EU and ISO certification means that the company's products can be sold seamlessly throughout the twenty-five member-nation region. With the possibility of expanding markets, however, comes the need to find additional sources of supply.

Fortunately for Michaud, the EU also supports beekeeping as a viable form of economic development in the world's emerging economies. The EU's push of regulation, and its pull of development funding, has encouraged companies like Bernard Michaud to expand their operations into the global environment. Thus, Michaud's project, described in Exhibit 8.5, is part of a multifaceted program emphasizing social equity, environmental protection, high product quality, and support for tradition along with expanding import-export markets.

Analysis. In GBC terms, the Michaud program stays at Step 2, local implementation. Apparently there are no exceptions to the stringent rules, no reason for local variations, no conflict between local beekeepers' desires or practices and what Michaud requires. The company's actions vis-à-vis developing-country suppliers are ethical and logical, take a broad view of beekeeping as a development activity, and help Michaud to avoid the quicksand of non-compliance with EU regional regulations and quality standards.

As a change management example, requiring EU compliance of their suppliers in developing countries is a very logical and developmental thing for Michaud to do—it's an action that is well-aligned with the company's values and strategy. Furthermore, it follows through with the founder's intense focus on bees and honey, quality and tradition. The program reaches Step 5 in the change proccess—guide and generate alignment—and demonstrates consistency with the company's history, mission, values, and operational approach.

Exhibit 8.5

Bernard Michaud Company

Quality Charter Program: "Beekeeping in Selected Territories"

Starting in 2002, Bernard Michaud Company introduced a quality charter program, "Beekeeping in Selected Territories," for many of its suppliers in Chile, Argentina, Brazil, and elsewhere. The aims of the program were:

- to develop "good practices in beekeeping, respectful of the product and environment,"
- to "guarantee the absence of contaminating residues in honey (antibiotics, chemical products)"
- to select "native areas protected from harmful and polluting elements,"
- to enhance "the image and value of producers' know-how,"
- to provide "additional income to producers," and
- to promote "honeys produced in [underdeveloped] areas or countries."

The company claims many benefits from its program, including regional economic development, enhancement of biodiversity (because of the importance of bees in plans pollination), and provision of reliable extra income for producers who abide by the quality standards.

Michaud buys honey from contracted producers and sells the product in the French and other European markets. Compliance with European Union directives is an especially important part of the Quality Charter Program:

The selected area must be protected from harmful and polluting elements due to:

- a big city (and its suburbs) of more than 500,000 inhabitants within a radius of 50 km., or of more than 150,000 inhabitants within a radius of 10 km.
- chemical and/or petroleum industries within a radius of 20 km.

(continued)

- a nuclear power station within a radius of 20 km.
- a rubbish dump or incinerator within a radius of 6 km.
- highways within a radius of 5 km. and/or four-lane roads within a radius of 3 km.
- an airport within a radius of 10 km.

Respect for Beekeeping Traditions

- compulsory use of traditional hives and frames (made of wood)
- use of plastic, aluminum, or polystyrene hives and plastic frames is forbidden
- beekeeping operations must be more than five years old
- extraction of honey must be made by cold centrifugation (without any added source of heat but room temperature)

Respect for Beekeeping Good Practice

- use of chemical bee repellents is forbidden during the honey crop
- use of antibiotics to treat bee diseases is forbidden during the period of honey production

Michaud monitors its suppliers to ensure than standards are being met, and performs analytical control tests itself to ensure that products labels with the Quality Charter designation are indeed free of residues.

Source: www.unglobalcompact.org (accessed September 20, 2004). Minor editing has been done to improve readability.

Aarhus: A Little Nut and A Big Problem

Aarhus United was founded in Denmark in 1871 and assumed its current name in a 2003 consolidation of fourteen companies engaged in production, sales, application development, support, brokering, and raw materials farming and acquisition. [7] Aarhus is a world leader in specialty vegetable fats and oils—it was the first, for example, to use palm kernel oil as a cocoa butter substitute to stabilize chocolate products across a broader range of temperatures.

One of Aarhus's key natural resources is the shea nut—sometimes called "woman's gold"—which is used to produce shea oil and butter for foods, soaps, chocolate, and cosmetics. Although several neighboring countries also engage in significant shea nut production and Nigeria is the leading exporter, Burkina Faso (the former Upper Volta) has the world's heaviest concentration of shea trees, and 300,000–400,000 women and girls labor to gather shea nuts in that extremely poor country.

Aarhus managers became concerned about media attention to child trafficking on cocoa plantations in the region, and wondered if the company had exposure to child labor issues in its shea nut supply chain. The problem was succinctly summarized by activist group Global March, citing a 2000 UNICEF study:

> [A]bout 200,000 children are trafficked each year in the West and Central Africa sub-region alone, with minors being purchased for as little as US$10 from Benin, Togo, Mali, Niger and Nigeria. They are then shipped to work with no pay in homes, cocoa and coffee plantations, fishing boats and mines in Cameroon, Gabon, Cote D'Ivoire, The Gambia and Equatorial Guinea. Some from Nigeria are even purchased to work as sex slaves.[8]

Burkina Faso and the shea nut gatherers had not been targeted for attention, but Aarhus wisely wondered about the company's exposure to this difficult and emotional issue. Cocoa plantations might be on one side of the road, and shea nut trees on the other. The proximity of the two activities left Aarhus and other shea butter users very vulnerable.

A company task force was created to study the problem. They proceeded as the company describes in its Global Compact entry:

> We decided that the definitions of ILO Convention 182 concerning worst forms of child labour should form the basis of absolutely unacceptable behaviour. All other identified forms of children involvement would have to be further assessed.
>
> We therefore gathered information, via our local West African offices, about the situation primarily as described in the media, by NGO's and at conferences but also from the observations made by our local offices. Our immediate conception of the situation hereafter was that collection of shea nuts did not involve child labour as defined in ILO convention 182. Evidence of child trafficking/slavery seemed to be related only to plantation work.
>
> To further test our conception of the situation, we decided to carry out a survey of the shea supply chain. A West African audit team as well as a

Danish audit team travelled 13,000–15,000 km by car, thus covering Mali, Ghana, Burkina Faso, Côte d'Ivoire, Benin and Togo. In addition to observations and interviews a simple questionnaire was used. The questionnaire was presented mainly to relevant "neutral" people such as teachers, local NGO's etc.

The result of the survey supported our immediate conception of the situation, namely:

- Forced labour/slavery was not involved in the shea supply chain.
- Children were involved in collecting shea nuts together with the rest of the family as a part of a family culture.
- Children were not prevented from going to school due to their participation in collecting shea nuts.[9]

Whew! No child trafficking in the shea nut supply chain! Aarhus executives were no doubt relieved, and many companies would have let the matter drop right there.

Aarhus leaders, however, were shaken by the deep poverty its observers reported in Burkina Faso, and decided to open a school to help improve things in the region. Two years of planning led to the brink of implementation, but there was one big problem. Executives worried that the school would not survive a downturn in company earnings if it was set up as a charitable project. Discussions with the Nordic branch of the United Nations Development Programme (UNDP) led to a substantially revised strategy, and "in December 2003 Aarhus United signed a partnership and cost-sharing agreement with UNDP for the project entitled 'National Multifunctional Platform Programme for the Fight Against Poverty.'"[10] The company's own website highlights the project as an indication that it is serious about Global Compact objectives:

Practically, Aarhus United has provided multi-functional platforms which generate electricity for the villages. The platforms use a diesel engine to power various tools, which provide affordable, energy-related services such as husking rice, grinding cereals, pumping water and generating electricity for lighting and for powering various electric tools—hence the term "multi-functional."

One of the aims of the platforms is to relieve women and girls of some of their daily work duties in their homes. The incomes they are able to generate also improve the women's economic and social status and alleviate poverty in the immediate community. Finally, the platforms also enhanced food hygiene and water quality, which improved the general health of the local community. At the same time, Aarhus United has decided to further optimise the supply chain, thereby potentially increasing the revenues of the locals.[11]

Analysis. From a GBC standpoint, this case is especially interesting as an example of the movement from Step 2 to Step 3 implementation. Aarhus acknowledged a potential problem, chose a reasonable universal standard, researched the situation, and decided that the problem did not affect the company. But their analysis made plain another underlying problem—the devastating poverty of workers at the bottom of their supply chain. From an initial wish to avoid the quicksand of child-trafficking accusations, Aarhus moved to a broader view of the problems of the region as a whole. Building a school seemed like a good idea, but what if the company could not sustain a sufficient level of giving? Time to move from GBC Step 2 to Step 3. Partnering with a powerful NGO, the company shifted its focus to practical economic development tools that are expected to become self-sustaining.

As a transitional change management example, Aarhus's Burkina Faso experience demonstrates a clear movement along the path of planned change, including the process of negotiating unexpected bumps and bungles. We don't know how the new generator project will be evaluated or if the company will decide to try further inroads against regional poverty. We can see, however, a commitment to principles that is translated into action, even if that action takes an unanticipated twist.

Connor & Associates: One Step at a Time

Perhaps a man with a personal fortune just shy of $1 billion might be excused from caring about the plight of a single underage worker in a faraway land. In fact, William E. Connor II was himself an underage worker, beginning work at his father's Hong Kong-based sourcing firm at the age of twelve. Now, under this industrious son's leadership, William E. Connor & Associates manages fully transparent global supply chains for some of the world's leading retailers, including Nordstrom's, Dillard's, Saks Fifth Avenue, and Harrods.[12]

A key marketing edge for Connor is the company's "on the ground" presence in various sites where goods are manufactured and shipped. The company's website describes a special take on supply chain management:

> We provide full and up to date information on markets throughout the world; identify and qualify suppliers and factories; provide comprehensive

160

Exhibit 8.6

William E. Connor & Associates

We are committed to the elimination of child labour in our own and our suppliers' businesses. To help implement this commitment, our company conducts social compliance audits of all factories from which we source merchandise. Using standards prescribed by SA 8000, we audit for matters such as the quality of the product being produced and working conditions. The audits consist of a plant inspection, a questionnaire and interviews with workers.

On March 15, 2001, we conducted a social compliance audit of one of our suppliers in southern China. During the plant inspection, we found that one of the operators working in the looping department looked very young. We checked the personnel records and discovered that she was below the minimum working age in China (16).

We therefore met with the supplier and requested them to follow the SA 8000 guidelines, i.e. to provide school fees and, until she reached the legal minimum working age, to give an allowance to the girl's family because of losing this job. The supplier also agreed to provide transportation to return the girl to her hometown, which was about 800 km away, and to reemploy the girl if she wished to work there again on completion of her studies and after she reached the legal minimum working age. Last December, we sent someone from our office to visit the girl. She had just finished her studies and was helping her family on the farm. She told us that she wished to return to the factory after the Chinese New Year. Later, we received a message from the supplier to the effect that the girl, who is now over the minimum working age, had returned to the factory as a looping operator. This was confirmed during our own follow up visit to the factory.

Source: www.unglobalcompact.org (accessed August 12, 2004).

product development assistance; coordinate raw material supply; provide web based order tracking; provide comprehensive on-site quality control; supervise logistics and multi-market merchandise programs; track quotas; monitor factory compliance and country of origin requirements; and provide human rights due diligence. In sum, we seamlessly manage the entire global supply chain.[13]

Connor bills itself as operating "on a zero-tolerance platform regarding any breach of legality or human rights." Discovering an underage worker in one of its supplier factories in China was, therefore, a big deal. On the Global Compact website, Connor describes its perspective and the problem it faced; see Exhibit 8.6.

Analysis. At first glance, we thought this was the simplest and easiest of the six Global Compact examples discussed in this chapter. The child's removal from the workplace seems obvious enough when placed in the context of Connor's code of conduct, which rests upon several key principles forbidding child or forced labor, corporal punishment or any form of coercion, and corruption of any sort. Discriminatory practices, while not forbidden, are frowned upon, and on this criterion Connor permits some local cultural variation in practice, while emphasizing non-discrimination as a stretch goal.

But wait—wasn't this an easy case only because the company had already gone through wrenching transformational changes that had been necessary to establish a no-tolerance policy and learn how to make it work? Connor's example, as it turns out, is the only one so far that exhibits the most advanced level of GBC and change management. And, it's the best illustration we've found so far of the idea that, *for a GBC company, some decisions become easier.* Not old enough to meet labor standards? Can't work here—sorry.

And there's more! The path Connor chose was respectful of the too-young worker, her family, and the supplier organization as well. If Connor's intent was simply to certify to its big-name retail clients that their products were not made by children, then the child could simply have been fired. But what about their sending her to school, replacing her income in the family, and guaranteeing her a job when she was old enough? For a company with Connor's mission, vision, and integration, all these steps were simply a natural outgrowth of living and working in difficult environments with a policy of zero tolerance for human rights violations. The case looks easy because all the hard work of organizational change had already been done.

Conclusion

Easy problems of implementation can quickly become quagmires. Shifting environments, the entry of new players, encountering resistance, and any number of other factors can cause the simple to become complex, the no-brainer to become nerve-wracking. GBC companies are not immune to these problems, but they do have effective defenses.

The broader vision of GBC executives makes it easier for them to scan their environments and recognize patterns amid the seemingly random events and circumstances. The thoughtful and careful approach GBC companies take with regard to change helps them sidestep the quicksand and tar pits that prevent long-term sustainability. The ethical and logical links they make between idea, action, and outcome can steer them away from self-deception and from unintended negative consequences. And, with the hard work of change under their belts, GBC executives can find it easier to make decisions that might have been ambiguous or impossible for companies not so well equipped.

Stay with us for more on implementation and stakeholder accountability in the next two chapters.

➤ 9 ◀

The Practice
of Accountability
GBC Measurement and Reporting

Global business citizenship is both a destination and an ongoing journey. It requires that an organization's economic, environmental, and social performance be evaluated and results communicated. Measurement and reporting thus are essential components of stakeholder accountability.

Accountability is the core principle of organizational reporting that provides key stakeholders with feedback on what the company learned during stakeholder dialogue and engagement and that shares the change management activities it has taken as a result. A primary goal of organizational reporting is to facilitate an ongoing stakeholder dialogue that informs the decision making of both the organization and its stakeholders. In this chapter we examine the "how and why" of accountability-based organizational performance measurement and reporting for a GBC company.

Accountability is a two-way street. As explained in earlier chapters, stakeholder engagement uncovers opportunities for the organization to change. Change management is the process for implementing change. Accountability includes the mechanism for feedback to stakeholders that closes the loop.

For example, managers may assess the current state of information that is being shared with stakeholders to find out what is needed, what is already being done, who is doing it, and how well it is being done—thus, to set objectives for further action. Then the task is to communicate these findings to people inside and outside the firm who are interested or who need to be informed, and to engage in dialogue with these relevant stakeholders as described in chapter 5. At the end of the C-H-A-N-G-E process, evaluation

---

Exhibit 9.1

Accountability

Accountability is the core principle of organizational reporting that provides key stakeholders with feedback on what the company learned during stakeholder dialogue/engagement and that shares the change management activities it has taken as a result.

---

allows managers to learn how well the actions taken have met their objectives and the expectations of their stakeholders. This information can then be communicated to and discussed with internal and external stakeholders and used to change organizational policies, processes, and/or practices as a new iteration begins.

GBC Reporting Goes Further

For GBC companies, being responsive to stakeholders' needs for information on company performance means moving beyond traditional reporting devices like annual reports and financial statements. Because such reports are externally mandated, managers too often see reporting requirements as burdensome and unnecessary busywork. Yet performance reporting can serve as a powerful strategic tool. By inviting external stakeholders to evaluate firm performance against their expectations, the company can gain invaluable feedback, thus:

- enabling management to integrate a range of economic, social, and environmental considerations into decision making;
- providing methodologically sound and comprehensive information on the full range of impacts of business activities; and
- enabling the monitoring, evaluation, and reasons for stakeholders' response to organizational behaviors/impacts.[1]

The idea of *triple bottom line reporting*—encompassing economic, environmental, and social impacts and performance—is evolving into comprehensive standards and guidelines for accountability. This emerging reporting paradigm alternatively refers to such reports as: social reports, environmental reports, 3BL (triple bottom line) reports, and sustainability reports. We will, for simplicity, hereafter refer to broad-based externally reported business performance data as "sustainability reports."

"Sustainability" carries none of the baggage of "bottom line" or "social reporting"; it covers a wide range of possible content, and it assumes a long-term, interconnected perspective.

The foundation of GBC is the set of principles and the codes adopted in Step 1 of the GBC model. For the GBC company, those principles must be translated into action, implemented, and learned from. Accountability for the GBC company therefore must align outcomes with principles.

Ford Motor Company is skilled at explicitly mapping its performance with its principles. Ford's approach, illustrated in Figure 9.1 (p. 168) from its 2003/2004 Corporate Citizenship Report, contains many GBC elements. For example, Ford explicitly aligned its business principles with its reporting categories. Further, it provided indicators for each reporting category, some of which are internal measures that are not shared publicly. It reported its actual performance on each category, highlighting the trend from the previous two years. Finally, Ford provided narrative explanations for unfavorable trends and in some cases its plans for improvement.

Following the performance report, Ford narrates a "closer look" at places, products, and issues that are especially challenging. For example, it explores the environmental issues associated with vehicle paint and how to minimize the impact of paint shops while improving product quality and reducing costs. It compares the newer waterborne paints versus the solvent-based paints historically used in their processes. Although reducing volatile organic compound emissions, waterborne paints have other undesirable impacts, including the need for larger painting facilities, resulting in higher energy use and carbon dioxide emissions. At the end of the day, Ford's analysis revealed a similar impact using either paint in terms of direct environmental effects. Ford's decision to remain with the solvent-based paint was thus based on reasonable research, and the company exhibits a willingness to share this information with interested stakeholders.

Now let's take a step back from Ford as a current example of accountability, and learn about how we've gotten to this point with corporate reporting.

Reporting Then: An Historical Perspective

The most common form of organizational reporting has focused on a firm's financial performance. The traditional view of financial performance reporting is a one-way communiqué to a limited set of stakeholders. Annual reports and quarterly financial statements are intended to support decision making by investors and other capital providers. Traditional financial reporting is governed by rule-based reporting principles—Generally Accepted Accounting Principles (GAAP) govern financial reporting in the

United States.[2] International Financial Reporting Standards (IFRS) became effective on January 1, 2005, and also focus on financial disclosures. IFRS are global accounting standards that seek a convergence and consistency of national accounting standards for financial reporting.[3] Because financial reporting principles are solely focused on fairly and accurately presented financial positions, financial results of operations, and cash flows, primarily to investors and lenders, financial reporting standards don't tell us enough of what we need to know for risk assessment and due diligence. These standards tell us nothing, for example, about product quality and safety, environmental impacts, or the regulatory climate.

For decades, financial reporting has been seen as woefully inadequate to meet legitimate stakeholder needs. As early as 1953, Howard Bowen recommended that companies create social audits to address their fulfillment of social responsibilities.[4] Even earlier, in 1940, a government report explored the ways and means of social performance measurement.[5] But the idea of non-traditional, non-financial reporting did not take off in any significant way until the early 1970s.

In the first days of social reporting, some companies experimented with this tool of stakeholder engagement and used something we might call *goal reporting and accounting*.[6] In short, this method involved a company setting its own goals in the social and environmental arenas, and then reporting, in whatever way it saw fit, on how it was doing on accomplishing those goals. Imagine if financial reporting were done like this![7] But as a way to start learning about accountability reporting, it's not that bad. At least this method helps managers to identify the particular vulnerabilities and stakeholder information needs they face, and to establish goals and measures of progress. Over the longer term, however, this method offers no consistency or comparability and can too easily degenerate into a public relations, image-creating device.

A classic example of pioneering practice to expand accountability in reporting in the realm of stakeholders and accountability is Migros Genossenschaftsbund AG of Switzerland, in its extensive experimentation with social reporting beginning in 1976. Migros tracked improvements in stakeholder perceptions of the company, but also discovered that incomplete or misinterpretable reports could generate stakeholder controversy.[8] In its eight-year experience with social reporting, the company produced three major reports and instituted a number of changes, but it didn't cover all the bases. In the first report, for example, Migros observed an unexplained difference in wages paid to male and female employees. The second report did not even mention the gender wage gap, to the annoyance of some stakeholders. The third report revisited the issue, noting very slow progress, but with a promise to continue efforts towards equitable compensation.

Figure 9.1 **Ford Motor Company:**
Our Performance Highlights: 2003 at a Glance

Measuring Performance Against Our Business Principles
(sample categories, indicators, and results)

PRINCIPLE CATEGORY	INDICATOR	2002/2003 RESULTS	Compared to '02
PRODUCTS AND CUSTOMERS	Initial quality (3 months in service), Ford U.S., problems per hundred vehicles	143/136	Better than 2002
We will offer excellent products and services	Vehicle dependability (4-5 years of ownership) Ford U.S., problems per hundred vehicles	354/287	Better than 2002
	Service satisfaction with dealer/retailer, Ford Brand, Europe, percent completely satisfied	50.8/54.0	Better than 2002
	Owner loyalty, Ford Brand, Europe, percent loyal to corporation	49.0/48.0	Worse than 2002
ENVIRONMENT	Ford U.S. fleet fuel economy, car and truck, miles per gallon	23.2/23.6	Better than 2002
We will respect the natural environment and help preserve it for future generations.	Worldwide facility CO_2 emissions per vehicle, metric tonnes	1.30/1.34	Worse than 2002
	Worldwide facility energy consumption per vehicle, million BTUs	12.7/12.9	Worse than 2002
	Global manufacturing water use, total, million cubic meters	92.8/90.0	Better than 2002
SAFETY	Lost-time case rate (per 100 employees)	2.1/1.8	Better than 2002
We will protect the safety and health of those who make, distribute, or use our products.	Severity rate (per 100 employees) – days lost per 200,000 hours worked	31.7/25.3	Better than 2002
COMMUNITY	Ford Motor Company Fund Contributions, $ million	84/78	Worse than 2002
We will respect and contribute to the communities around the world in which we work.	Corporate contributions, $ million	47/43	Worse than 2002
QUALITY OF RELATIONSHIPS	Employee satisfaction, Pulse survey, overall, percent satisfied	61/61	Same as 2002
We will strive to earn the trust and respect of our investors, customers, dealers, employees, unions, business partners, and society.	Total purchases from minority-owned businesses, U.S., $ billion	3.2/3.4	Better than 2002
FINANCIAL HEALTH	Shareholder return, percent	(39)/79	Better than 2002
We will make our decisions with proper regard to the long-term financial security of the company.	Net income (loss), $ billion	(1.0)/0.5	Better than 2002

INTEGRATING OUR BUSINESS PRINCIPLES

During 2003, Ford's business groups were charged with reflecting the Business Principles–adopted in 2002—in their 2004 business plans and scorecards. This was a key step toward integrating the Principles into our most fundamental business practices.

We develop new scorecards each year. Senior management members of the Strategy and Business Governance group set corporate direction and strategic priorities, establish goals

(continued)

and allocate resources, which in turn set the parameters for business operation plans. Each business plan is translated into a scorecard. On a single page, scorecards define the key priorities, success drivers, targets and responsibilities for achieving business results and provide managers with progress indicators....

In early 2004, we began a review of the various business groups' scorecard metrics to assess how they reflect the Business Principles and to continue the process of defining key performance indicators for each Principle. The table (above) includes some scorecard metrics that are common across business units and some indicators that we have reported on previously. Other scorecard metrics are internal measures that are not shared publicly.

Building the Business Principles into the business planning and scorecard processes is an important step toward incorporating them into the business. But we recognize that much remains to be done to raise awareness of the Principles among our 328,000 employees, explore the Principles' significance in day-to-day decision making and make them part of the fabric of our culture. That is our continuing challenge.

Source: The data are examples of Ford's accountability reporting and are extracted from a table entitled "Measuring Performance Against Our Business Principles," p. 6 in Ford Motor Company's 2003 Corporate Citizenship Report. The text comes from p. 7 of the same report.

As with Migros, reporting on the triple bottom line of economic, environmental, and social performance is a vehicle by which a firm can demonstrate components of accountability—stakeholder engagement, transparency, responsiveness, compliance, assurance, and learning. Through the evaluations of stakeholders, a firm can learn by receiving and incorporating their responses into organizational behaviors. But, as mentioned in chapter 5, a company must either act on what it learns from stakeholders or justify its lack of responsiveness. Reporting without responsiveness leaves companies like Migros open to controversy.

Reporting Now: A Current Perspective

Moving from traditional financial reporting to broad-based sustainability reporting can be daunting to visualize, much less accomplish. Organizations themselves are experimenting with both content and format, reporting in a more holistic way to describe the "footprint," or total impact, of the activities of the firm on the environment, the stakeholder network, and societies at large.

The method on the forefront of progressive non-traditional reporting is sustainability reporting, which focuses on the dimensions of economic, social, and environmental performance. Sustainability reporting is gaining credibility and is getting ever more informative and useful. Again using Ford Motor Company as an example, Figure 9.2 illustrates how Ford aims to move toward expanded processes of accountability and away from a sole focus on traditional

Figure 9.2 **Ford Motor Company Expands Commitment to Accountability**

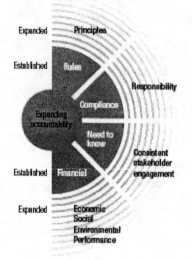

CHANGING EXPECTATIONS—EXPANDING ACCOUNTABILITY

Society's concept of corporate accountability is expanding in response to a number of factors, including:

- Stakeholder concerns that the global reach of corporations exceeds the ability of existing institutions to govern them effectively
- The well-publicized failure of certain companies in the recent past that has eroded public trust in corporations
- Evolving corporate commitments to sustainability, with a corresponding need to define how companies can be accountable to these commitments.

Ford is expanding its commitment to accountability in four major areas.

1. BUSINESS PRINCIPLES—Governance using Business Principles builds on established rules (policies, standards, codes, etc.). However, rules cannot cover every eventuality. Our adoption of Business Principles acknowledges the complexity of our business environment and the many, often competing factors that go into our decisions and behaviors. Through our Business Principles, we provide employees with the means to address dilemmas inherent to business decision making.
2. RESPONSIBILITY—Compliance with all legal requirements everywhere we do business is essential, but not always sufficient. Going beyond compliance by adhering to global, voluntary standards for our activities can be more efficient and further protect our employees, customers, other stakeholders, and our reputation. . . .
3. CONSISTENT STAKEHOLDER ENGAGEMENT—A "need to know" approach to communicating with stakeholders relies on a one-way flow of information, often after the fact. Expanded accountability includes stakeholders early in decisions likely to affect them and involves two-way communication. Systematic engagement re-

(continued)

170

veals stakeholder expectations, improves the quality of information available to make decisions, and increases the transparency of our actions and their consequences.

4. ECONOMIC, SOCIAL, AND ENVIRONMENTAL PERFORMANCE—Taking account of our economic, environmental, and social performance—and publicly reporting on that performance—embraces the fact that we have more than just financial impacts and must measure, integrate, and communicate these impacts.

Source: Ford Motor Company 2003, pp. 12–13.

financial reporting and limited, sporadic communication to stakeholders on a need-to-know basis. Experimentation by Ford and other leading-edge companies in reporting format, including online reporting, will no doubt eventually evolve to more frequent, and ultimately real-time, performance reporting.

Both of these aspects of reporting—content and format—present significant challenges for today's executives with respect to what to measure, how much to tell, and when and how to tell it. In the following sections we examine several major efforts to systematize multi-stakeholder performance reporting.

Accountability Tools: An Internal Focus

The first two accountability tools presented, the Balanced Scorecard and the SIGMA Project, provide internal and strategic decision-making support. The second two, the AA1000 Process Standards and the Global Reporting Initiative, provide guidance for external stakeholder engagement and external performance reporting. The Balanced Scorecard was a first step toward expanding and coordinating data collection to focus the organization on strategic implementation. Later, the SIGMA scorecard was developed to focus more specifically on GBC strategies.

The Balanced Scorecard

Introduced in the mid-1990s, the Balanced Scorecard (BSC) has been widely adapted in large companies as a means to improving accounting systems to contribute more effectively to the strategic planning process.[9] It is a driver model—that is, the BSC requires that the organization identify the "drivers" of success with respect to each of four perspectives: financial, customer, internal, and learning and growth. Each perspective can be characterized by questions that flow from the organizational vision and strategy:

Financial—"What returns do our shareholders expect, and how can we meet those expectations?"

Customer—"What do our customers expect of our products and services, and how can we meet those expectations to achieve our goals?"

Table 9.1

A Balanced Scorecard Illustration

Financial
  • Return on investment
  • Market share
  • Growth rates
  • New product introductions

Customer
  • Retention rates
  • Customer satisfaction
  • Product safety

Internal Business Process
  • Product quality measures
  • Customer service processes
  • Cost controls

Learning and Growth
  • Intellectual capital
  • Training and development
  • Knowledge management

Internal—"To satisfy our customers, at which processes must we excel?"

Learning and Growth—"To achieve our goals, how must the organization learn and improve?"[10]

Implementation of the Balanced Scorecard requires the company to design performance metrics that help to answer the questions in each perspective. For example, the customer success factor might translate into tracking the percent of repeat purchasers, new product introductions, or other standard customer satisfaction measures. Table 9.1 provides a sample BSC along with typical drivers that might be measured and monitored within each perspective.

BSC drivers, or performance metrics, can be qualitative or quantitative; the key is that they are readily interpretable.[11] The BSC's gift was the impetus it provided for business leaders to think beyond traditional financial performance measurement. As adaptations of BSC have evolved, other dimensions have been added. A lack of specific focus on people is one of the drawbacks noted by subsequent adopters of the BSC, and so the concept of BSC has been leveraged to include other stakeholder dimensions. Thousands of companies worldwide have incorporated the Balanced Scorecard to measure and manage multi-dimensional business performance, thus generating a host of measures and examples of how to make this approach work for strategic gain.[12]

The SIGMA Project—Sustainability: Integrated Guidelines for Management

An adaptation of the Balanced Scorecard, the SIGMA Project was developed in the United Kingdom (UK) beginning in 1999 as a collaborative venture between government (UK Department of Trade and Industry, and UK Department of Environment, Transport, and the Regions), NGOs (Forum for the Future and AccountAbility), and the private sector. The aim was to move beyond the approach of the Balanced Scorecard toward a measurement and reporting schema that could support emerging ideas of *sustainability* as a business goal.

The SIGMA Project developed a set of tools and guidelines to help organizations address sustainability issues, and to include them in their strategic processes. The SIGMA Scorecard is also a four-quadrant driver model describing what success would look like from the four perspectives of sustainability, stakeholders, internal, and knowledge/skills. The scorecard links social, environmental, and economic perspectives into one framework to facilitate prioritization of assets and decision making. As does the BSC, the SIGMA Scorecard operates at any level in the organization (corporate, functional, business unit, department, and individual) and works best when integrated across levels. Each perspective can be characterized by questions that flow from organizational goals regarding sustainability:

Sustainability—"How do we understand success for the organization in terms of sustainable development and the goal of organizational sustainability? What measures of social, economic, and environmental performance are relevant—in line with the organization's values, vision, and mission?"

Stakeholders—"How must the organization engage with, and be accountable to, its stakeholders in order to achieve its contribution to sustainable development?"

Internal processes—"How must the organization's management activities and processes operate in order to satisfy its stakeholders and achieve its contribution to sustainable development?"

Knowledge and skills—"How must the organization learn, innovate, and improve in order to excel at its management activities and processes and achieve its contribution to sustainable development?"[13]

The SIGMA Scorecard also requires identification of critical success performance metrics, or drivers, for each perspective. As mentioned before, SIGMA includes a specific focus on stakeholders while the Balanced Scorecard is less focused on all stakeholders. Another interesting difference between the two tools is that, although the Balanced Scorecard broadens the assessment of the company's impacts, the SIGMA Scorecard continually emphasizes the company's contributions to sustainable development, a goal that is bigger than the company's narrow self-interest and truly worthy of a global business citizen.

Accountability Tools: An External Focus

It's good for managers to know what's happening in their own organizations—but then the information has to be transmitted outward, to stakeholders. The approaches described next provide guidance for external stakeholder engagement and external performance reporting.

Global Reporting Initiative

The Global Reporting Initiative (GRI) is an international body of corporate and NGO representatives committed to developing guidelines for broad-based corporate reporting.[14] GRI has not promulgated a code, performance standard, or management system, nor does it provide instruction for designing management reporting systems or offer methodologies for preparing reporting, monitoring, or verification of reports. Rather, it provides comprehensive guidelines for *communicating* organizational performance in a way that ensures comparability, consistency, relevance, reliability, transparency, and verifiability. The GRI Sustainability Reporting Guidelines are to economic, social, and environmental performance reporting what Generally Accepted Accounting Principles are for financial performance reporting. The GRI has promulgated a specific framework for reporting on an organization's economic, environmental, and social performance.[15] As the foremost global reporting standard for triple bottom line performance, the GRI guidelines include:

- reporting principles and specific content requirements
- promotion of comparability across organizations
- support for benchmarking
- facilitation of stakeholder engagement

Inclusivity is a significant component of stakeholder engagement.[16] It refers to "reflection at all stages of the process over time of the views and needs of all stakeholder groups."[17] Note that this standard does not say "reflection on the views and needs of stakeholders that help us or agree with us." Recall the stakeholder salience model from chapter 5 and you'll realize that a GBC company will consider stakeholders who may be dependent, involuntarily harmed, or perhaps even illegitimate.

Stakeholders should be consulted regarding what is reported, how it is reported (indicators, format, frequency), and to whom sustainability reporting is directed. The inclusivity principle in sustainability reporting recognizes that various stakeholders have diverse decision-making needs that can benefit from specific information not needed by all. For example, employees benefit from knowing the description of programs to support their continued employability and to manage career endings, while this information is of no direct interest to suppliers. And, while information needs of diverse stakeholders can overlap, as in the description of significant environmental impacts of principal products and services, they can also be distinct. Failure to include information that stakeholders need would violate the inclusivity principle of sustainability reporting, resulting in less relevance to decision-makers than is advocated by these initiatives.

A sustainability report according to GRI guidelines includes the following four sections:

- Organization strategy
- Operating profile
- Governance and management systems
- Performance indicators

GRI guidelines identify core and supplemental indicators to produce a balanced report on the organization's economic, environmental, and social performance.[18] The 50 Core Indicators, listed in Table 9.2, include 10 on economic impacts, 16 on environmental impacts, and 24 on social impacts (11 on labor, 7 on human rights, 3 on community impact, and 3 on product responsibility).

Using Ford as our example again, the information available through GRI reports now includes such interesting facts as these:

- Ford Asia Pacific witnessed a 23 percent increase in favorable ratings on their employee stress survey.
- 2001 was the first year since 1918 that Ford had no traumatic fatalities of employees.
- Total charitable giving reached an all-time high in 2001 of $139 million for projects focused on education, the environment and community development.
- Every Ford salaried employee is offered up to 16 hours of paid time per year to work on community service projects.
- Since 2000, Ford has improved its EU fleet average [carbon dioxide] emissions by 2 percent.[19]

Table 9.2

GRI Sustainability Report Core Indicators

Dimension	Focus	Indicator
Economic	Customers	EC1: Net sales
		EC2: Geographic breakdown of markets
	Suppliers	EC3: Cost of all goods, materials, and services purchased
		EC4: Percent of contracts that were paid in accordance with agreed terms, excluding agreed penalty arrangements
	Employees	EC5: Total payroll and benefits (including wages, pension, other benefits, and redundancy payments) broken down by country or region
	Capital providers	EC6: Distributions to providers of capital broken down by interest on debt and borrowings, and dividends on all classes of shares, with any arrears of preferred dividends to be disclosed
		EC7: Increase/decrease in retained earnings at end of period
	Public sector	EC8: Total sum of taxes of all types paid broken down by country
		EC9: Subsidies received broken down by country or region
		EC10: Donations to community, civil society, and other groups broken down in terms of cash and in-kind donations per type of group
Environmental	Materials	EN1: Total materials used other than water, by type
		EN2: Percent of materials used that are wastes (processed or unprocessed) from sources external to the reporting organization
	Energy	EN3: Direct energy use segmented by primary source
		EN4: Indirect energy use
	Water	EN5: Total water use
	Biodiversity	EN6: Location and size of land owned, leased, or managed in biodiversity-rich habitats
		EN7: Description of the major impacts on biodiversity associated with activities and/or products and services in terrestrial, freshwater, and marine environments

	Emissions, effluents, and waste	EN8: Greenhouse gas emissions
		EN9: Use and emissions of ozone-depleting substances
		EN10: NOx, SOx, and other significant air emissions by type
		EN11: Total amount of waste by type and destination
		EN12: Significant discharges to water by type
		EN13: Significant spills of chemicals, oils, and fuels in terms of total number and total volume
	Products and services	EN14: Significant environmental impacts of principal products and services
		EN15: Percent of the weight of products sold that is reclaimable at the end of the products' useful life and percent that is actually reclaimed
	Compliance	EN16: Incidents of and fines for non-compliance with all applicable international declarations/ conventions/treaties, and national, sub-national, regional, and local regulations associated with environmental issues
Social	Employment	LA1: Breakdown of workforce by region/country, status, employment type, and by employment contract.
		LA2: Net employment creation and average turnover segmented by region/country
	Labor/ management relations	LA3: Percent of employees represented by independent trade union organizations or other bona fide employee representatives broken down geographically, or Percent of employees covered by collective bargaining agreements broken down by region/country
		LA4: Policy and procedures involving information, consultation, and negotiation with employees over changes in the reporting organization's operations
	Health and safety	LA5: Practices on recording and notification of occupational accidents and diseases, and how they relate to the ILO Code of Practice on Recording and Notification of Occupational Accidents and Diseases
		LA6: Description of formal joint health and safety committees comprising management and worker representatives and proportion of workforce covered by any such committees
		LA7: Standard injury, lost day, and absentee rates and number of work-related fatalities (including subcontracted workers)
		LA8: Description of policies or programs on HIV/ AIDS

(continued)

177

Table 9.2 *(continued)*

Dimension	Focus	Indicator
Training and education		LA9: Average hours of training per year per employee by category of employee
	Diversity and opportunity	LA10: Description of equal opportunity policies or programs, as well as monitoring systems to ensure compliance and results of monitoring
		LA11: Composition of senior management and corporate governance bodies (including the board of directors), including female/male ratio and other indicators of diversity as culturally appropriate
	Strategy and management	HR1: Description of policies, guidelines, corporate structure, and procedures to deal with all aspects of human rights relevant to operations, including monitoring mechanisms, and results
		HR2: Evidence of consideration of human rights impacts as part of investment and procurement decisions, including selection of suppliers/contractors
		HR3: Description of policies and procedures to evaluate and address human rights performance within the supply chain and contractors, including monitoring systems and results of monitoring
		HR4: Description of global policy and procedures/programs preventing all forms of discrimination in operations, including monitoring systems and results of monitoring
	Freedom of association and collective bargaining	HR5: Description of freedom of association policy and extent to which this policy is universally applied independent of local laws, as well as description of procedures/programs to address this issue
	Child labor	HR6: Description of policy excluding child labor as defined by the ILO Convention 138 and extent to which this policy is visibly stated and applied, as well as description of procedures/programs to address this issue, including monitoring systems and results of monitoring
	Forced and compulsory labor	HR7: Description of policy to prevent forced and compulsory labor and extent to which this policy is visibly stated and applied as well as description of procedures/programs to address this issue, including monitoring systems and results of monitoring

Community	S01: Description of policies to manage impacts on communities in areas affected by activities, as well as description of procedures/programs to address this issue, including monitoring systems and results of monitoring
Bribery and corruption	S02: Description of the policy, procedures/management systems, and compliance mechanisms for organizations and employees addressing bribery and corruption
Political	S03: Description of policy, procedures/management systems, and compliance mechanisms for managing political lobbying and contributions
Consumer health and safety	PR1: Description of policy for preserving customer health and safety during use of products and services, and extent to which this policy is visibly stated and applied, as well as description of procedures/programs to address this issue, including monitoring systems and results of monitoring
Products and services	PR2: Description of policy, procedures/management systems, and compliance mechanisms related to product information and labeling
Respect for privacy	PR3: Description of policy, procedures/management systems, and compliance mechanisms for consumer privacy

Source: GRI Sustainability Reporting Guidelines (2002), accessible at www.globalreporting.org/.

Note: GRI indicators have code numbers referring to their order in the guidelines and the dimension to which they apply. Thus, EC = economic indicators and EN = environmental indicators. In the social dimension, indicator labels are as follows: LA = labor practices, HR = human rights, SO = other social domains, and PR = product-related indicators.

Many companies are now publishing sustainability reports. As of October 2005, GRI is aware of 729 organizations that use the GRI guidelines to some extent, although there is no way for an exhaustive list to be compiled, as reporting is generally voluntary. Of these reporters, seventy-nine are U.S.-based. GRI says that over forty of them are reporting "in accordance" with GRI guidelines, meaning that their reports are in conformity with GRI content guidelines (mandatory indicators) and that the report has been "signed-off" on by the CEO or a board representative. These numbers appear modest, but they are growing. GBC companies may be more likely to adopt the GRI framework because they understand the importance of external reporting which meets a broadly accepted set of characteristics that the GRI is working diligently to codify.

179

GRI's performance indicators represent a significant step forward in accountability reporting, but they will go even further as GRI supports the development and use of two types of *integrated* performance metrics:

1. *Systemic indicators*—relating the activity of an organization to the larger economic, environmental, and social systems in which it operates. An example provided by GRI is net job creation as a proportion of total jobs created in a region in which it operates.
2. *Cross-cutting indicators*—directly relating two or more dimensions of economic, environmental, and social performance as a ratio. Eco-efficiency measures are an example. These measures illustrate the magnitude of the impact of change of one indicator on the value of another, as in the amount of emissions (environmental) per monetary unit of savings in operating costs (economic).[20]

GRI continues to develop and evolve. The next revision of the GRI Reporting Guidelines is scheduled for release in 2006, following an extensive two-year, multi-stakeholder program to study and revise the reporting guidelines and overall framework. Additionally, the GRI aims to facilitate compliance with international accountability standards, including the Organization for Economic Cooperation and Development (OECD) Reporting Guidelines for Multinational Enterprises. According to GRI, "The ability of the GRI Guidelines to bring expression and accountability to international standards and codes such as the OECD Guidelines has been widely recognized."[21] An easy-to-use guide for using the GRI Guidelines to demonstrate commitment and progress with the Global Compact Principles, the Millennium Development Goals, and the OECD Guidelines for MNE's is forthcoming, promising additional support for GBC companies striving for compliance with diverse global accountability standards.

AccountAbility1000

As we stated in chapter 5, the AA1000 Framework was designed to help companies manage the entire accountability process. Here we take a look at how to achieve accountability through transparency for the economic, social, and environmental impacts of a business.

Following the release of the initial AA1000 framework, the Institute for Social and Ethical Accountability (formerly ISEA, now called AccountAbility) has coordinated the development of several specialized modules. The first module, the AA1000 Assurance Standard, was released in March 2003. It is the equivalent of Generally Accepted Auditing Standards (GAAS) for auditing and verification of social and environmental reporting, and is designed to be used to audit the reports issued under Global Reporting Initiative (GRI) guidelines and company-specific formats. According to AccountAbility, "The AA1000 Assurance Standard uses three principles to assess reports:

- *Materiality:* does the sustainability report provide an account covering all the areas of performance that stakeholders need to judge the organisation's sustainability performance?
- *Completeness:* is the information complete and accurate enough to assess and understand the organisation's performance in all these areas?
- *Responsiveness:* has the organisation responded coherently and consistently to stakeholders' concerns and interests?"[22]

The first two of these Assurance Principles mirror the traditional financial auditing standards while incorporating additional relevant dimensions. The third, responsiveness, assesses specifically what is truly different about sustainability reporting—the mantle of responsibility for meeting the legitimate expectations of stakeholders accepted by the GBC company.

Future AA1000 modules will address two important areas[23]:

1. *Governance and Risk Management*—a means to respond to increasing demands to demonstrate effective management of social and environmental risks.
2. *Measuring and Communicating the Quality of Stakeholder Engagement*—This module will provide a standard to assess whether, and to what extent, the legitimate interests of stakeholders have been taken into account, and to what extent conflicting interests among different stakeholder groups have been resolved. AccountAbility proposes to measure the procedural quality of stakeholder engagement on three dimensions: (1) procedural quality (how the engagement was conducted, and whether consistent with its declared purpose); (2) responsiveness (evidence of organizational learning from the engagement); and (3) quality of outcomes (evidence of resulting costs/benefits to the organization and its stakeholders).[24]

These two modules are scheduled for release by the end of 2005. The website states that "new modules will be introduced over time to reflect developments in the field of accountability and the needs of our members and accountability professionals."[25]

The practices of nonfinancial performance measurement and reporting will go through extensive periods of experimentation before the accounting criteria of consistency, relevance, comparability, and verifiability will be possible. This process is already at work and will certainly continue.

Challenges of Accountability Reporting

Reporting sustainability performance remains challenging in several important ways. First, consistency and comparability across organizations are not ensured by existing reporting standards because the format and content of sustainability reports remain voluntary in most of the world.[26] Second, no single template can satisfy every company's needs with respect to accountability reporting because the circumstances, the stakeholder set, the internal processes and assets, the competitive strategy, and so much more will constitute a unique profile.

Learning, then, becomes critically important in developing the measurement and reporting pieces of accountability. We will say more about learning at the systemic level in chapter 11, but for now, we just note that organizations that embrace GBC face at least the following learning challenges:

- Integrating sustainability issues (economic, social, and environmental) into strategic decision-making processes.
- Identifying, understanding, and managing the impacts and risks of their activities.
- Recognizing opportunities for improving performance relating to organizational impacts and initiating change management interventions.
- Incorporating "stakeholder knowledge" (responses, concerns, preferences, expectations) into organizational decision making.

Conclusion: Memo to Global Business Citizens

First you have to talk with stakeholders. Then you have to act on what you learned. And then you have to tell them what they need to know. Sounds simple, but of course it isn't. The good news is that as stakeholders are demanding more trustworthiness, more accountability, and more performance from companies, managers are indeed learning how to get it right.

Accountability is a bedrock concept for GBC companies, but it is not a rigid rule of content and form. Instead it reflects the hybrid nature of GBC strategy. Accountability gives companies a way to chart a course to sustainability by remaining attuned to stakeholder needs and expectations. This requires, of course, some consistency in local implementations, and very likely some experimentation when conflicts and inconsistences arise. If done well, accountability generates systematic learning for the firm, along with the trust that is so essential to company survival and success.

➤ 10 ◀

Cases in Implementing
Stakeholder Accountability

We have explored GBC implementation from the internal perspective of organizational change and from the external perspective of stakeholder engagement. Now it's time to turn our attention outward to accountability/transparency practices. These are the crucial tools that managers and companies can use to negotiate the tricky waters of culture conflicts, integrity management, cross-border variations in custom and law, and a host of other problems faced by multinationals in today's global environment.

The framework for this chapter, shown in Table 10.1, combines the key components of accountability, derived from the last chapter, with the four steps of the GBC process. Cases chosen from the Global Compact database and from various company sources are slotted into the framework to illustrate the relationships.

Implementing Stakeholder Accountability

Accountability and transparency earn a lot of lip service from the business press. U.S. laws such as the Sarbanes-Oxley Act have raised the bar for accountability, leaving many companies scrambling to comply, and the European Union is also struggling with regulations that will open up corporate governance and decision-making processes. GBC accountability takes the law into account but goes beyond to focus on mission-driven accountability to stakeholders. Even the best stakeholder engagement practices are a waste of time unless the company is prepared to act on what it hears and learns, and then to report reliably on accomplishments, progress, and problems. Here we investigate illustrative cases of accountability practices, including compliance, independent assurance, transparency, and formal reporting.

Table 10.1

Accountability Processes and Global Business Citizenship

Accountability processes	GBC steps			
	Code of conduct	Local adaptation	Conflicts and experimentation	Systematic learning
Compliance		Beauty Essential, Thailand; SA8000 certification	Royal Dutch Shell, human rights tool. Oman, South Africa	
Independent assurance				
Transparency				
Reporting		GAP social report 2003, labor rights		Interface, sustainability report

Note: The GBC steps across the column headings are intended to represent a progression of actions toward becoming a global business citizen. The row headings, however, are not in progression but are discrete. Any or all of them could be present in a particular case.

Compliance and Local Adaptation: Beauty Essential Co., Ltd.

Exporting is a powerful incentive for companies in developing regions to search out global standards and learn to comply with them. North American and European markets, though not especially growth markets, are still the locus of most of the world's wealth and offer the best likelihood of high-margin sales. Meeting global standards may require not only pledges to not violate basic human rights, but also technological and process innovations that ultimately bring the company closer to par with its competitors in more developed regions.

Beauty Essential Co., Ltd., of Thailand had already been certified compliant with ISO 9002 and ISO 14001 standards, in 1998 and 1999, respectively. ISO 9002 is a set of quality assurance guidelines that apply to manufacturers, installers, and servicers of products. ISO 14001 standards apply to environmental practices, specifying what constitutes a complete and effective environmental management system.

But their chief branded customers—including Calvin Klein, Tommy Hilfiger, and Nautica—demanded more. Labor practices had come under severe attack worldwide (remember Nike and the Vietnam footwear industry?), and big-name companies were under the gun to certify their supply chains as non-oppressive to workers. Complying with SA 8000 standards, promulgated by Social Accountability International, would give the company the essential proof they needed to continue exporting to U.S. and European markets.

SA 8000 standards, as we saw in chapter 9, require compliance with internationally accepted labor rights principles, a factory-level compliance system, independent verification, stakeholder involvement, and public reporting. The labor principles cover child labor, forced labor, health and safety, freedom of association, collective bargaining, discriminatory practices, abusive punishment, working hours, compensation, and management systems that integrate the standards into everyday practice.

Because of prior certification efforts, Beauty Essential had already instituted many of the changes needed to comply with SA 8000. Their one difficulty was endemic in the Thai environment—a very high overtime burden. Workers averaged more than 84 hours of work per week, including more than the Thai legal limit of 36 hours of weekly overtime. SA 8000 required "no more than 48 hours per week with at least one day off for every seven day period; voluntary overtime paid at a premium rate and not to exceed 12 hours per week on a regular basis."[1] Management correctly anticipated that workers would bitterly resist any innovation that would lower their incomes. So, instead of arbitrarily reducing hours, Beauty Essential began process improvements to enhance productivity.

Time-and-motion studies illuminated inefficiencies in the production lines, and ergonomic principles were applied to reduce worker strain and fatigue. Sequencing, tools, and entire workstations were redesigned. Supervisors demonstrated the new processes and answered all questions from their workers, then began training. Employees quickly realized that they could equal or better their old salaries with many fewer hours of work.

Vetted by the independent certifying agency Bureau Veritas Quality International (BVQI), Beauty Essential achieved SA8000 certification in 2000.

The result? The company claims better output, fewer hours worked, stable income for workers, SA8000 certification for the export market, and—as an unplanned bonus—higher quality products![2]

Compliance, Conflicts, and Tool Development: Royal Dutch Shell

This isn't the same old story about Shell and the Brent Spar oil rig, or about Shell in Nigeria when the Ogoni spokesman Ken Saro-Wiwa and eight colleagues were summarily executed and Shell chose not to intervene. But these stories form the background of Shell's subsequent attempts to restructure, assert more centralized control over far-flung units, and attend more closely to the needs and issues of stakeholders.

The experimentation step of the GBC process is of course essential whenever local norms conflict with universal principles or with expected company practices. In addition, experiments are needed when a single global principle is defined, interpreted, and possibly violated in multiple ways across various cultures. Nowhere more than here is the value of a flexible GBC process more apparent.

On the face of it, a principle endorsing universal human rights seems straightforward enough. But think about it: Shell's group of companies operates in 145 countries and employs more than 115,000 people. The geographic range alone covers the earth's face and includes cultures where women can't participate in public life, where brutal dictators execute their enemies on a whim, where rigid class hierarchies and religious dictates are enforced with violence, where dire poverty ensures that child labor is routine, and where people can be imprisoned for advocating a labor union. Oddly enough, most cultures don't violate all or even most of the internationally accepted standards of human rights. But a great many cultures violate one or a few. What is a company like Shell to do?

Working with a template from the Danish Institute for Human Rights (DIHR), Shell developed a data-gathering and assessment instrument to be used country by country to identify the most likely human rights violations and the ease with which guidelines could be adopted and implemented. In the first test of the instrument, in South Africa, Shell and DIHR also wanted to learn whether the data tool could be readily integrated into Shell management systems and practices. After simplifying and redesigning the instrument to get the bugs out, Shell went to Oman, at the other end of the African continent, for a second field test.

Shell reported that the preliminary tests showed "that the tool is capable of detecting the most important human rights concerns in relation to each company's location and type of operation."[3]

The end result? Shell gets a tool that lets them find the human rights hot buttons before they get burned. It remains to be seen what use Shell will make of such a tool. And, eventually, the rest of the world will get the benefit of what Shell and the Danish Institute have learned from their experiments.

Experiment in Monitoring and Transparency: The Gap

In 1996, television personality Kathy Lee Gifford made a plea to her public. She wanted them to trust that she would never hire children or abuse workers in any way to produce her "Kathie Lee" line of clothing and accessories, sold at Wal-Mart. The facts, via the magic of supply chain ethics and global media and to Gifford's shock, had told quite a different story. As reported by the National Labor Committee, a labor-rights organization, Kathie Lee's clothing was made in Honduras and El Salvador by children, in Saipan and China under grueling and cruel working conditions, and in Manhattan and Los Angeles with below-minimum wages and forced overtime.

The "No Sweat" campaign, engineered by then-U.S. secretary of labor Robert Reich, was a multi-sector effort to come up with standards for monitoring and controlling supply chains for labor practices. An important outcome of "No Sweat" was the creation of the Apparel Industry Partnership Fair Labor Association, an industry-wide effort to establish and implement labor standards. Wal-Mart, meanwhile, got on board late in the process, with a self-monitoring scheme that turned out to be not terribly effective at identifying labor problems in its supply chain.

Other companies besides Wal-Mart were skewered in a massive global campaign against sweatshops. We have already seen one of Nike's responses via the Vietnam footwear industry case. Major brands involved in the controversy included Abercrombie & Fitch, Cacique, Dana Buchman, Elisabeth, Guess, Lands' End, Lane Bryant, Lerner New York, Levi Strauss, Liz Claiborne, Nordstrom, Victoria's Secret, and the companies of The Gap Inc.— Gap, GapKids, Banana Republic, and Old Navy. The Gap's response to the controversy was multifaceted, with one very important component being the release in 2004 of the company's first-ever social responsibility report.

Gap is a $16 billion, 150,000-employee multinational corporation. It sources its popular clothing lines from fifty nations, using more than 3,000 contractors and subcontractors. Gap began its involvement in the sweatshops issue in 1992 when it developed its first supplier code of conduct. Monitoring and compliance, as always, proved to be exceedingly difficult, and for years not much progress was made.

The Gap story goes a long way toward answering standard concerns about the unintended negative consequences of reducing sweatshop labor. In 1995, when the company discovered "low pay, excessive overtime, and union-busting" in a Salvadorean contractor, they severed relations. Labor groups, however, encouraged Gap executives to stay, keep the jobs alive, and work with the contractor to make changes. So, Gap partnered with three prominent NGOs to develop ways to improve working conditions. Getting serious about accountability, and partnering with NGOs, made it possible for Gap to report "significant progress" in 2003 toward its goal of "supplier monitoring for compliance with company standards."[4]

At present, Gap's Global Compliance function is headed by an executive vice president and directed by a vice president, and employs more than ninety full-time vendor compliance officers (VCOs) and support staff. The compliance officers are mostly natives of the regions or countries they monitor. They speak the language and have had relevant work experience. When a manufacturer makes overtures to become a Gap supplier, the approval process swings into action, with these three steps, which may take as long as a year to complete:

1. A manufacturer's written commitment: A manufacturer must sign our compliance agreement, stating its commitment to abide by our Code of Vendor Conduct. The manufacturer is required to provide a profile of each facility it plans to use for our order and its workers. The manufacturer must also agree to allow us unrestricted access to factory workers, working and living facilities, and employment records.

2. Our initial evaluation visit: Once the required paperwork has been reviewed, a VCO schedules a visit. A detailed assessment of factory conditions is conducted based on the eight sections of our code. Any violations are documented. Our policy is that no garment factory is approved without an inspection by one of our VCOs.

3. A decision by our compliance team: After analyzing the paperwork and the results of the evaluation, our Global Compliance staff determines whether the manufacturer is able to comply with our code. At this point, the manufacturer and applicable factories may be approved—meaning orders can be placed—or additional corrective action may be required. Follow-up evaluations may be needed. If a manufacturer does not satisfactorily correct the problems, or is unable or unwilling to make necessary changes, it will be rejected. Approved garment factories are then monitored on an ongoing basis.[5]

The vendor compliance officers are extremely important in this monitoring process. As Gap employees, they carry the clout of a positive or negative recommendation. In the process of evaluating one new factory in Guatemala, the VCO told managers they had to correct poor ventilation and provide safety equipment for workers who handled chemicals. The problems had not quite been dealt with at the time of the VCO's follow-up visit, so more feedback was given and a third inspection arranged. Only after the factory was in compliance with the supplier code did the VCO send his report to the Global Compliance staff for approval.[6]

Factories are monitored at least once a year, and more often if managers are working to correct serious violations. Gap reports, "We will stay with a manufacturer as long as we believe it is committed to making ongoing improvements. . . . In 2003, we terminated our business with 136 factories for serious or excessive breaches of our Code of Vendor Conduct."[7]

The two-page chart on pages 14–15 of Gap's 2003 report is a remarkable piece of transparency. Summary data on code violations in 3,009 "active" or approved factories are detailed across eleven major regions of the globe. For example, more than 50 percent of the 464 factories in greater China were not in compliance with local laws and had inadequate hazardous materials storage practices. In Northern Asia, more than 50 percent of 200 factories had obstructed stairwells, aisles, or exits, creating a safety hazard should workers need to exit the building quickly. In sub-Saharan Africa, over half of the 118 factories were using unsafe machinery. Relatively few contracts were terminated, however; 42 in China, only 1 in North Asia, and 4 in southern Africa.

Remember, Gap's strategy is to save the jobs and work with the manufacturer as long as it perceives a good-faith effort to improve working conditions. Gap has reported on widespread and difficult problems in its monitoring of suppliers, leaving it wide open to stakeholder criticism and possibly more legal action. Nevertheless, providing such data is the very essence of transparency.

Stakeholder representatives were convened to review the report before its publication. The company chose to include some tough feedback:

- If significant progress is to be made in the areas of wages and hours, freedom of association and other problematic issues, sourcing strategies need to be rethought, and the drive to reduce costs at any expense must end.
- More work needs to be done on the concept and application of the living wage.
- Gap needs to drive adoption of a universal code of conduct and move to external monitoring.
- Multinationals don't emphasize empowering workers. Many workers don't even know what rights they have.
- While it's encouraging that Gap Inc. has accepted freedom of association and collective bargaining as unassailable rights, they need to improve their enforcement in this area.[8]

All this reporting could end up going nowhere, with unpredictable consequences for Gap's reputation and stakeholder credibility. Remember the story of Migros's discovery of a sizeable pay differential between men and women workers and their failure to address the issue in their second social report. Gap, likewise, could well be inviting another round of negative media publicity.

On the other hand, if transparency works the way it should, Gap will have acquired powerful allies in its efforts to remain both competitive and supportive of labor rights. Gap has now partnered with a coalition of faith-based, nonprofit, and socially responsible investing (SRI) firms to further develop and implement its goals of routine supplier monitoring, independent assurance, and transparent reporting on labor issues. These partners, commenting on Gap's first social responsibility report, have this to say:

> This report contains a great deal of information that many companies have not provided publicly, and includes valuable insights from a company that we believe is sincerely struggling with these complex issues. . . . We expect that in the future, the company will provide the public with factory specific data to permit stakeholders to better understand the complexities of compliance and to measure Gap Inc.'s performance over time."[9]

This is high praise from groups that could just as easily be adversaries. Gap's partners include Calvert Group Ltd., Domini Social Investments LLC, and the Interfaith Center of Corporate Responsibility, all of which have decades of experience in corporate social responsibility advocacy, evaluation, and reporting. Their vote of confidence is an impressive sign of Gap's good faith. Gap seems intent on making serious progress, but we shall see.

Interface, Inc.'s Sustainability Reporting

Interface, Inc., the largest global supplier of carpets and industrial-grade flooring, was founded in 1973 by Ray Anderson, who still serves as chairman of the board. In the 1970s, Interface pioneered the development and marketing of modular carpet tiles. Based in LaGrange, Georgia, and with corporate offices in Atlanta, Interface now boasts "sales in 110 countries and manufacturing facilities on four continents. In addition to carpet tiles and broadloom carpet marketed under several brands, Interface also manufactures and markets specialty fabrics, architectural products such as raised access flooring, and a variety of chemicals used in commercial office installations."[10] Annual sales run close to $1 billion, and both the stock price and financial returns have experienced more volatility than the industry average (the industry is office furnishings).

Interface's business description in the Domini 400 Social Index explains that modular carpet is a more environmentally friendly choice than ordinary rolled carpet. Worn or damaged tiles can be easily replaced without dumping the entire carpet.[11] But Interface has gone far beyond the initial modular concept in reducing its environmental footprint. And, as we emphasize in this case study, the company is not only innovating in environmentally sound products and services, they are also sharing vast amounts of knowledge and learning through their online sustainability reports.

Before moving to the reports themselves, let's explore the motivation for the transformative choices that Interface has made. Ray Anderson, entrepreneur, was transformed personally into Ray Anderson, visionary environmentalist, through an experience he describes as "a spear through the heart"—reading Paul Hawken's book, *The Ecology of Commerce*. Donella Meadows describes his experience this way:

> Hawken's book opens with a description of the night he stood up to receive an award for his own company's environmental excellence. Looking at the impact of his business on the earth, Hawken realized that he deserved no such award—and no company did.
>
> The book goes on to list the many ways in which the human economy violates the laws of the planet. We mobilize an increasing amount of stuff from the earth's crust and spit it out as waste. We pour poisons into our own life support systems. We draw down an unreplenished supply of fossil fuels and in the process derange the atmosphere.
>
> Anderson, an engineer from Georgia Tech, got the message. His carpet tiles are nylon and polyvinyl chloride, made from oil through polluting processes. They last forever in landfills. His business is not an asset to the planet and it's not sustainable.
>
> That was the spear through the heart.[12]

The outcome? Anderson heard Hawken's message as the challenge it was meant to be. In a stunning speech to his staff, he announced a new vision for the company, one that has galvanized employees and generated many creative ideas and projects. The goals are big, including dramatic energy efficiency, using only renewable energy sources, zero production waste, cradle-to-cradle product recycling, and the idea of putting back more than they take from the earth.

Sustainability as Good Business Practice

Perhaps the first thing one notices about Interface's sustainability report is that financial, environmental, and social performance data are melded into a single coherent document. Many companies that do social reporting or environmental reporting issue their reports as documents separate from financial statements, but for Interface, the idea of sustainability is economic, environmental, and social performance all rolled into one. It is triple bottom line reporting magnified by hundreds of measures and data sources:

For Interface, sustainability is more than surface appearance. It's a belief that is built into our business model. It's an underlying corporate value, ensuring that business decisions are weighed against their potential impact on the economic, natural and social systems we touch. It's a means for our associates to deliver superior value to our customers and to our shareholders.[13]

Interface's sustainability policies and practices are broad-ranging. They include charitable support for local communities, an active supplier diversity commitment, and a great deal more. The range of activities is suggested in their seven major commitments, as shown in Exhibit 10.1.

These commitments are not just vague by-and-by goals; there is a stated intention to achieve global leadership on each commitment by the year 2020! If you peruse the report itself, you'll see that realistic intermediate goals are also laid out and tested.

The natural environment is Interface's most innovative and remarkable arena for sustainable action. Beginning with the guidance of The Natural Step principles and those of the Coalition for Environmentally Responsible Economies (CERES), and adding the guidelines of the Global Reporting Initiative (GRI) and ISO 14001, Interface has developed a detailed set of short-term, intermediate, and long-term objectives for environmental protection and enhancement. All the bases are covered, from supplier certification to retaining responsibility for product impacts, including the abandonment in 2001 of printed sustainability reports!

The process of identifying the company's current status with respect to a particular goal can be burdensome and time-consuming, but it is the necessary first step toward meeting the goal. For each of its goals, Interface describes the initial evaluation process and traces the progress made. For example,

Our goal is to have no negative or toxic effect on natural systems. In 1997, Interface worldwide inventoried all existing air stacks and wastewater discharges from each facility. Data on emissions were collected stack by stack. Interface's Chairman, Ray Anderson, called for a study of the most stringent applicable regulations or limitations for air and water emissions worldwide. This internal data was used to compare each stack and pipe to the most stringent pollutant regulations found. The study included "criteria pollutants" and selected greenhouse gases. Each facility worldwide was challenged and is actively working to meet the "most stringent" regulations found. We are eliminating stacks and emission sources through process elimination and process redesign, as well as alternate energy sources, including green energy.[14]

Exhibit 10.1

The Seven Faces of Mt. Sustainability
Interface, Inc.

1. Eliminate Waste: Eliminating the concept of waste, not just incrementally reducing it;

2. Benign Emissions: Focusing on the elimination of molecular waste emissions. Eliminating waste streams that have negative or toxic effects on natural systems;

3. Renewable Energy: Reducing the energy demands of Interface processes while substituting nonrenewable sources with sustainable ones;

4. Closing the Loop: Redesigning Interface processes and products into cyclical material flows;

5. Resource-Efficient Transportation: Exploring methods to reduce the transportation of molecules (products and people) in favor of moving information. This includes plant location, logistics, information technology, video conferencing, e-mail, and telecommuting;

6. Sensitivity Hookup: Creating a community within and around Interface that understands the functioning of natural systems and our impact on them; and

7. Redesign Commerce: Redesigning commerce to focus on the delivery of service and value instead of material. Encouraging external organizations to create policies and market incentives promoting sustainable practices.

Source: http://www.interfacesustainability.com/seven.html (accessed January 6, 2005).

And the result? The company reports, "Worldwide, Interface . . . identified and inventoried 247 air emissions stacks and 19 waste water effluent pipes at its manufacturing locations. . . . As of December 2003, Interface had

165 stacks and 10 effluent discharges remaining."[15] The sustainability report contains many specific details on exactly how the goals are being met; companies with similar issues should be able to learn a great deal from the Interface experience.

"Cradle to cradle" product recycling is an environmental concept championed by innovative architect William McDonough in his book of that name and in his consulting work with Interface and other companies.[16] The cradle-to-cradle notion, intentionally crafted as an alternative to the more popular cradle-to-grave thinking, is captured in Interface's four-part principle for reducing environmental impacts:

REDUCE • REUSE • RECYCLE • REDESIGN

McDonough's ideas focus on *redesign,* beginning with the notion that "waste is food," that is, every output of manufacturing, including the entire product itself, should be thought of and *designed* as raw materials for some subsequent process.

Interface is pioneering—once again—in the design of carpet using an increasing percentage of post-consumer waste, the reclamation of discarded carpet, and the development of technologies to recycle 100 percent of the reclaimed materials. "Nylon molecules are very precious," says Anderson. "We want to spend the rest of our days harvesting yesteryear's carpets and recycling them, with zero scrap going to the landfill and zero emissions into the ecosystem—and run the whole thing on sunlight."[17] The carpet taken back by Interface is recycled into other products, donated to charitable organizations (if it's still useable), or used as fuel for the steam generators. Not all are ideal solutions, and the reclamation process is neither foolproof nor widespread yet, but that is the nature of experiments and innovation. Interface just keeps trying until it gets it right.

Efficiencies of Environmental Protection

A key message of Interface's sustainability reporting is that innovation eventually pays off in reduced costs and/or higher profits or margins. Here are examples of just some of the savings the company reports from its environmental protection efforts:[18]

- Eliminating wasted water, materials, and inventory: $231 million over 8 years.
- Energy consumption per linear yard of manufactured fabric is down 31 percent since 1996.

- 35 percent reduction in energy needed to produce carpet since 1996.
- 12 percent of 2003's total energy consumption comes from renewable sources.
- Water intake per square meter of carpet is down 78 percent in modular carpet facilities and down 40 percent in broadloom facilities from 1996.
- Frequency of workplace injuries reduced by nearly 47 percent since 1999.
- A single U.S. facility has saved over $10,000 each year in water costs after installing an $8.50 brass nozzle.

Profits, however, have been volatile for a number of years. Even the best company can't sustain smooth growth in a crowded, commodity-oriented industry that is so dependent on the state of the economy. But Interface has retained their market lead and has survived, so perhaps that in itself is enough good news for now.

Wrap-Up on Interface's Sustainability Reporting

We commend Interface's sustainability reports to you as interesting and instructive reading. They've got it all: mission, vision, and values; code of conduct; stakeholder engagement processes; measurement and reporting; independent monitoring and verification; organizational learning; and, not least by any means, a substantial contribution to systemic learning via their candor and completeness in presenting challenges, opportunities, trials, and results. The reports are valuable as a conduit for relevant stakeholder information, but even more, they are role models for other companies looking to become more transparent and accountable.

Interface's vision of being a thought-leader among the world's companies is ambitious, and its goals with respect to environment, people, and profits are equally so. Is it perhaps too ambitious to aim to be a sustainable company? According to president and CEO Dan Hendrix, "We at Interface believe that by striving for sustainability we are discovering better ways to make a bigger profit."[19]

Conclusion: Accountability Processes

This chapter has illustrated the steps of GBC and the processes of stakeholder accountability with a variety of cases. Accountability practices were apparent in Beauty Essential's SA 8000 certification, Shell's development of a human rights assessment tool, the Gap Inc.'s first foray into social responsibility reporting, and the remarkable environmental design and reporting efforts of Interface, Inc.

195

As with earlier case chapters, there are many more examples of global companies that are making the effort, but there's only so much room to tell their stories. You might look up NovoNordisk, the BTC pipeline project, or Aviva Corporation for additional illustrations of how companies are experimenting with internal and external accountability practices. By all means, check out the Global Compact Website, the Global Reporting Initiative, SocialAccountability, and the numerous other sources of company information on responsible business practices. And do continue to look for evidence that the cases you read about represent real efforts to create sustainable business practices.

And now, on to the final step of GBC—systemic learning and the benefits that result to reputation, image, and identity.

➤ 11 ◀

System-Level Learning and the Payoff in Reputation

Did you see the light comedies *50 First Dates* and *Groundhog Day*? The protagonists in each movie were doomed to repeat certain events over and over, stuck in a time warp, because they could not remember and thus learn from past experience. For companies, learning is serious business. Previous chapters have focused on how GBC companies learn to develop codes that are consistent with values, learn to implement policies and practices with appropriate local adaptations, and learn from experiments and conflicts. Organizational learning is reinforced in the measurement and reporting of performance, the subject of chapter 9. GBC companies strive to integrate all these levels and types of learning into a comprehensive learning process that makes decisions a bit easier the next time similar issues and problems emerge.

But there's more to learn about learning. In this chapter, we extend Step 4 of the GBC process to the level of the business system and the larger institutional environment to show how companies learn from their peers through benchmarking and become role models and change agents in the larger socioeconomic systems by sharing their processes and experiences with other organizations. Such system-level learning enhances the legitimacy and sustainability of the global economic system. It might also be the ultimate "carrot" that makes GBC worthwhile for companies—being a good role model can be something to aspire to.[1] Later in the chapter we show how GBC processes and behaviors tie the processes of learning and role modeling to the vital corporate issues of reputation, image, and identity.

Knowledge Management and GBC Learning

Most successful business organizations continually renew and reinvent themselves, their strategies, products, services, and processes, based on what they

---

Exhibit 11.1

Knowledge Management and GBC

Knowledge management involves collecting and integrating information with both tacit and explicit knowledge in the minds of organizational members, so that it can be shared and used appropriately.

A hot trend in information systems is the idea of a formally structured knowledge bank, available to everyone in a company, where employees can enter tacit knowledge or lessons learned or questions to share with others throughout the organization. Such a database can be especially helpful for managers who have their operations, sales, or plant management knowledge down cold, but who may not have experience with stakeholder pressures or ethical conflicts. A knowledge management process that incorporates GBC is especially valuable to spread GBC knowledge to those who need it most but who don't necessarily have any other access to it.

Levi Strauss is pioneering GBC-relevant knowledge management systems. After a decade of implementing its Supplier Terms of Engagement, Levi Strauss's area managers for human rights decided that to avoid reinventing the wheel in every situation, they would establish a database of suppliers, issues, problems, and solutions. For any manager who wants such information, the database is available in read-only format. However, those managers who are involved in supply chain management and in particular supplier conduct certification can enter new information into the database, correct mistakes, input questions, and generally keep the site up to date.

---

learn from their engagement with stakeholders, the outcomes of firm behaviors, and the reception their accountability practices receive. Innovation is the most critical benefit from knowledge management; sustainable organizations successfully transform learning into business value.[2]

This final step of the GBC process has its confusions. Isn't learning something that happens at *each* step, from the articulation of values to their implementation in the field? What do managers have to do to learn? What do organizations have to do? If you're sharing everything you learn, how can you possibly stay competitive?

For GBC companies, achieving Step 4, organizational learning that is system-wide, means that learning is incorporated into all phases of the GBC process, from articulating values to establishing a code of conduct, from identifying needed organizational changes to putting them into practice, from engaging stakeholders responsibly to being transparent and accountable to them, from implementing guidelines and policies locally to solving unique

Figure 11.1 **Normative and Instrumental Payoffs from GBC Learning**

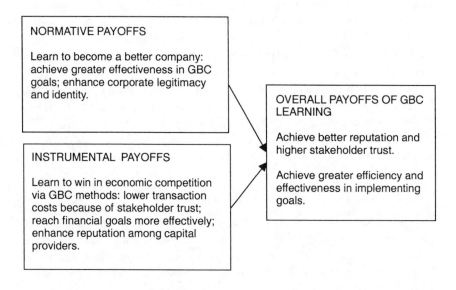

cross-border or cross-cultural problems. In addition, GBC learning goes beyond the firm's self-interest and helps the organization learn to model desirable behavior to other companies.

Analysis—identification of all the bits—and *synthesis*—putting them back together in meaningful patterns that inform future decisions and actions—well, that's what learning is all about. And it's not just individuals who learn. Organizations too can learn when managers design processes to collect the lessons learned and then communicate them systematically throughout the organization. Learning can be extended outside the organization too, and we'll see that there are often good reasons to do so.

System-Level Learning

We see two partially overlapping reasons why GBC companies need to attend to systemic learning as they implement their values and principles. First, the company can learn in order to become a "better" company, one that exhibits consistency between its values and actions and between its internal identity and external reputation. Second, the company can learn in order to become a winner in global competition. These two types of payoffs, and their overlap, are illustrated in Figure 11.1.

199

The normative and instrumental payoffs of learning are only partly over-lapping in GBC thinking because there are situations when ethics demands that a company do or not do certain things that might be economically ben-eficial, at least in the short run. Also, there are times when a company's strategic goals and orientation will not permit it to participate fully in various forms of inter-organizational and systemic learning. For example, a GBC com-pany will not accept the idea that child labor is necessary though undesirable, because this idea is in violation of a fundamental ethical principle that children should not be exploited and should have full access to education. And, a GBC company may rightly refuse to reveal product and market knowledge, not to mention its strategy, because it will get into competitors' hands.

How Does a GBC Company Learn?

Companies strive to create organizational learning from all sources, including their own experiences and outcomes, benchmarking the outcomes of peer orga-nizations, stakeholder interactions (direct and secondary), and industry and market-based sources. Basically, learning can be viewed as externally or inter-nally generated, and both sources are critical components of long-term success.

What facilitates learning within, between, and among organizations and with stakeholders? Inside an organization, it's no secret that learning is fos-tered by open communications, information sharing, teamwork, and incen-tives that reward these behaviors. Sanctions are particularly powerful enforcers within a learning environment. For example, if you're working in a firm where "no good deed goes unpunished," do employees have any incentive to learn about being helpful and cooperative? Conversely, if managerial evaluation has a substantial component of ethics, responsibility, and other GBC attributes, isn't there a stronger likelihood of such a company truly learning to act as a global business citizen?

One way of thinking about how and whether to collaborate with others is to consider how much you have in common, and how much you need each other. We saw these variables at work in the discussion of forms of collabo-ration in stakeholder engagement processes in chapter 5. In the emerging global economy, it's difficult to imagine that any company has all necessary knowledge and skills within its own organization. Progressive companies are learning to draw effectively from a wide range of knowledge sources in pursuit of their goals and objectives, including nontraditional sources, espe-cially those housed within their various stakeholder communities.

Barriers to inter-organizational learning include a variety of cross-cultural confusions and misunderstandings as well as the need to maintain competi-tive confidentiality. In addition, as we have seen, stakeholders may be hostile

Table 11.1

Expectations versus Evaluations
(Who is learning?)

	What should the firm be doing according to management?	What should the firm be doing according to stakeholders?
How is the firm doing according to management?	Performance-based (management)	Response-based (management)
How is the firm doing according to stakeholders?	Assurance-based (stakeholders)	Engagement-based (management and stakeholders)

or aggressive, requiring companies to alter their usual approaches to stakeholder engagement and learning. And, as we know, the existence of hostile stakeholders and the resulting damage of a bad encounter can certainly sour the deal for future learning, unless managers are careful not to generalize from one bad experience to all future experiences.

What's the Link from Accountability and Stakeholder Engagement to Learning?

Learning results from accountability in at least four ways, based on the evaluations versus expectations approach that is illustrated in Table 11.1. We want to make it clear that these types of learning are not mutually exclusive. Indeed, a firm aspiring to be a global business citizen will very likely progress through, and accommodate to, all four types of learning.

In the journey toward implementation of GBC, the first step is *performance-based learning*. This mode is well-established in all organizations, where management evaluates the actual performance of the firm vis-à-vis its own goals and objectives. For example, financial budgeting and reporting help a company to achieve performance-based learning. Managers compare what they intended to accomplish to what they actually accomplished, and make adjustments and reallocations to operating plans in order to move toward their stated objectives.

The second type of learning in the GBC model emerges when managers evaluate how organizational performance stacks up against stakeholder expectations through *response-based learning*. Often this learning comes from unintentional and/or catastrophic events, such as the Valdez oil spill and the related public backlash against Exxon. It can be accomplished by one-way information channels, such as stakeholder responses reported through the media and received by the organization. At this point, responsiveness and transparency are not necessarily occurring, and the learning may still be characterized as organization-centric. Accountability therefore has not yet been achieved.

When the organization realizes that stakeholders have a right to receive information about its impacts on them (socially and environmentally as well as economically), the third type of learning, *assurance-based learning,* can be achieved through external reporting. In this way, external parties can evaluate the actual performance of the firm with respect to management goals and objectives. The learning here benefits the stakeholders. For example, sustainability reports facilitate investment decisions for socially and environmentally conscious investors. The value of the information reported is, of course, enhanced by the assurance provided by external independent audit.

The company that aspires to GBC will ultimately want to achieve the *engagement-based learning* that occurs when management *and* stakeholders evaluate the actual performance of the firm vis-à-vis stakeholder expectations. This fourth type of learning allows the organization to analyze difficult problems within a framework of stakeholder expectations and to seek solutions that achieve maximum satisfaction among conflicting interests. This is only possible when stakeholders are fully engaged in two-way, ongoing dialogue on critical and emerging issues regarding the day-to-day impacts of the firm.

Benchmarking: How GBC Firms Learn to Learn

Benchmarking, or comparing organizational performance to that of competitors or to best practice, is a widely practiced path to improvement. Benchmarking is used to determine how the firm measures up within its industry sector, or against peers that are similar on other relevant dimensions, so that it can build capacity to successfully meet emerging challenges in innovative and commercially successful ways.

Benchmarking, like any comparative evaluation tool, has its difficulties, especially for companies seeking GBC stature. The problem is that industry best practices on a particular issue may be undesirable from the standpoint of ethical principles. It doesn't help the company much to know, for example, that everybody else in the industry uses subcontractors with questionable workplace safety or a history of hiring child labor. Best practices always need to be evaluated according to aspirational standards as well as the actual level of performance.

There are numerous valuable resources for benchmarking accountability and GBC activities. The executive trying to navigate the rapids of global business will appreciate the wide range of information available from sources such as those shown in Table 11.2.

Table 11.2

Benchmarking Sources for GBC

Business for Social Responsibility	www.bsr.org	U.S.-based association of 1,400 companies committed to sustainable business practices. Annual conferences include governance trends and practices, accountability, and implementation. Website provides link to Global Business Responsibility Resource Center online database which includes over 100 social responsibility issue areas, company leadership practices, sample policies, standards, and recent developments.
Council of Institutional Investors	www.cii.org	An organization of large public and corporate pension funds that seeks to encourage funds, as major shareholders, to take active roles in corporate affairs. Its website includes an annual list of financially underperforming corporations, and information on how companies have responded to shareholder resolutions that received majority votes within the past year.
Institute for Social and Ethical AccountAbility (ISEA)	www.accountability.org.uk	A UK-based membership organization of accountability professionals who have produced a process standard for the practice of accountability. It provides information on practice and theory of accountability management worldwide through regular publications and a website. ISEA publishes a quarterly journal, *AccountAbility Quarterly*.
Investor Responsibility Research Center (IRRC)	www.irrc.org	A not-for-profit organization that provides research, software, and consulting on corporate governance, shareholding, and social issues. IRRC provides company profile information and portfolio screening for benchmarking, identifying, and analyzing major corporate social responsibility issues facing institutional investors at U.S. companies. It maintains an active website.
Kinder Lydenberg Domini (KLD) database	www.kld.com	KLD is a private investment management firm that pioneered and still produces extensive social scoring for hundreds of large companies. Its company database is available for purchase.
SustainAbility	www.sustainability.com	A U.K. think-tank dedicated to business sustainability issues. Its website provides research reports on accountability practices, business case evidence, and reporting.

As an example of the benchmarking resources available and the recent applications of benchmarking to GBC, consider the Global Compact's 2004 Guidelines for "Communications on Progress" (COP). You'll recall that many of the cases presented in this book are drawn originally from the United Nations Global Compact website and are posted there by companies as examples of how they are trying to implement the Global Compact's ten principles. The new COP guidelines require an annual statement of continuing commitment to the principles, an annual update on the cases that the company posted in previous years, and measurement of progress based on the Global Reporting Initiative (GRI) guidelines.[3] We'll see more of this in the next chapter. Here, in Exhibit 11.2, the Global Compact describes the intent and process of members' COP toward meeting the principles of business conduct.

One often hears the gloomy phrase "a race to the bottom" when global business standards are being discussed. Our take on what's happening with corporate benchmarking and role modeling is quite different. We believe there will be a "race to the reasonable and responsible," as more and more companies seek to earn the label of global business citizen. The principle of accountability to stakeholders is driving this transformation already. And, efforts like the Global Compact, the GRI, the internal SIGMA discussed in chapter 9, and the knowledge management systems that are being created will make possible the system-wide learning that is so necessary for sustainable capitalism.

Georg Kell, Executive Head of the United Nations Global Compact, and his colleague David Levin, put it this way: "[T]he Global Compact is conceived as a value-based platform designed to promote institutional learning with few formalities and no rigid bureaucratic structures."[4] Such inter-organizational networks are already invaluable for organizational learning, and they will become more so as globalization continues its inexorable transformations. Along the way, GBC companies will find that their images, identities, and reputations take a turn for the better.

Reputation, Image, and Identity the GBC Way

Reputation is called an intangible asset, but it has very tangible consequences for organizations. It affects revenues, stock price, employee recruitment and retention, the ability to locate company facilities, treatment by government regulators, willingness of stakeholders to dialogue, and many other aspects of organizational activity. Despite the popular appeal of the term "reputation management," a company's reputation cannot be managed in the usual sense of the word because *reputation is assessed by stakeholders,* who use many facts, accounts, and observations to evaluate a firm's performance and assign it a reputation *on stakeholder terms.*

Exhibit 11.2

Global Compact Guidelines for "Communications on Progress"

Global Compact participants are expected to communicate with their stakeholders on an annual basis about progress in implementing the Global Compact principles through their annual reports, sustainability reports, or other corporate communications. Participants are also expected to submit a short description and a URL link to these communications on the Global Compact and/or Global Compact local network website.

To safeguard the integrity of the initiative as a whole, only those participants who communicate progress will be allowed to continue their participation in the Global Compact.

1. Communications on Progress (COPs). COPs should include the following three elements:
    a. Statement of continued support for the Global Compact in the opening letter, statement or message from the Chief Executive Officer, Chairman or other senior executive.
    b. Description of practical actions that participants have taken to implement the Global Compact principles during the previous fiscal year.
    c. Measurement of outcomes or expected outcomes using, as much as possible, indicators or metrics such as those developed by the Global Reporting Initiative.

Note: COPs should be integrated in participants' already existing communications with stakeholders, such as annual reports or sustainability reports. In the event that a participant does not publish an annual report or a sustainability report, a COP can be issued through other channels where employees, shareholders, customers and other stakeholders expect to read about the company's major economic, social and environmental engagements.

2. Link to and Description of COPs. Participants are expected to submit a brief description and, where an online version exists, a URL link to their COP on the Global Compact website and/or Global Compact local network website. In the event that an online version of the COP does not exist, participants can submit an electronic version of their COP as an attachment with a description of how they are communicating the content to their stakeholders.

(continued)

Exhibit 11.2 *(continued)*

The Global Compact Office accepts COPs in all languages by allowing companies to post links to their respective reports on the Global Compact website and/or Global Compact local network website. The development of local Global Compact networks will offer opportunities to facilitate this process.

COPs are important demonstrations of participants' commitment to the Global Compact and its principles. It is also a tool to exercise leadership, facilitate learning, stimulate dialogue and promote action.

Last updated on 10 September 2004

Source: http://www.unglobalcompact.org/Portal/Default.asp (accessed January 7, 2005).

When trying to assess the tangible effects of organizational intangibles, it helps to distinguish three related concepts: identity, image, and reputation.

Organizational Identity

An organization's *identity* is the essential set of values that define and differentiate it from other organizations, the equivalent of "character" in the human person. Identity is sometimes found in the organization's vision and mission, which Dowling calls the "soul of corporate reputation,"[5] but identity need not be written down and may not, in fact, be consistent or even well understood. Fundamental organizational values are embedded in organizational culture and may run counter to what is written in the vision or mission statements. For example, Enron had a great sounding mission, all about treating everyone with respect and acting with the highest integrity, but its top managers literally destroyed the company with their many unethical actions.

Organizational Image

The *image* of the organization is what it projects about itself to its stakeholders. Corporate communications are clear messages about what the organization elects to say about its values, contributions, and responses to various events. In contrast to product advertising, most corporate-level marketing focuses on fundamental values that the corporation wants stakeholders to associate with it, such as reliability (UPS), low prices (Wal-Mart), or commitment to good ecological practices (Weyerhauser). In crisis communications, executives are urged to project an image of truthfulness and caring about what happens to innocent parties when an accident occurs. It goes without saying that a corporation's image and its identity may not be consistent. For example, Archer-Daniels-Midland tries to project an image of concern about providing healthy food to the hungry, but its identity as an organization willing to sacrifice customer welfare for higher profits was revealed in its extensive participation in price-fixing schemes in the late 1990s, and its ultimate payment of $500 million in fines plus jail sentences for three ADM executives.[6]

Organizational Reputation

Reputation is different from identity and image—it is how the stakeholders evaluate the organization. In a sense, reputation is the most important vehicle stakeholders have for giving feedback to the company about its values, actions, and impacts. So an organization can have many reputations—it may have one reputation for good financial returns so investors are favorable, but poor community responsiveness or low levels of compliance with regulations, or a hard-nosed attitude about not striving for a diverse workplace. Scholars have rightly pointed out that *Fortune*'s "Most Admired" List, an annual ranking of companies by CEOs and analysts, is slanted by its overwhelming focus on financial performance.[7] Reputation is actually multidimensional because the stakeholders, who create corporate reputations through their perceptions, have many different interests.

The aggravating part about corporate reputation is that managers cannot control it, although they can influence it. This is not the case with identity and image. The organization can define its identity by targeting what is "most central, enduring, and distinctive" about it, according to Albert and Whetten.[8] The organization generally controls its image via communications strategies and conscious selection of messages to project through the media to its stakeholders. People generally expect a company to be congruent in its identity and image, and hope for an authentic communication of values. But reputation? No. Managers simply aren't in charge.

While the organization cannot control its reputation, it can use the tools of GBC to strengthen its relationships with strong stakeholder engagement practices and to provide information about how stakeholders will be judging its reputation through stakeholder engagement and dialogue. One of the biggest advantages of being a GBC company is "increasing the odds" of having a good reputation.

Much has been researched and written about the value of a good corporate reputation.[9] The most frequently cited benefits include attracting and retaining talent, having the credibility to form alliances with strategic partners, increasing sales, and enhancing stock value. But ultimately, the value of a good reputation is stakeholder trust, confidence, and support.[10]

The Importance of Trust

Trust is perhaps best defined as *the willingness to make oneself vulnerable to another.* Vulnerability is tough talk for managers who thrive on competence and autonomy, and for companies that have grown accustomed to being skewered in the mass media. But think about it: companies are always asking stakeholders to trust them not to cheat or steal, not to sell products that explode randomly, not to foul the earth, and not to harm the local community. When such things happen more than once, maybe twice, stakeholders lose any reason to trust a company, and the demand for information and accountability—particularly through regulatory channels—is bound to increase. Trust, then, is a surrogate for monitoring. A trusted company does not wait for overwhelming pressure before it releases information that stakeholders need to make good decisions.

Trust is established when several conditions are met in a relationship:

- The parties learn enough about each other to be confident that there are no intentions to harm.
- The parties have enough experience in the relationship to be confident that there will be no actual harm.
- The parties believe, and have no reason not to believe, that each will regard the other's interests with respect.

What follows from the establishment of trust among stakeholders and companies is just common sense, backed up by organizational research. When trust is there, it is a predictor of organizational effectiveness, including increased employee satisfaction, reduced transaction and litigation costs, and the ability to recover in a crisis. Without trust, everything is harder, takes longer, and is more uncertain. So much for the "expense" of stakeholder engagement and accountability!

Factors Influencing Reputation and Trust

There are several key factors that influence reputation and the consequent trust that stakeholders have in a company. These include alignment of shared purpose, the company's value proposition, the CEO's personality and presence, and the degree to which the company is transparent in its relevant operations and outcomes.

Alignment of shared purpose means simply that the mission, vision, and values of the firm are fully articulated in the company's strategy and actions. A clear and effective shared purpose acts as a compass for decision making, and it centers decisions and actions on the firm's reputation and identity. It guides and influences corporate behavior (rather than saying lofty things but doing something quite different). The experience of stakeholders must at least equal the promise made to them. Enron's fall was especially bitter to the community of Houston, where Enron executives had substantial reputations for community involvement, philanthropy, innovative practices, and exciting job opportunities.

The value proposition is the way in which the company understands and communicates its core competencies and what makes it unique and successful. This is a matter of aligning identity with image, telling the truth about who and what the company really is. Such alignment alone won't guarantee a good reputation, but focusing on the things that are valued by stakeholders can differentiate a company from its rivals and create lasting value in terms of reputation and trust.

The view from the top. The CEO's personality and behavior can be a strong influence on corporate reputation. If the CEO cannot communicate the firm's mission, brands, or values, some other organization or stakeholder group with communications capability can and will. Furthermore, the CEO ordinarily has a large say in management succession practices, thus setting the tone for the firm's entire culture and public presence not just now, but also in the future.

Transparency, being willing to disclose information and engage in stakeholder dialogue, is a key way that companies can demonstrate their trustworthiness and thus establish valuable reputations. No, companies don't have to tell all. There are legitimate trade secrets and strategic plans that don't need to be broadcast. But when stakeholders have a legitimate interest in a company's inputs, processes, or outputs, sharing this information sends a strong signal that the company is trustworthy and trusts its stakeholders.

Other factors are thought to influence corporate reputation as well. Branding, product and service lines, and pricing structures are some of the ordinary business practices that can make or break a company's reputation. Rent-to-own companies, for example, have good branding, extensive product lines, and a pricing policy that may exploit the desires of those who live from paycheck to paycheck. Not bad at making money, perhaps, but there's plenty to worry about in terms of fair dealing.

The nature of the industry itself can affect a company's reputation, too. Oil and chemical firms, no matter how hard they may try (and some have tried very hard), are not fully trusted on environmental performance by the general public. It's just a dirty and dangerous business.

Media coverage, finally, is a relatively uncontrollable factor that can affect reputation in a flash. The public relations office will work hard to communicate news and events in the company's favor, but the spin that the public sees is very much in the court of the reporter, editor, publisher, and broadcaster. Years ago, Ashland Oil Company experienced a disastrous spill of diesel fuel that polluted three rivers in the tri-state area of Pennsylvania, West Virginia, and Ohio. Remarkably, the CEO immediately granted interviews to all news media to announce that the company was investigating the spill, and meanwhile it was establishing walk-in offices to accept the claims of any stakeholders whose interests had been damaged by the spill. The effect was electrifying, and the trust in this company was palpable. They followed through on all their promises, and you will not find this company's name in the roster of corporate rogues—at least not on account of this spill.[11]

In a more recent example, when Ford's popular SUV, the Explorer, was identified with an excessively high rate of rollover deaths and injuries, controversy shifted back and forth for awhile between Ford and its strategic partner, Bridgestone-Firestone. Was it the tires that were defective, was the vehicle poised too high off the ground, or were customers underinflating the tires? Ford eventually initiated a massive recall to replace all of the Firestone tires. Bridgestone-Firestone, meanwhile, stonewalled and blamed the whole problem on Ford. Ford was later exonerated by the U.S. National Highway Traffic Safety Administration, earning credits to its image *and* reputation.[12] GBC behavior is essential to maintaining a good corporate reputation, but as this case shows, it can take awhile for the effects to become visible.

Types of Trust and Reputation

The trust that derives from a good reputation is of two types.[13] *Fragile trust* is delicate and easily shattered because it is based on too little or ambiguous evidence. *Resilient trust,* by contrast, is long-term and well-grounded, and can survive a ripple or two of difficulty. A couple on their second date may have established fragile trust, but they haven't yet gained the experience with each other to have resilient trust. A long-time couple, however, can weather grumpiness, disappointments, and failure because the overall record tells each party that the other is trustworthy and will not try to cause harm, until and unless the balance of evidence shifts.

Company-stakeholder relationships may also have fragile and/or resilient trust. Indeed, one of the key objectives of stakeholder engagement is to build a sufficient stock of resilient trust so that stakeholders will not jump ship at the first hint of trouble. Too many firms seem content, however, with fragile trust, if any at all, and they put themselves at risk of mismanaging their reputations and consequently their ability to call upon stakeholder assistance or loyalty in difficult times.

Companies that mismanage their reputations often do so with behaviors such as:

- Focusing on a single stakeholder rather than being aware of how their multiple stakeholders perceive them and what they each value. GBC companies, because of their commitment to stakeholder dialogue and accountability, will be in touch with their broad stakeholder interests and needs rather than be blindsided.
- Airing one's dirty laundry in public. The contentious fighting between management and organized labor has not allowed these two groups to establish any resilient trust. Think also of the enormous damage done to the relationship between Ford and Firestone when accusations began flying over the Explorer and its radial tires.
- Treating employees as second-class citizens, or worse, as labor units or variable costs. Do you know of any companies that have badly managed downsizings—or that downsize only to meet quarterly financial targets? Is there any good reason why employees of such companies should trust them?
- Deliberately upsetting the company's customers by not keeping commitments. The authors of this book have a collective million frequent flyer miles, but ask us how much difficulty we have had in trying to use them!
- Poor or no measurement. Most companies understand what it takes to secure a good financial reputation, but in other domains, there's a lot of confusion. Not understanding what impacts its reputation, or the use of poor measures across stakeholder groups, can cause a company to lose its stakeholders' trust because it fails to address their information needs adequately or because it misinterprets what stakeholders want from the firm.
- Collecting information from stakeholders, but not acting on what they have been told, is behavior that stakeholders view as manipulative, an attempt to create image without changing identity. Companies can wreck their reputations by not fostering change management initiatives to correct or address the legitimate concerns of stakeholders.

Conclusion

Learning for GBC companies is going to be continuous and will require regular attention; this should be no surprise. Any company that wants to remain competitive in a rapidly changing environment has to do no less than this.

What is different about GBC learning? Aside from GBC's focus on guiding values and principles, perhaps the most distinctive feature of GBC learning is its systemic aspect. A GBC company is willing to learn in a broad-based network and is willing to be a role model for others when it has done something well or learned something important.

Effective learning, in turn, helps a GBC company earn its valuable reputation, polish its image, and understand its identity. All in all, the desirable state is that reputation, image, and identity be well aligned. GBC companies have a leg up on this goal because their managers are not going to manipulate the truth through false imaging, or to act toward stakeholders in untrustworthy ways.

It just makes sense: When identity is acted out in organizational structure and process, when image accurately reflects identity, and when stakeholder relations are built and maintained on trust, a good reputation follows—worth its weight in gold.

➤ 12 ◀

The Promise of Global
Business Citizenship

The end of our journey in this book opens the door to a new era of global business citizenship. In this final chapter, we summarize the book's main messages and outline the individual, organizational, and systemic implications of the GBC undertaking. We end with some questions to guide the next round of thinking and action toward developing and sustaining our corporations as global business citizens.

GBC for Managers and Their Companies: Themes Revisited

In the preface, we laid out six interrelated messages that were developed in the book. In most instances we traced the implications of these messages across three levels of analysis—the individual, the organizational, and the systemic. These messages were:

1. The status quo isn't so great. Managers, companies, institutions, and societies face increasing difficulties with no end in sight.
2. Trust is essential for individuals, organizations, economies, and societies, but it is easily lost.
3. Ethics and values make a difference in business as in personal life. There is no "great divide" between ethics and business.
4. GBC—global business citizenship—offers firms a hybrid strategy to implement ethics and values within and across borders, neither a "when in Rome" approach of ethical relativism nor an imperialistic top-down headquarters approach.
5. Although GBC is a new idea, the tools for implementing it in organizations already exist. These tools include personal attributes and

training; stakeholder engagement; organizational change management; and accountability and sustainability reporting.

6. Learning to apply these tools to the big ideas of GBC promises to
change the status quo in positive, desirable ways.

In Table 12.1 we map these themes and levels of analysis and show which
chapters of the book focused on them in most depth.

The big lesson of GBC is that managers and companies already know a
great deal about what they need to do to make their organizations and the
capitalist system as a whole sustainable. Managers already know that neither
they nor their firms can thrive without partnering with others; they already
know that causing undue harm to others is both ethically wrong and prag-
matically undesirable.

The challenge managers face today is in *implementing a GBC vision and
acting as if stakeholders really do matter.* It's that shift of perspective that is
key—perhaps startling, but certainly fresh and inspiring.

GBC Payoffs: Why Global Business Citizenship
Makes a Difference

Managers are first and foremost responsible for guiding the company to achieve
its goals—market dominance, innovation leadership, low-cost production, enhanced reputation, or whatever. Managers are usually judged and compen-
sated on how well they achieve these goals. This congruence between
organizational goals and the individual goals of managers is well-known.

But there's more. The normal *instrumental* pay-offs of achieving business
goals are complemented by *normative* pay-offs when those business goals
are met in a manner consistent with universal ethical principles. Indeed, that's
an important message of GBC. Furthermore, when organizational and individual goals are met in a normatively acceptable manner, the entire socioeconomic system benefits.

In Table 12.2, we summarize a number of pay-offs that can accrue to
managers, companies, the economy, and societies when GBC principles are
fully integrated into business practice.

These pay-offs are not only discrete and identifiable; there are also important cross-level linkages. Managers are critical actors who coordinate the
organization's goal attainment with the outcomes that are desired by individual stakeholders and by the collective business community. For example,
employees' personal goals are intertwined with their sub-unit's performance
and the organization's performance as a whole. Consequently, managers must
be aware of the organizational culture they create, and specifically whether

Table 12.1

Themes of Global Business Citizenship

Themes	Chapters	Individual Level	Organizational Level	Systemic Level
The status quo isn't so great.	1, 2	Managers are stuck in a performance vise with too many challenges and responsibilities; they feel trapped and powerless, faced with fear, uncertainty, doubt.	Firms face ever-harder competitive pressure in a more complex and turbulent environment. Bad actors in the global economy—the ruthless rule-breakers—are hard to rein in.	Problems abound within and across nations: shrinking governments, cross-border economies, massive poverty, a growing divide between rich and poor, violence, and environmental degradation.
Trust is essential, but easily lost.	2, 3	Trust makes life easier for managers. To keep trust alive, agreements must be kept, duties fulfilled, and expectations met.	Trust lowers transaction costs and earns social capital for the firm. To keep trust alive, stakeholders must be satisfied.	Trust makes the social system possible. To keep trust alive, institutions must permit and support its fulfillment by persons and organizations.
Ethics and values make a difference in business.	2, 3, 4	Personal character: Most managers aren't evil and want to do the right thing. Ethics belongs in business decision-making and action.	Organizational guidance: Vision, mission, values, principles, codes, and policies all help a firm's employees develop and use good ethical judgment.	Institutional enforcement: Law, regulation, courts, and even industry self-regulation can and do support ethical conduct for individuals and organizations, for the betterment of societies and institutional systems.

(continued)

215

Table 12.1 (continued)

Themes	Chapters	Individual Level	Organizational Level	Systemic Level
The GBC process gives firms a hybrid strategy.	3		GBC—global business citizenship—offers a hybrid strategy for firms to help them be trustworthy on standards, adaptable in implementation, and systematic in their learning.	
We already have the tools for achieving GBC benefits.	5, 6, 7, 8, 9, 10	Personal tools: buy-in, commitment, courage; the language of rights, duties, and justice; management communication and authority channels; peer support; knowledge of planning and decision-making.	Organizational implementation tools: • Stakeholder engagement (Ch. 5, 6) • Organizational development and change management (Ch. 7, 8) • Accountability and sustainability reporting (Ch. 9, 10)	Systemic tools: Stakeholder activism; investor/customer pressures; supranational regulatory agreements; and stable nation-level civil institutions.
Applying these tools to GBC promises to change the status quo.	11, 12	For people, and especially managers: A better and more moral life, a sense of efficacy, a solid reputation, and an ability to learn and grow. (Ch. 11)	For companies: A good reputation based on earning stakeholders' trust; the creation of sustainable businesses; and the possibility of competitive advantage; and organizational learning.	For the globe: Global business citizenship is the path to sustainable capitalism, bringing innovation and wealth creation to all.

Table 12.2

GBC Payoffs

Level of Analysis	Motivations for Global Business Citizenship	
	Instrumental	Normative
Organizational motivations: What can a company gain from implementing GBC?	• Stakeholder engagement pays off financially via higher satisfaction, less conflict, good public opinion, and reasonable public policies, which can create competitive advantage relative to less responsible companies.	• Stakeholders themselves will be better off—happier, healthier, with more of their interests met.
	• There can be a first mover advantage for companies that successfully adapt; awards, reputation, consumer approval, regulatory relief, etc.	• If customers can rely upon the firm to be responsible, they will be safer and have less reason for concern, and they may also have lower total costs because the value of trust is built into pricing.
	• When market leaders demonstrate GBC, others in the industry must eventually follow or face the costs of lagging.	• Building organizational reputation based on trust allows all stakeholders to reduce the costs of their transactions with the firm.
	• There are fewer surprises with a firm's broad range of NGO alliances and its transparent performance measures.	• Creating trusting coalitions with stakeholders can help everyone—firm and stakeholders—achieve their goals and sustain their rights.
	• Public policy makers are less likely to impose regulatory constraints and costs if businesses are self-regulating and public pressures remain low.	• A responsible corporation can fulfill its duties to be a good citizen in the societies in which it operates.
Personal motivations: What can individual managers gain from implementing GBC?	• Managers can produce convincing and credible arguments for senior managers and the board of directors, and thus be more successful within the firm.	• Responsible members of the business community can step forward as role models and not leave leadership to their colleagues who are less responsible.
	• GBC systematizes ethics and social responsibility inside corporations, giving managers a language, a set of processes, and the flexibility needed for making responsible and ethical choices.	• GBC represents good ethical behavior. Managers will be able to pass the "morning mirror" and "front page" ethics tests, that is, maintain self-respect and good reputation.

(continued)

217

Table 12.2 (continued)

Motivations for Global Business Citizenship

Level of Analysis	Instrumental	Normative
Systemic motivations: How does GBC help to ensure the survival of democratic capitalism?	• Actively addressing the needs of the disadvantaged will create better working conditions, better distribution of resources so that the disadvantaged will more quickly become active participants in the entire economic system.	• Fostering human rights helps to create and uphold the democratic and lawful processes on which capitalism relies.
	• Less bribery and extortion will make the business system more efficient and effective, and will support the rule of law (contract enforcement, property rights, etc.) that capitalism requires.	• Public policies are likely to converge at a higher standard around the globe, if businesses demonstrate that they can be trusted to act in the public interest.
		• Less bribery and extortion creates better conditions for establishing social justice and guarding human rights.
	• GBC will unleash greater human and organizational creativity so that the private sector will thrive.	• Greater human and organizational creativity sustains the capitalist system and promotes human liberty.
	• Supporting human rights and social justice will reduce conflict, bolster stability and predictability, and enhance the business environment.	• Stakeholders have a right to act as moral agents, making informed decisions based on free and full information. Accountability processes sustain this right.

Source: Logsdon and Wood, 2004.

218

that culture supports or inhibits the personal motivations toward business citizenship. Similarly, the collective interests of business are affected by the actions of organizations that support or run counter to business citizenship. For example, organizations that act as trustworthy economic partners in business transactions reduce criticism of the business institution and the need for stakeholder monitoring.

The Old Rules No Longer Work

More than a hundred years ago, the industrializing nations of the West began to experience the social dislocations and political transformations arising from big business, big cities, and ultimately big government. The tensions between community and society, *gemeinschaft und gesellschaft,*[1] were a principal concern of citizens and civil society. This local versus national conflict of values and social organization has now gone global, transforming into pitched battles between Jihad and McWorld,[2] resonating in contradictory yearnings for the Lexus and the olive tree,[3] threatening both local traditions and cultures *and* the stable, beneficent environments upon which business growth and success depend.

It is possible, however unthinkable, that these tensions will resolve via mass human and environmental destruction or through social and political chaos. It seems certain, however, that most of us will attempt to avoid these unappealing options. One answer is to permit a single superpower to act as "king of the mountain" in setting and enforcing rules. Another answer is to support some form of negotiated world government, a United Nations with clout. Yet another is simply to believe that free markets will eventually make necessary a level playing field complete with democratic governments, and so we can wait out the transition without concern.

These answers just won't work. No nation is capable of exercising the kind of power and authority required for governing the world. Likewise, the possibility of negotiated world governance appears remote, principally because of strong preferences for national sovereignty as well as the vast differences among nations in economic viability and political stability. And, in contrast to the ideology of market capitalism, free markets can *contribute* to these dislocations and conflicts and cannot alone provide socially acceptable solutions.

In the absence of any realistic supranational authority, global businesses themselves are providing, and will increasingly continue to provide, both solid ground rules and adaptive multicultural and culture-specific implementation. The concept of global business citizenship takes the older, societally based notion of corporate social responsibility into the global arena where

219

national sovereignty no longer suffices for basic rule-setting and enforcement. The idea is that global businesses are realizing, and will increasingly realize, that the opportunism of present-day economic and political inequities around the globe must eventually yield to a more stable environment where the rules are known, the pathways of experimentation and learning are accepted, and the rule-breakers can be caught and penalized.

Is It Too Late to Self-Regulate?

In the nineteenth century, Alexis de Tocqueville warned in his usual far-seeing way that businesses could become mini-aristocracies, with owners and managers routinely taking advantage of their power to exploit workers. Democracy's rising demand for cheap goods would encourage this development, Tocqueville felt, although in 1840 he thought this was "the most confined and least dangerous" of the corporation's political threats to society. But he delivered this sober warning:

> The friends of democracy should keep their eyes anxiously fixed in this direction; for if ever a permanent inequality of conditions and aristocracy again penetrates into the world, it may be predicted that this is the gate by which they will enter.[4]

If Tocqueville had foreseen the rise of the modern global corporation, he might have made his warning even more emphatic. Indeed, Tocqueville's gloomy prediction has already been fulfilled in the minds of some scholars and analysts. Marjorie Kelly, editor of *Business Ethics* magazine, argued in her book, *The Divine Right of Capital,* that it is too late to try self-regulatory concepts such as corporate social responsibility, or even business citizenship, because the aristocracy of business has become a permanent fixture in the world and is creating more wealth for the wealthy, more burdens for the very poor. Her recommendation is that people assert their moral agency and their autonomy of action and demand more transparency and more opportunity to participate in corporate governance and operational oversight.[5] David Korten, similarly, has developed a compelling argument that corporate capitalism in the global environment is out of control, trampling human rights and the natural environment alike, and needs to be reined in by "an awakened civil society."[6]

Our position is that it is *not* too late to change the course of capitalism in the world—for the organizations of capitalist enterprise to better adapt their orientation to local situations while retaining the integrity of universal principles.[7] We have seen throughout this book that many businesses are already moving from exploitation of the cheapest labor and the least restrictive environmental rules toward imposition of more consistent, predictable, ethically sound standards of interaction with humans and the natural environment. It seems inevitable that routinization of global business will involve commonly accepted standards of human rights and experiments with social justice, and that global businesses—because of their reach and power, and because there is no countervailing public force—will be blazing these trails.

Power Imbalances and the Need for Self-Regulation

If the movement we observe toward business self-regulation does not continue for some reason, we can all expect a great deal more turmoil in the global environment. Multinational corporations are bigger and more powerful than ever before, and in the absence of effective government controls, they can easily outweigh their more vulnerable stakeholders. Severe power imbalances between companies and their stakeholders threaten the application of moral principles, the continuity of social institutions, and the ability of people to act as moral agents.

Moral principles themselves can be distorted by serious power imbalances because the demands of those principles for universality and reversibility need not be met. For a moral principle to be considered just, it must be applicable and acceptable as a reason for anyone's action in all similar situations, that is, it must be *universalizable*. Furthermore, persons or organizations using a just principle must be willing to have that same principle used by others, even if it is disadvantageous to the initial actors. That is, a principle must be *reversible*. It's not difficult to see that an imbalance of power among social actors can lead to the more powerful ones using principles that they do not allow others to use, thereby creating injustices and distortions in the moral justification of action.

Power imbalances likewise can threaten the continuity of social institutions by introducing unjust differences in people's access to resources and the distribution of society's burdens. Just think of the old saying, "The rich get richer and the poor get poorer," to see this point clearly. Many thinkers have pointed out that such dichotomy in societal wealth, access, and struggles can lead readily to unstable political regimes and responses by the less powerful ranging from sabotage to outright warfare.

Finally, severe power imbalances eventually make it impossible for the conditions of human agency to exist, much less any form of social justice, neither fair processes nor fair distribution. "Conditions of moral agency" is "ethics-speak" for the very simple idea that when you're starving, you don't worry too much about whether you *should* steal that loaf of bread. Human

221

agency—the ability to make rational moral choices—depends on having at least minimum survival needs met. If some stakeholders become ever more vulnerable in the face of the power and growth of multinational enterprises, their ability to make moral choices also diminishes.

The stakes are high. Global business citizenship is the self-regulatory approach to correcting such power imbalances and guarding against abuse when they do exist. For capitalism to fulfill its promise and for businesses to thrive in the new economy, power must always be accompanied by the responsibility to exercise it wisely. The lessons of GBC help managers and their companies to do just this.

Problems to Watch Out For

There are numerous traps to be avoided and difficult problems yet to be solved. At the systemic level, one issue is that business citizenship may become an unexamined vehicle for cultural imperialism. Another is that business citizenship has no clear mechanisms yet for governing behaviors and relationships among the various levels of citizenship—local, national, supranational, global—or even within a single layer. And too, it is not at all clear that the corporate form and its supporting legal structures can tolerate, much less encourage, consistent citizenlike behaviors. Yet another issue is the rise of supranational structures (WTO, EU, ASEAN, OPEC, NAFTA, etc.) and the declining importance of national boundaries, with the consequent possibility of the rise of global autocracy or a continuation of the current weakening of ethnic cultures. Still another issue is the time perspective taken on institutional transformations—we believe that rapid change toward acceptance of general principles of global business citizenship is now occurring, but the full implications of these events may not be seen for decades.

At the organizational level, the usual problems apply: leadership, mission and vision, goal-setting and strategy, organizational change and development, accurate environmental scanning, team-building, motivation, incentives, and measurement. In addition, implementing GBC requires, as we have seen, strict attention to stakeholder engagement and accountability processes, because the new reality of the global economy is that there is no place to hide.

At the individual level, managers may feel that another big batch of burdens is being added to their already strained shoulders. We have encouraged you to think about GBC as a bundle of opportunities, but we do recognize that in times of cost-cutting and hypercompetition, it can seem a stretch. Remember, though, that incremental, barely noticeable changes can ultimately be as powerful as major transformations, and the small changes may actually have a better chance of taking root in ordinary practice.[8] Above all, if people in organizations encourage each other's movements toward global business citizenship, many of the presumed barriers will simply dissolve into unrealized fears.

These and other stumbling blocks, of course, are fair game for further thinking. But they are not going to halt the progress of global businesses toward a saner, healthier, more ethical global business climate. Like any other business problem, they'll just take time and effort and attention. Out of the ordinary challenges of business can come the extraordinary transformations of GBC.

In the End, a New Beginning

Business citizenship is a necessity for the survival and health of the global institution of business, and individual enterprises can and should use business citizenship to maintain and enhance their positions as the broader society changes. No particular firm is essential to the business institution, but the business institution itself is necessary to societies because of its vital functions.

Business citizenship represents a private pathway to a collective good. As with any collective good, temptations exist for actors to shirk or hold back in hopes that other actors will incur the costs of achieving the collective good, which then benefits all actors.[9] Those actors that choose to incur the costs, however, are more likely to reap the long-term benefits, as other actors fail to adapt and do not survive, or as other actors are not prepared to reap first-mover advantages as societal expectations change.

However, if citizenship for business organizations is considered only a "voluntary" concept with a limited content of local charity or self-interested strategic advantage, it has no chance to correct power imbalances or to guard against them, and so becomes self-defeating, illogical, and unworkable. Balancing the demands of liberty and justice is a task for *all* institutions—business, government, education, family, and religion. We believe that global business is moving toward the goals of liberty and justice for all—toward fulfilling their duties as business citizens—because these are the conditions necessary not only for the sustenance of human autonomy and quality of life, but also for the sustainability of capitalism itself.

As businesses apply systematic learning and share their knowledge with others, the impacts of experimentation and adaptation will be magnified far beyond the individual firm and its communities. Rights and obligations are becoming more clearly defined as companies understand the impacts of their behaviors and as they work to tip the balance of impact in the direction of higher quality of life for the peoples of the world.

For example, consider the case of developing economies. It is apparent that many businesses identify more with global hypernorms—consistent universal standards—than with particular local rules and customs. As this process of identification with common standards continues, it seems inevitable that those "stretch goals," such as environmental protection, ethical conduct, and human rights, will become expectations. When this happens, many of the current practices in developing economies—bribery and corruption, illegal seizure of assets, contract-breaking, human rights problems, and so on—will no longer be viable as companies within those economies try to compete abroad, and as global companies bring their practices and policies to these economies.

Other systemic effects of the spread of business citizenship are likely. These effects include higher standards of living, especially for the poor; growth of the free market system; environmentally sustainable practices; and survival of the earth's many diverse species, including humans. The GBC lens shows us that human rights, environmental protection, and universal access to fair processes are key to the survival of the capitalist dream. The GBC toolkit shows us that the problems of business citizenship are understandable and to a large extent manageable.

The true enemies of capitalism are not those who regulate or moderate. No right goes without limit. Instead, the enemies of capitalism are the poverty, ignorance, corruption, short-sightedness, and exploitation that prevent the world's peoples from being free moral agents and living lives of dignity and respect. Capitalism depends on free choice, on full and accurate information. Together we must smoke out the enemies of capitalism, eliminate them, and build a new understanding of business-society relationships in the global context.

Global business citizenship is a viable path to economic success and social stability, and an opening of opportunity and justice for all the world's peoples. You have stuck with us to the end, and so we're pretty sure that you are on board. Your company may take a bit more effort, but the investment is worth it many times over.

Notes

Notes to Chapter 1

1. Carroll 1987.
2. We want to thank Dr. Phil McGraw for popularizing this phrase, which cuts through so much rationalization and gets right to the heart of things.
3. "Opportunism" is used here to mean "moral hazard," or taking advantage of an opportunity to profit by breaking the law or ethical norms. We don't mean to suggest the more positive and general "taking advantage of opportunities."
4. Research on "strategic uses of regulation" has provided numerous historical examples of U.S. companies or industries using the regulatory powers of government to serve their own strategic purposes. For example, the content of the U.S. Pure Food Law of 1906 was dramatically influenced by private interests in the dairy (versus margarine) and wine (California versus New York) industries, and by the lobbying of H.J. Heinz, who alone had the pressure retort canning technology that would preserve acidic foods without chemical additives (see Wood 1986). More recently, the European Union has issued carbon emissions regulations that offer some companies a competitive advantage in terms of top-line products that are compliant. ("Ready for Carbon Controls?" 2003).
5. For a complete discussion of U.S. market failures, see Stone 1982.
6. The idea of "sustainable capitalism" is borrowed from the language of environmentalism and suggests that capitalism, as is true of any large-scale system, requires appropriate balance between inputs and outputs in order to survive long term.
7. See, for example, Korten 1999; and Friedman 2000.
8. Donaldson and Dunfee 1999.

Notes to Chapter 2

1. The "butterfly effect," with many variations of the same basic idea, comes from Lorenz 1993.
2. Friedman 2000, p. 9.
3. The figures are from various publications and information sources of the Social Investment Forum. See Social Investment Forum-2 (accessed January 23, 2005) for current 2003 figures; Federal Reserve Bank of Boston (accessed November 11, 2004) for 1995 figures; and Social Investment Forum-1 (accessed November 11, 2004) for 1985 figures.

225

4. The European Union has adopted a gradual approach to creating minimum corporate governance standards. An E.U. Commission Action Plan to update governance standards was published in May 2003. Short-term goals (2003–2005) focus primarily on board of directors membership and responsibilities and on strengthening shareholder rights. See Woffenden and Dennison 2004. Updates can be found on the E.U. website, www.europa.eu.int/comm/internal_market. The U.S. Sarbanes-Oxley Act does require that foreign companies doing business in or listed on a stock exchange in the United States comply in the same way that U.S.-based corporations must. U.S.-E.U. discussions continue on harmonizing accounting rules and corporate governance standards. See, for example, Bruce 2003.

5. For example, Friedman (2000, p. 402) writes about "the Super-Empowered Angry Man," a creation of globalized high-tech, with destructive capability ranging from internet hacking to nuclear suitcase bombs, whose common intent is to "spit in the face of Americanization-globalization and stomp on it, by using the system against itself."

6. See Arrow 1973, and Sen 1999.

7. Huston Smith, *The World's Religions* (San Francisco: HarperCollins 1991), p. 399.

8. Even in such cases, however, the U.N. may intervene at the request of the government in power, to restore order.

9. See, for example, Targett 2003; Low 2003; and Uhrquart 2003.

10. Haufler 2001.

11. Some scholars have recently termed this dichotomy the "separation thesis." See, for example, Wicks 1996.

12. Empirical studies are examined in Wood and Jones 1995; Frooman 1997; and Margolis and Walsh 2001.

13. Elkington 1997.

14. A detailed field study of twenty-three companies in the footwear, apparel, and retail industries is found in Mamic 2004.

15. See Nelson and Prescott 2003, quote from p. 7.

Notes to Chapter 3

1. We don't want to belabor political theory here, but readers who are interested in our full analysis are directed to Wood and Logsdon 2001, which explores the changes in political ideology that tend to accompany movements from accepting citizenship as an idea that applies only to individual members of nations toward accepting the citizenship of organizations who operate across multiple national borders. For even more depth, see also Logsdon and Wood 2002, and Wood and Logsdon 2002.

2. We do not want to argue here for a "One World" of common experience. We do want to emphasize a huge potential for common awareness of each other's life circumstances, never before possible.

3. Nickel 1987, p. xi.

4. There are direct parallels between minimalist citizenship ideas and ethical egoism.

5. See Quinn and Jones 1995.

6. Etzioni 1993; see also Walzer 1994.

7. White 1998.

8. Ethical relativism can be seen as immoral, or violating moral norms. It can also be viewed as amoral, meaning apart from, or aside from, moral norms.

9. See http://www.interfaithcalendar.org for dates and definitions of the world's major religious holidays.

Notes to Chapter 4

1. Quote from Carasco and Singh 2003. The original study referenced is Berenbeim 2003.

2. Some readers will recognize these values as the ones promoted by Blanchard and Bowles (2000) in their blockbuster fable, *Big Bucks!*

3. Bluemstein and Pulliam 2003.

4. The relevant definitions of "principle" from *Webster's New World Dictionary & Thesaurus* include: "the ultimate source, origin, or cause of something"; "a fundamental truth, law, doctrine, or motivating force, upon which others are based [moral principles]", and "(*a*) a rule of conduct, esp. of right conduct (*b*) such rules collectively *c*) adherence to them; integrity; uprightness [a man of principle]."

5. See Business for Social Responsibility (accessed November 27, 2004). The original source is General Motors-3 (accessed November 27, 2004).

6. General Motors-1 (accessed November 27, 2004).

7. General Motors-3 (accessed November 27, 2004).

8. With globalization, Japan is changing along with the rest of the world. Traditional and mutual lifetime loyalty between employee and company has begun to crumble, and divorce rates are rising.

9. Adapted from Trevino and Nelson 1995. Another version is found in Moses 2002.

10. See, for example, Küng 1998 and Küng 1993.

11. See, for example, Faithnet (accessed January 31, 2005).

12. Global Compact.

13. "The Ten Principles" (accessed August 17, 2004).

14. Kelly 2002.

15. This paragraph is taken from Logsdon and Wood 2005. For an extended discussion, see Sethi 2003.

16. For a more extended illustration, see Logsdon and Wood 2005.

17. Indeed, our executive MBA students tell us that Johnson & Johnson never has a management *meeting* without the Credo being available for instant reference should a question of ethics arise.

18. These structures are part of the U.S. 1991 Sentencing Guidelines as they apply to corporate crime. Following passage of these guidelines, virtually all large U.S. corporations adopted all of these structures, which can be grounds for large reductions in fines for companies when their employees commit crimes. Implementing the guidelines also offer some protection for prosecution for high-level executives.

19. See Ethics Officers Association (accessed January 5, 2005). These high-level positions may be staff, as in General Counsel or Controller, or they may be line, as in Chief Auditor or Chief Financial Officer.

20. Years ago, one of us pursued an offer from an H.J. Heinz manager to interview executives and write a case on Heinz's leadership in the dolphin-free tuna campaign. The interviews never happened and the case wasn't written because Heinz lawyers could not be assured that the venture was completely risk-free for the company.

Notes to Chapter 5

1. Institute for Social and Ethical Accountability 1999b.

2. Mitchell, Agle, and Wood 1997.

3. Susskind, Fuller, Ferenz, and Fairman 2003.
4. ABB Group-3 (accessed January 5, 2005).
5. ABB Group-2 (accessed January 5, 2005).
6. ABB Group-3 (accessed January 5, 2005).
7. ABB Group-1 (accessed July 27, 2005).
8. United Nations-2 (accessed September 14, 2004).

Notes to Chapter 6

1. The quote is from Global Compact (accessed October 29, 2004). Other sources for this section are QA-Talk (accessed October 29, 2004); and ANBA (accessed October 29, 2004).
2. "HP's Supplier Code of Conduct" (accessed October 24, 2004).
3. Catholic Agency for Overseas Development (accessed October 29, 2004). See also Warden, no date.
4. Hewlett-Packard(accessed October 29, 2004).
5. Holcim-1 (accessed October 31, 2004).
6. Union Cement recently changed its name to Holcim Philippines following Holcim Group's purchase of a majority interest. We will refer to the company as Union Cement to avoid confusion.
7. Holcim-2 (accessed October 31, 2004).
8. Holcim-3 (accessed October 31, 2004).
9. Fussler, Cramer, and van der Vegt 2004, p. 69.
10. McDonough and Braungart 2002.
11. This quote is from Volvo's story on the Global Compact website (accessed October 29, 2004).
12. Ibid. Other sources for the Volvo story include Gasforeningen (accessed November 12, 2004), and Think the Earth (accessed November 12, 2004).
13. Logsdon 1991.
14. Hartford Web Publishing-2 (accessed November 12, 2004).
15. Ibid.
16. Hartford Web Publishing-1 (accessed November 12, 2004).
17. Saigon.com (accessed November 12, 2004).
18. International Business Leaders Forum(accessed November 12, 2004).
19. Vietnam Business Links Initiative (accessed November 12, 2004).
20. "Living in a World with HIV/AIDS" (accessed November 13, 2004).
21. Ghanaian Chronicle (accessed November 13, 2004).
22. "AngloGold Report to Society 2003, HIV/AIDS" (p. HA2) (accessed November 12, 2004).
23. Biz.Yahoo (accessed November 13, 2004).
24. Global Compact (accessed August 17, 2004).
25. Ghanaweb.com (accessed November 13, 2004).
26. Biz.Yahoo (accessed November 13, 2004).
27. Danfoss Group Global (accessed November 12, 2004).
28. Global Compact (accessed November 10, 2004).

Notes to Chapter 7

1. Novo Nordisk (accessed September 13, 2003).
2. Maitland 2002.

3. Burke, Seashore, Tannenbaum, Worley, and. Zhang 2001.

4. Maurer 1996.

5. Ackerman-Anderson and Anderson 2001; Hallstein 2003; Maurer 1996; Mink, Esterhuysen, Mink, and Owen 1993; and Kotter 1996.

6. Gioia 1992.

7. Reeves 2002.

8. Ibid.

9. Available at Novartis under Investor Relations (accessed December 19, 2003).

10. Tavis, Lee A. "Novartis: The United Nations Global Compact Initiative," a business case created as a learning document for the United Nations Global Compact Learning Forum, p. 3.

11. Tavis, no date, p. 15.

12. Lehrer 2002.

13. Guth and Lublin 2003.

14. Fisher 1994.

15. Moran, Hogeveen, Latham and Russ-Eft 1994.

16. Johnson 1995.

17. Maurer 2002a.

18. Ibid., p. 2.2.

Notes to Chapter 8

1. This latter framework is borrowed from Ted Murray; see, for example, Murray 1976.

2. Sounds just like the ultimate goal of global business citizenship, right? In truth, it's not accidental that we have chosen most of our case examples from the Global Compact initiative. The quote here and the ones that follow in the bullet list are from Global Compact (accessed September 4, 2003).

3. The quote is from World Bank Group (accessed September 17, 2004). Other sources for this case include: for general company information EDF Energy-1 (accessed September 17, 2004); for a profile of EDF's corporate responsibility policy, EDF Energy-2 (accessed September 17, 2004); for a discussion of EDF's employee volunteer programs, Employee Volunteering (accessed September 17, 2004); and for more specifics on Yeelen Kura, European Union (accessed September 17, 2004) and World Bank Group (accessed September 17, 2004).

4. Sources for this case, besides the Global Compact website, include: for financial and strategic analysis, Business Line (accessed September 17, 2004) and India Infoline (accessed September 17, 2004); for an extensive write-up and analysis of the low-flush toilet case, Environmental Information Center (accessed September 17, 2004); and for a look at Hindustan's product line, Hindustan Sanitaryware (accessed September 17, 2004).

5. Sources for this case, besides the Global Compact website, include: for general and corporate responsibility information on the company's website, Bouygues Telecom-2 and Bouygues Telecom-3 (accessed September 19, 2004); for the company's environmental policy, Bouygues Telecom-1 (accessed September 19, 2004). On the French recycling law, see London 1993, and Kulik 1994.

6. Beyond the Global Compact website, sources for this case include: for company history and general information, Bernard Michaud S.A (accessed September 20, 2004); for results of an industry conference on EU beekeeping, Beekeeping-1 (accessed September 20, 2004); for examples of beekeeping as an economic devel-

opment activity, Beekeeping-2 and Universiteit Utrecht (both accessed September 20, 2004); and for the EU standards on beekeeping and honey, BeeSource.com (accessed September 20, 2004).

7. Beyond the Global Compact website, sources used in preparing this case include: for financial and business information, Hoovers (accessed August 17, 2004); for the company's story about Burkina Faso, Aarhus United-3 (accessed August 17, 2004); for general company history, Aarhus United-3 and Aarhus United-5 (both accessed August 17, 2004); for Aarhus's mission and vision statements, Aarhus United-7 (accessed August 17, 2004); for its commitment to a balanced scorecard strategy, Aarhus United-6 (accessed August 17, 2004); for facts on Burkina Faso, Central Intelligence Agency (accessed August 17, 2004); for market data and analysis on the shea nut industry, Raise.org (accessed September 4, 2004); for a more extensive discussion of shea nut production as economic development, United Nations-1 (accessed September 4, 2004); and for the facts on child labor in cocoa production, Global March Against Child Labour, BBC News, Global Exchange, Save the Children UK, Integrated Regional Information Networks, United States House of Representatives, and Jubilee-Kids (all accessed September 4, 2004).

8. Quote is from Global March Against Child Labour (accessed September 16, 2004).

9. "From Child Labour Survey to Win-Win Project," Aarhus United A/S, from the Global Compact website (accessed August 17, 2004).

10. Aarhus United-1 (accessed August 17, 2004).

11. Aarhus United-2 (accessed September 4, 2004).

12. Aside from the Global Compact website, sources used in writing this case include: for company and founder information, Forbes (accessed September 17, 2004); for the company's mission and responsibility statements and a brief history, W.E. Connor-1 and W.E. Connor-2 (both accessed September 17, 2004); for the code of conduct and compliance statement, W.E. Connor-3 (accessed September 17, 2004).

13. W.E. Connor-2 (accessed September 17, 2004).

Notes to Chapter 9

1. Dierkes and Antal 1986, p. 108.

2. The OECD has proposed financial accounting guidelines similar to GAAP to be applied to multinational enterprises.

3. The International Accounting Standards Board is the standard-setting body of the International Accounting Standards Committee (IASC) Foundation (site accessed January 11, 2005).

4. Davenport 1998; Steiner and Steiner 2003, p. 196; Bowen 1953.

5. Kreps 1940.

6. The term comes from the work of Dierkes 1980. See also Dierkes and Antal 1985b.

7. Actually, when Western companies first entered Eastern Europe and Russia in the very early 1990s, this seemed to be precisely how financial reporting was done in those locales, much to the dismay of Western accounting and financial experts.

8. Dierkes and Antal 1985a.

9. Kaplan and Norton 1996.

10. Ibid.

11. Lewellyn and Logsdon 2005.

12. Kaplan and Norton 2001.

13. "The SIGMA Guidelines Toolkit" (accessed January17, 2005). Extracts from the SIGMA Guidelines Toolkit are reproduced with the permission of the British Standards Institution (BSI). Further information on BSI publications can be found at http://www.bsi-global.com.

14. The original thirty-six-member GRI Stakeholder Council included representatives from Brazil, Ivory Coast, United States, Australia, Philippines, Canada, France, Hong Kong, UK, Sweden, India, Germany, Denmark, Japan, South Africa, Kenya, Thailand, Argentina, Spain, Korea, Hungary, the Netherlands, and Norway. Organizations represented included Baxter International Inc., BMT Asia Pacific Ltd., Westpac Banking Corporation, the International Labor Rights Fund, BASF, the Trade Union Advisory Committee to the OECD, Unilever, General Motors, Modus Vivendi, Social Accountability International, the Federation of Thai Industries, Budapest Power Plant Ltd., and Norway's Statoil ASA, among others.

15. Global Reporting Initiative 2002.

16. This paragraph and the next two from Lewellyn and Logsdon 2005.

17. Institute for Social and Ethical Accountability 1999a.

18. The framework suggests additional indicators that are encouraged, but not required, for the reporting organization to be in compliance with the guidelines (not included in this analysis).

19. Ford Motor Company 2002.

20. Global Reporting Initiative-1 (accessed September 12, 2004).

21. Global Reporting Initiative-2 (accessed September 12, 2004).

22. AccountAbility (accessed September 12, 2004).

23. Personal communication with Jeannette Oelschlaegel, Standards Researcher, ISEA, August 31, 2004.

24. Institute for Social and Ethical Accountability (accessed September 12, 2004); Zadek 2001.

25. Institute for Social and Ethical Accountability (accessed September 12, 2004).

26. At least five countries require environmental reports for some industries or size of company: Denmark, France, The Netherlands, Norway, and Sweden. In France, social and environmental performance is required for firms listed on the stock exchange (Kolk 2003). Many other countries strongly encourage voluntary reporting.

Notes to Chapter 10

1. Social Accountability International (accessed November 13, 2004).

2. The details of this case are compiled from Fessler et al. 2004, p. 138; and from Rohitratana, no date (accessed November 13, 2004).

3. Fessler et al. 2004, p. 112.

4. Gap, Inc. 2003, p. 7 (accessed November 14, 2004).

5. Gap, Inc. 2003, pp. 10–11 (accessed November 14, 2004).

6. Gap, Inc. 2003, p. 11 (accessed November 14, 2004).

7. Gap, Inc. 2003, p. 12 (accessed November 14, 2004).

8. Gap, Inc. 2003, pp. 19–20 (accessed November 14, 2004).

9. Gap, Inc. 2003, p. 28 (accessed November 14, 2004).

10. The Corporation (accessed January 8, 2005).

11. Domini 400 Social Index (accessed January 8, 2005).
12. Sustainability Institute (accessed January 8, 2005).
13. Interface Sustainability-1 (accessed January 6, 2005).
14. Interface Sustainability-3 (accessed January 8, 2005).
15. Ibid.
16. McDonough and Braungart 2002.
17. Sustainability Institute (accessed January 8, 2005).
18. Interface Sustainability-2 (accessed January 6, 2005).
19. Interface Sustainability-4 (accessed January 6, 2005).

Notes to Chapter 11

1. It is worth noting that some companies may choose to play more quiet roles, because with the spotlight comes unwanted and sometimes unfair scrutiny. Even so, GBC companies can be role models for others without making a big deal out of it.
2. We acknowledge without replication the extensive work of Peter M. Senge and his colleagues on organizational learning. See, for example, Senge 1990.
3. Global Compact (accessed January 7, 2005).
4. Kell and Levin 2003, p. 152.
5. Dowling 2001.
6. See, for example, "Archer Daniels Midland to Pay $400M," (accessed February 25, 2005).
7. See Business & Society's "Showcase Issue on Empirical Research," 1995, for extensive analysis of the "financial halo" in Fortune's "Most Admired" data.
8. Albert and Whetten 1985.
9. See, for example, Dowling 2001; Schreiber 2002; and the annual "Corporate Reputation Watch" survey sponsored by Hill & Knowlton, Korn/Ferry, and Opinion Research Corporation (accessed February 25, 2005).
10. Dowling 2001.
11. Oberman and Wood 1994.
12. See, for example, White and Power 2002.
13. Ring 1996.

Notes to Chapter 12

1. Tonnies 1957.
2. Barber 1995.
3. Friedman 1999.
4. Tocqueville 1956.
5. Kelly 2001.
6. Korten 1995.
7. Other scholars of note agree; see, for example, Handy 1998; and Sen 1999.
8. See, for example, Meyerson 2001.
9. Olsen 1965.

Bibliography

Aarhus United 1: No date. "From Child Labour Survey to Win-Win Project." Available at www.unglobalcompact.org (accessed August 17, 2004).

Aarhus United-2: http://www.aarhusunited.com/AU/Web/AarhusUnited.nsf/ (accessed September 4, 2004).

Aarhus United-3: http://www.aarhusunited.com/AU/Web/AarhusUnited.nsf/links/ 3CA44B4CD7565173C1256EE10049032B (accessed August 17, 2004).

Aarhus United-4: http://www.aarhusunited.com/AU/Web/AarhusUnited.nsf/links/ 8DF36E87A28F33E6C1256E82003B9E22 (accessed August 17, 2004).

Aarhus United-5: http://www.aarhusunited.com/AU/Web/AarhusUnited.nsf/links/ 7EDB8B09FA5E249EC1256D5100434C08 (accessed August 17, 2004).

Aarhus United-6: http://www.aarhusunited.com/AU/Web/AarhusUnited.nsf/links/ 418A968B4A61978AC1256D5600297A3F(accessed August 17, 2004).

Aarhus United-7: http://www.aarhusunited.com/AU/Web/AarhusUnited.nsf/links/ E93735C0F5B997EFC1256D51002A4972 (accessed August 17, 2004).

ABB Group-1: http://library.abb.com/GLOBAL/SCOT/scot266.nsf/VerityDisplay/ 9A26C161A8BC5C2BC1256FEB0049648E/$File/ABB_SR04en_finish _140705.pdf (accessed July 27, 2005).

ABB Group-2: http://www.abb.com (accessed January 5, 2005).

ABB Group-3: http://www.abb.com/global/abbzh/abbzh251.nsf!OpenDatabase&db=/ global/seitp/seitp255.nsf&v=499A&e=us&c=74168F7A72D50E7EC1256 C6A00487101 (accessed January 5, 2005).

AccountAbility: http://www.accountability.org.uk (accessed September 12, 2004).

Ackerman-Anderson, Linda, and Dean Anderson. 2001. *The Change Leaders Roadmap*. San Francisco, CA: Jossey-Bass).

Albert, Stuart, and David Whetten. 1985. "Organizational Identity." In Larry L. Cummings and Barry M. Staw (eds.), *Research in Organizational Behavior*, vol. 7. Greenwich, CT: JAI Press, 263–95.

ANBA: http://www.anba.com.br/ingles/noticia.php?id=1038 (accessed October 29, 2004).

"AngloGold Report to Society 2003, HIV/AIDS," available at http://test.anglo gold.co.za/subwebs/InformationForInvestors/ReportToSociety03/index.htm (accessed November 12, 2004).

"Archer Daniels Midland to Pay $400M," an Associated Press report posted June 17, 2004, at http://www.forbes.com/feeds/ap/2004/06/17/ap1421326.html (accessed February 25, 2005).

Arrow, Kenneth. 1973. "Social Responsibility and Economic Efficiency." *Public Policy* 21: 303–17.

Barber, Benjamin R. 1995. *Jihad vs. McWorld*. New York: Times Books.

BBC News: http://news.bbc.co.uk/2/hi/africa/1389185.stm (accessed September 4, 2004).

Beekeeping-1: http://216.239.41.104/search?q=cache:AAh6xXbrDPUJ:web.uniud.it/eurbee/Proceedings/beekeeping%2520in%2520EU.pdf+beekeeping+EU&hl=en (accessed September 20, 2004).

Beekeeping-2: http://www.delsur.cec.eu.int/en/whatsnew/Alternative_income_by_beekeeping.htm (accessed September 20, 2004).

BeeSource.com: http://www.beesource.com/pov/organic/orghdr.gif (accessed September 20, 2004).

Berenbeim, Ronald. 2003. "Global Ethics." *Executive Excellence* 17, 5: 7.

Bernard Michaud S.A.: http://www.lunedemiel.fr/michaud/copymichaud/uk/index.php3 (accessed September 20, 2004).

Biz.Yahoo: http://biz.yahoo.com/iw/040715/069979.html (accessed November 13, 2004).

Blanchard, Ken, and Sheldon Bowles. 2002. *Big Bucks!* New York: Morrow.

Bluemstein, Rebecca, and Susan Pulliam. 2003. "Leading the News: WorldCom Was Widespread—Ebbers, Many Executives Conspired to Falsify Results In Late 1990s, Probes Find." *The Wall Street Journal* (June 10): A3.

Bouygues Telecom-1: http://www.bouygues.fr/us/groupe/environnement.asp (accessed September 19, 2004).

Bouygues Telecom-2: http://www.bouygues.fr/us/groupe/mecenat.asp (accessed September 19, 2004).

Bouygues Telecom-3: http://www.bouygues.fr/us/groupe/presentation.asp (accessed September 19, 2004).

Bowen, Howard R. 1953. *Social Responsibilities of the Businessman*. New York: Harper.

Bruce, Robert. 2003. "Now How Does It All Fit Together?" *Financial Times* (Sept. 15): 2.

British Standards Institute: http://www.bsi-global.com (accessed various dates as noted in footnotes).

Burke, W. Warner, Edith W. Seashore, Robert Tannenbaum, Christopher G. Worley, and S. Zhang. 2001. "Statement of the Board." In Linda Ackerman-Anderson and Dean Anderson, *The Change Leader's Roadmap*. San Francisco: Jossey-Bass, xxi.

Business for Social Responsibility: http://www.bsr.org/CSRResources/IssueBrief Detail.cfm?DocumentID=48982 (accessed November 11 and 27, 2004).

Business Line: http://www.blonnet.com/iw/2004/06/06/stories/2004060600500900.htm (accessed September 17, 2004).

Carasco, Emily F., and Jang B. Singh. 2003. "The Content and Focus of the Codes of Ethics of the World's Largest Transnational Corporations." *Business and Society Review* 108, 1: 71–94.

Carroll, Archie B. 1987. "In Search of the Moral Manager." *Business Horizons* 30, 2: 7–16.

Catholic Agency for Overseas Development: http://www.cafod.org.uk/get_involved/ campaigning/clean_up_your_computer/whats_wrong_with_my_computer (accessed October 29, 2004).

Central Intelligence Agency: http://www.cia.gov/cia/publications/factbook/geos/ uv.html (accessed August 17, 2004).

"Corporate Reputation Watch," an annual survey sponsored by Hill & Knowlton, Korn/ Ferry, and Opinion Research Corporation, available at http://www.hillandknowlton .com/crw/index/press_releases/1 (accessed February 25, 2005).

Danfoss Group Global: http://www.danfoss.com (accessed November 12, 2004).

Davenport, Kim. 1998. "Corporate Citizenship: A Stakeholder Approach for Defining Corporate Social Performance and Identifying Measures for Assessing It." Unpublished doctoral dissertation (Ann Arbor, MI: The Fielding Institute.

Dierkes, Meinolf. 1980. "Corporate Social Reporting and Performance in Germany." In Lee E. Preston (ed.), *Research in Corporate Social Performance and Policy*, vol. 2. Greenwich, CT: JAI Press, 251–89.

Dierkes, Meinolf, and Ariane Berthoin Antal. 1985a. "Corporate Social Reporting and Auditing: Theory and Practice." In Gunther Teubner (ed.), *Corporate Governance and Directors' Liabilities*. Berlin: deGruyter.

———. 1985b. "The Use and Usefulness of Corporate Social Reporting." *Accounting, Organizations and Society* 10, 1: 29–34.

———. 1986. "Whither Corporate Social Reporting: Is It Time to Legislate?" *California Management Review* 28, 3: 106–21.

Domini 400 Social Index: http://www.domini.com/dsi400/pop_dsi400.asp ?slct=5&cn=Interface%2C+Inc. (accessed January 8, 2005).

Donaldson, Thomas, and Thomas W. Dunfee. 1999. *Ties That Bind: A Social Contracts Approach to Business Ethics*. Cambridge, MA: Harvard Business Press.

Dowling, Grahame R. 2001. *Creating Corporate Reputations : Identity, Image, and Performance*. New York: Oxford University Press.

EDF Energy-1: http://www.edfenergy.com/ (accessed September 17, 2004).

EDF Energy-2: http://www.edfenergy.com/index.asp?template=corporate/ index.html&language=en&mode=production (accessed September 17, 2004).

Elkington, John. 1997. *Cannibals With Forks: The Triple Bottom Line of 21st Century Business*. Oxford: Capstone.

Employee Volunteering: http://www.employeevolunteering.org.uk/casestudies/ details.asp?id=165 (accessed September 17, 2004).

Environmental Information Center: http://www.cleantechindia.com/eicimage/ 210101_17/hindustan.htm (accessed September 17, 2004).

Ethics Officers Association: http://www.eoa.org/EOA_Resources/Reports/ Org_Structure_of_ChiefEO(72004).pdf (accessed January 5, 2005).

Etzioni, Amatai. 1993. *The Spirit of Community: Rights, Responsibilities, and the Communitarian Agenda*. New York: Crown.

European Union: http://www.europa.eu.int/comm/internal_market (accessed various dates as noted in footnotes).

Faithnet: http://www.faithnet.org.uk/A2%20Subjects/Ethics/catergoricalimperative .htm (accessed January 31, 2005).

Federal Reserve Bank of Boston: http://www.bos.frb.org/commdev/c&b/2002/summer/SRI.pdf (accessed November 11, 2004).

Fisher, Anne. 1994. "How to Make a Merger Work." *Fortune* 129, 2: 66–69.

Forbes: http://www.forbes.com/finance/lists/54/2003/LIR.jhtml?passListId
=54&passYear=2003&passListType=Person&uniqueId=6FTY&datatype=Person
(accessed September 17, 2004).

Ford Motor Company. 2002. *Connecting with Society...Our Learning Journey; 2001
Corporate Citizenship Report* (Dearborn, MI: Ford Motor Company.

Ford Motor Company. 2003. *Connecting with Society: 2002 Corporate Citizenship
Report.* Dearborn, MI: Ford Motor Company.

Friedman, Thomas L. 1999. *The Lexus and the Olive Tree.* New York : Farrar, Straus,
Giroux.

———. 2000. *The Lexus and the Olive Tree.* New York: Anchor Books.

Frooman, Jeff. 1997. "Socially Irresponsible and Illegal Behavior and Shareholder
Wealth." *Business & Society* 36, 3: 221–9.

Fussler, Claude, Aron Cramer, and Sebastian van der Vegt (eds.). 2004. *Raising the
Bar: Creating Value with the United Nations Global Compact.* Sheffield, UK:
Greenleaf Publishing.

Gap, Inc. 2003. "Social Responsibility Report 2003." Available at http://
www.gapinc.com/public/SocialResponsibility/socialres.shtml (accessed November 14, 2004).

Gasforeningen: http://www.gasforeningen.se/661/626d_1.html (accessed November
12, 2004).

General Motors-1: http://www.gm.com/company/gmability/sustainability/reports/04/
300_company/311_vis_vis.html (accessed November 27, 2004).

General Motors-2: http://www.gm.com/company/investor_information/corp_gov/
guidelines.html (accessed November 27, 2004).

General Motors-3: http://www.gm.com/company/investor_information/corp_gov/
winning_integrity.html (accessed November 27, 2004).

Ghanaian Chronicle: http://www.ghanaian-chronicle.com/231013/page2e.htm (accessed November 13, 2004).

Ghanaweb.com: http://www.ghanaweb.com/GhanaHomePage/NewsArchive/
artikel.php?ID=68069 (accessed November 13, 2004).

Gioia, Dennis A. 1992. "Pinto Fires and Personal Ethics: A Script Analysis of Missed
Opportunities." *Journal of Business Ethics* 11: 379–89.

Global Compact: http://www.unglobalcompact.org/Portal/Default.asp (accessed various dates as noted in footnotes).

Global Exchange: http://www.globalexchange.org/campaigns/fairtrade/cocoa/448.html
(accessed September 4, 2004).

Global March Against Child Labour: http://www.globalmarch.org/child-trafficking/
news-articles/thebittertasteofchocolate.htm (posted July 2001; accessed September 4 and 16, 2004).

Global Reporting Initiative. 2002. *Sustainability Reporting Guidelines on Economic,
Environmental, and Social Performance.* Amsterdam: Global Reporting Initiative.

Global Reporting Initiative-1: http://www.globalreporting.org (accessed September
12, 2004).

Global Reporting Initiative-2: http://www.globalreporting.org/news/updates/
article.asp?ArticleID=336 (accessed September 12, 2004).

Guth, Robert A., and Joann S. Lublin. 2003. "Microsoft Ushers Out Era of Options."
Wall Street Journal (July 9): A1.

Hallstein Dick. 2003. *Managing Change.* Consulting Partners, Inc. Personal communication, used with permission.

Handy, Charles B. 1998. *The Hungry Spirit: Beyond Capitalism : A Quest for Purpose in the Modern World*. New York: Broadway Books.

Hartford Web Publishing-1: http://www.hartford-hwp.com/archives/54/105.html (accessed November 12, 2004).

Hartford Web Publishing-2: http://www.hartford-hwp.com/archives/54/109.html (accessed November 12, 2004).

Haufler, Virginia. 2001. *A Public Role for the Private Sector.* Washington, DC: Carnegie Endowment for International Peace.

Hewlett-Packard: http://www.hp.com/hpinfo/newsroom/press/2004/041021a.html (accessed October 29, 2004).

Hindustan Sanitaryware: http://www.hindwarebathrooms.com/about/ (accessed September 17, 2004).

Holcim-1: http://www.holcim.com/CORP/EN/b/GCK/oid/1610644572/channel_id/-8261/module/gnm0/jsp/templates/editorial/editorial.html (accessed October 31, 2004).

Holcim-2: http://www.holcim.com/CORP/EN/oid/46180/module/gnm50/jsp/templates/editorial/editorial.html (accessed October 31, 2004).

Holcim-3: http://www.unioncement.com/social_res.htm (accessed October 31, 2004).

Hoovers: http://www.hoovers.com/aarhus-united/—ID__90982—/free-co-factsheet.xhtml (accessed August 17, 2004).

"HP's Supplier Code of Conduct," available at http://www.hp.com/cgi-bin/hpinfo/oovpf_hpinfo.pl (accessed October 24, 2004).

India Infoline: http://www.indiainfoline.com/view/230703a.html (accessed September 17, 2004).

Institute for Social and Ethical Accountability. 1999a. *AA1000: Overview of Standards, Guidelines, and Tools.* London: Institute for Social and Ethical Accountability.

———. 1999b. *Accountability 1000 (AA1000) Framework.* London: Institute for Social and Ethical Accountability.

———. 2002. *AA1000 Series: Consultation Brief.* Available at www.accountability.org.uk (accessed September 12, 2004).

Integrated Regional Information Networks (IRIN): http://www.irinnews.org/report.asp?ReportID=37391&SelectRegion=West_Africa&SelectCountry=GHANA-NIGERIA (accessed September 4, 2004).

Interface Sustainability-1: http://www.interfacesustainability.com/comp.html (accessed January 6, 2005).

Interface Sustainability-2: http://www.interfacesustainability.com/pletsus.html (accessed January 6, 2005).

Interface Sustainability-3: http://www.interfacesustainability.com/seven.html (accessed January 8, 2005).

Interface Sustainability-4: http://www.interfacesustainability.com/visi.html (accessed January 6, 2005).

Interfaith Calendar: http://www.interfaithcalendar.org (accessed November 11, 2004).

International Accounting Standards Committee Foundation: http://www.iasb.org/about/constitution.asp (accessed January 11, 2005).

International Business Leaders Forum: http://www.iblf.org/csr/csrwebassist.nsf/content/f1c2b3a4b5.html (accessed November 12, 2004).

Johnson, Jim. 1995. "Chaos: The Dollar Drain of IT Failures." *Application Development Trends* (January): 41–47.

Jubilee-Kids: http://www.jubilee-kids.org/oldsite/news/hot.html (accessed September 4, 2004).

Kaplan, Robert S., and David P. Norton. 2001. "Transforming the Balanced Scorecard from Performance Measurement to Strategic Management: Part II." *Accounting Horizons* 15, 2: 147–60.

———. 1996. *The Balanced Scorecard.* Boston: Harvard Business School Press.

Kell, Georg, and David Levin. 2003. "The Global Compact Network: An Historic Experiment in Learning and Action." *Business and Society Review* 108, 2: 151–81.

Kelly, Arthur L. 2002. "Italian Tax Mores." In Thomas Donaldson, Patricia H. Werhane, and Margaret Cording (eds.), *Ethical Issues in Business: A Philosophical Approach,* 7th edition. Upper Saddle River, NJ: Prentice Hall, 98–100.

Kelly, Marjorie. 2001. *The Divine Right of Capital: Dethroning the Corporate Aristocracy.* San Francisco, CA: Berrett-Koehler.

Kolk, Ans. 2003. "Trends in Sustainability Reporting for the Fortune Global 250." *Business Strategy and the Environment* 12, 5: 279–91.

Korten, David C. 1995. *When Corporations Rule the World.* San Francisco, CA: Berrett-Koehler.

———. 1999. *The Post-Corporate World: Life After Capitalism.* San Francisco: Berrett-Koehler.

Kotter, John P. 1996. *Leading Change.* Boston, MA: Harvard Business School Press.

Kreps, Theodore J. 1940. *Measurement of the Social Performance of Business,* Monograph No. 7, *An Investigation of Economic Power for the Temporary National Economic Committee.* Washington, DC: U.S. Government Printing Office.

Kulik, Ann. 1994. "French Take New Approach to Solid Waste Planning." *World Wastes* 37, 7: 14–16.

Küng, Hans. 1993. *Global Responsibility: In Search of a New World Ethic.* New York: Continuum.

———. 1998. *A Global Ethic for Global Politics and Economics.* New York: Oxford University Press.

Lehrer, Jim. 2002. "View from the Top." *The NewsHour with Jim Lehrer,* Washington, DC: PBS Broadcasting (July 12).

Lewellyn, Patsy G., and Jeanne M. Logsdon. 2005. "Sustainability Reporting: The Global Reporting Initiative and Corporate Accountability." Working paper.

"Living in a World with HIV/AIDS, Information for Employees of the U.N. System and Their Families," available at http://www.unaids.org/EN/other/functionalities/Search.asp (accessed November 13, 2004).

Logsdon, Jeanne M. 1991. "Interests and Interdependence in the Formation of Social Problem-Solving Collaborations." *Journal of Applied Behavioral Science* 27, 1: 23–37.

———. 2004. "Global Business Citizenship: Applications to Environmental Issues." *Business & Society Review* 109, 1: 67–87.

Logsdon, Jeanne M., and Donna J. Wood. 2002. "Business Citizenship: From Domestic to Global Level of Analysis." *Business Ethics Quarterly* 12, 2: 155–88.

———. 2004. "Implementing Global Business Citizenship: Multi-Level Motivations and an Initial Research Agenda." In John Hooker and Peter Madsen (eds.), *International Corporate Responsibility: Exploring the Issues.* Pittsburgh, PA: Carnegie Mellon University Press: 423–46.

———. 2005. "Global Business Citizenship and Voluntary Codes of Ethical Conduct." *Journal of Business Ethics* 59, 1: 55–67.

London, Caroline. 1993. "Environmental Risk." *Euromoney* (September): 53–56.

Lorenz, Edward. 1993. *The Essence of Chaos.* Seattle: University of Washington Press.

Low, Charles. 2003. "Industry Self-Regulation Benefits All." *Canadian Business and Current Affairs* (July).

Maitland, Alison. 2002. "Inside Track—Truants, Nerds and Supersonics." *Financial Times* (November 18): 14.

Mamic, Ivanka. 2004. *Implementing Codes of Conduct: How Businesses Manage Social Performance in Global Supply Chains.* Sheffield, UK: Greenleaf Publishing.

Margolis, Joshua, and James P. Walsh. 2001. *People and Profits? The Search for a Link Between a Company's Social and Financial Performance.* Mahwah, NJ: Lawrence Erlbaum.

Maurer, Rick. 1996. *Beyond the Wall of Resistance.* Austin, TX: Bard Press.

———. 2002a. *Building Capacity for Change Sourcebook.* Washington, DC: Maurer & Associates.

———. 2002b. *Why Don't You Want What I Want? How to Win Support for Your Ideals Without Hard Sell, Manipulation, or Power Plays.* Austin, TX: Bard Press.

McDonough, William, and Michael Braungart. 2002. *Cradle to Cradle: Remaking the Way We Make Things.* New York: North Point Press.

Meyerson, Debra. 2001. *Tempered Radicals: How People Use Difference to Inspire Change at Work.* Boston, MA: Harvard Business School Press.

Mink, Oscar, Pieter W. Esterhuysen, Barbara Mink, and Keith Owen. 1993. *Change at Work: Process for Transforming Organizations.* San Francisco, CA: Jossey-Bass.

Mitchell, Ronald A., Bradley R. Agle, and Donna J. Wood. 1997. "Toward a Theory of Stakeholder Identification and Salience: Defining the Principle of Who and What Really Counts." *Academy of Management Review* 22, 4: 853–86.

Moran, Linda, Jerry Hogeveen, Jan Latham, and Darlene Russ-Eft. 1994. *Winning Competitive Advantage.* Tampa, FL: Zenger Miller.

Moses, Jeffrey. 2002. *Oneness : Great Principles Shared by All Religions,* 1st rev. and expanded ed.. New York: Ballantine Books.

Murray, Edwin A., Jr. 1976. "The Social Response Process in Commercial Banks: An Empirical Investigation." *Academy of Management Review* 1, 3: 5–15.

National Centre for Volunteering: http://www.employeevolunteering.org.uk/casestudies/details.asp?id=165 (accessed September 17, 2004).

Nelson, Jane, and Dave Prescott. 2003. *Business and the Millennium Development Goals: A Framework for Action.* Available at www.iblf.org.uk (accessed January 23, 2005).

Nickel, James W. 1987. *Making Sense of Human Rights: Philosophical Reflections on the Universal Declaration of Human Rights.* Berkeley: University of California Press.

Novartis: http://www.novartis.com (accessed December 19, 2003).

Novo Nordisk: http://www.novonordisk.com/sustainability/economic_viability/default.asp (accessed September 13, 2003).

Oberman, William D., and Donna J. Wood. 1994. "Oil on Troubled Waters: The Ashland Spill." In Wood, Donna J. *Business & Society,* 2nd ed. Englewood Cliffs, NJ: HarperCollins College, 1–49.

Oelschlaegel, Jeannette. 2004. Personal communication with Standards Researcher, ISEA, (August 31).

Olsen, Mancur, Jr. 1965. *The Logic of Collective Action: Public Goods and the Theory of Groups.* Cambridge, MA: Harvard University Press.

QA-Talk: http://www.qa-talk.com/news/del/del126.html (accessed October 29, 2004).

Quinn, Dennis P., and Thomas M. Jones. 1995. "An Agent Morality View of Business Policy." *Academy of Management Review* 20, 1: 22–42.

Raise.org: http://www.raise.org/natural/pubs/shea/shea.stm (accessed September 4, 2004).

"Ready for Carbon Controls?" *Country Monitor* 11, 19 (2003): 5.

Reeves, Arin. 2002. "CEOs Speak Out on the Business Case for the 21st Century: Diversity in Dollars and Sense." *Diversity & the Bar* (November): 9–18.

Renewable Energy for Europe: http://europa.eu.int/comm/energy/en/renewable/idae_site/deploy/prj058/prj058_1.html (accessed September 17, 2004).

Ring, Peter Smith. 1996. "Fragile and Resilient Trust and Their Roles in Economic Exchange." *Business & Society* 35, 2: 148–76.

Rohitratana, Kaewta. No date. "SA8000: Tool to Improve Quality of Life." Available at http://www.cepaa.org/Document%20Center/sa8000%20in%20Thailand%20Beauty%20E (accessed November 13, 2004).

Saigon.com: http://www.saigon.com/~nike/news/ny110897.htm (accessed November 12, 2004).

Save the Children UK: http://www.savethechildren.org.uk/scuk/jsp/resources/details.jsp?id=477&group=resources&section=project&subsection=details&pagelang=en (accessed September 4, 2004).

Schreiber, Elliot S. 2002. "Why Do Many Otherwise Smart CEOs Mismanage the Reputation Asset of Their Company?" *Journal of Communication Management* 6, 3: 209–19.

Sen, Amartya. 1999. *Development as Freedom.* New York: Oxford University Press.

Senge, Peter M. 1990. *The Fifth Discipline: The Art & Practice of the Learning Organization.* New York: Currency Doubleday.

Sethi, S. Prakash. 2003. *Setting Global Standards: Guidelines for Creating Codes of Conduct in Multinational Corporations.* Hoboken, NJ: John Wiley and Sons.

"Showcase Issue on Empirical Research." 1995. *Business & Society* 34, 2.

Smith, Huston. 1991. *The World's Religions.* San Francisco: Harper Collins.

Social Accountability International: http://www.sa8000.org/SA8000/SA8000.htm (accessed November 13, 2004).

Social Investment Forum-1: http://www.socialinvest.org/areas/general/investors/individuals.htm (accessed November 11, 2004).

Social Investment Forum-2: http://www.socialinvest.org/Areas/News/120403release.htm (accessed January 23, 2005).

Steiner, George A., and John F. Steiner. 2003. *Business, Government, and Society: A Managerial Perspective,* 10th ed. Boston, MA: McGraw Hill.

Stone, Alan. 1982. *Regulation and Its Alternatives.* Washington, DC: Congressional Quarterly Press.

Susskind, Lawrence E., Boyd W. Fuller, Michele Ferenz, and David Fairman. 2003. "Multistakeholder Dialogue at the Global Scale." *International Negotiation Journal* 8, 2: 235–66.

Sustainability Institute: http://www.sustainer.org/dhm_archive/index.php?display_article=vn671andersoned (accessed January 8, 2005).

Targett, Simon. 2003. "European Fund Leaders Plan Code of Conduct: Self-Regulation: Industry Hopes Voluntary Compliance Will Build Public's Trust." *Financial Times* (September 15): 27.

Tavis, Lee A. No date. "Novartis: The United Nations Global Compact Initiative," a business case created as a learning document for the United Nations Global Compact Learning Forum. Available at www.unglobalcompact.org.

The Corporation: http://www.thecorporation.com/people/ray-anderson.php (accessed January 8, 2005).

"The SIGMA Guidelines Toolkit," available at http://www.projectsigma.com/Toolkit/ SIGMASustainabilityScorecard.pdf (accessed January 17, 2005).

"The Ten Principles." Available at http://www.unglobalcompact.org/Portal/Default.asp (accessed August 17, 2004).

Think the Earth: http://www.thinktheearth.net/thinkdaily/report/rpt_r02.html (accessed November 12, 2004).

Tocqueville, Alexis de. 1956. *Democracy in America*. Specially edited and abridged for the modern reader by Richard D. Heffner. New York: New American Library.

Tonnies, Ferdinand. 1957. *Community & Society* (Gemeinschaft und Gesellschaft). Translated and edited by Charles P. Loomis. East Lansing: Michigan State University Press.

Trevino, Linda K., and Katherine A. Nelson. 1995. *Managing Business Ethics: Straight Talk About How to Do It Right*. Hoboken, NJ: John Wiley and Sons.

Uhrquart, Donald. 2003. "Save Self-Regulation, Urges Shipping Bureau." *The Business Times Singapore* (June 30).

United Nations-1: http://www.un.org/ecosocdev/geninfo/afrec/vol15no4/154shea.htm (accessed September 4, 2004).

United Nations-2: http://www.un.org/esa/sustdev (accessed September 14, 2004).

United States House of Representatives: http://www.house.gov/lantos/caucus/ TestimonyCohen061703.htm (accessed September 4, 2004).

Universiteit Utrecht: http://www.bio.uu.nl/~sommeijer/promabos.html (accessed September 20, 2004).

Vietnam Business Links Initiative: http://www.vcci.com.vn/sub/vbli/default.htm (accessed November 12, 2004).

W.E. Connor-1: http://www.weconnor.com/VISITORS_SECTION/aboutconnor.html (accessed September 17, 2004).

W.E. Connor-2: http://www.weconnor.com/VISITORS_SECTION/services.html (accessed September 17, 2004).

W.E. Connor-3: http://www.weconnor.com/VISITORS_SECTION/workplace.html (accessed September 17, 2004).

Walzer, Michael. 1994. *Thick and Thin: Moral Argument at Home and Abroad*. Notre Dame, IN: Notre Dame University Press.

Warden, Graeme. No date. "IT Firms Take Heat for 'Sweatshop' Labor," available at http://news.zdnet.com/2100-9584_22-5148328.html (accessed October 29, 2004).

White, Joseph B. 1998. "Global Mall: 'There Are No German or U.S. Companies, Only Successful Ones.'" *Wall Street Journal* (May 7): A–1, A–11.

White, Joseph B., and Stephen Power. 2002. "Federal Regulator Won't Probe Safety of Ford Explorer." *Wall Street Journal* (February 13): A4.

Wicks, Andrew C. 1996. "Overcoming the Separation Thesis: The Need for a Reconsideration of Business and Society Research." *Business & Society* 35, 1: 89–118.

Woffenden, Ken, and Giles Dennison. 2004. "The EU Enters the Corporate Governance Arena." Available at http://practicallaw.com (accessed January 8, 2005).

Wood, Donna J. 1986. *Strategic Uses of Public Policy: Business and Government in the Progressive Era*. Boston: Pitman Publishing.

Wood, Donna J., and Raymond E. Jones. 1995. "Stakeholder Mismatching: A Theoretical Problem in Empirical Research on Corporate Social Performance." *International Journal of Organizational Analysis* 3: 229–67.

Wood, Donna J., and Jeanne M. Logsdon. 2001. "Theorising Business Citizenship." In Jörg Andriof and Malcolm McIntosh (eds.), *Perspectives on Corporate Citizenship* (London: Greenleaf): 83–103.

———. 2002. "Business Citizenship: From Individuals to Organizations." In R. E. Freeman and S. Venkataraman (eds.), *Ethics and Entrepreneurship*. Charlottesville, VA: The Society of Business Ethics: 59–94.

World Bank Group: http://info.worldbank.org/etools/bspan/PresentationView .asp?PID=1109&EID=506 (accessed September 17, 2004).

World Business Council for Sustainable Development. 2003. *Sustainable Development Reporting: Striking the Balance*. Geneva: WBCSD (January).

Zadek, Simon. 2001. "AA1000S—Guidelines for the 2nd Generation of Corporate Responsibility: Stakeholder Engagement for Learning, Innovation & Accountability." Paper presented at the Business for Social Responsibility annual conference (November).

242

About the Authors

Donna J. Wood holds the David W. Wilson Chair in Business Ethics at the University of Northern Iowa. She earned her Ph.D. in sociology from Vanderbilt University. She has many publications and awards for her innovative, influential work. She is founder and past-president of the International Association for Business and Society, and is also past-president of the Society for Business Ethics and the Social Issues Division of the Academy of Management. Her current interests include global business citizenship, business ethics, corporate social performance, and stakeholder theory.

Jeanne M. Logsdon is a Regents Professor at the University of New Mexico and holds the Jack and Donna Rust Professorship in Business Ethics. She earned a Ph.D. in business and public policy at the University of California at Berkeley in 1983. She is a founding member, past president, treasurer, and conference program chair of the International Association of Business and Society. She has served as chair of the Social Issues in Management Division of the Academy of Management. She recently completed a term as editor of the premier academic journal, *Business & Society.*

Patsy G. Lewellyn is a Certified Public Accountant. Following a ten-year career in public accounting, she earned an M.B.A. (1982) and D.B.A. (1987) in quantitative analysis at Louisiana Tech University. She held the John M. Olin Chair Professor in Enterprise Development at the University of South Carolina Aiken where she was a professor of accounting from 1990 to 2004. She is a founding member, former treasurer and conference program chair, and past-president of the International Association for Business and Society.

Kim Davenport is the Vice President of Change and Process Management for First Data Corporation (FDC) in Denver, Colorado. Her responsibilities include supporting the senior leadership team of a 900-person business unit in creating and implementing its business strategy, ensuring alignment of the strategy with the organizational structure, staff development, and business processes through use of six sigma, employee training and change management tools. Prior to working for First Data, she had a thirteen-year career at AT&T and BellSouth Corporation. She has published numerous articles and co-authored a book on total quality management. Her education includes a bachelor's degree in journalism from the University of Kentucky, a master's degree in organizational development from the American University, and a Ph.D. in human and organizational systems from the Fielding Institute. She is also a graduate of the Gestalt Institute of Cleveland's Organization Systems and Development Program.

Index

Note: The abbreviation "GBC" used in subentries stands for "Global business citizenship"